HEIRLOOM

This book is dedicated to the
small organic farmer, the miller,
the community-supported baker,
and the fervent locavore.

Time-Honored Techniques,
Nourishing Traditions, and
Modern Recipes

HEIRLOOM

Sarah Owens

Photographs by Ngoc Minh Ngo

ROOST BOOKS

Contents

Introduction
A Considered Approach to Food / vii

Introduction

A CONSIDERED APPROACH TO FOOD

As much as I love a juicy-ripe, thick slice of heirloom tomato, this is not just another book singing the praises of heirloom tomatoes. While those beloved plump orbs of the nightshade family are indeed a fine place to begin our exploration into the superior flavor that most heirloom plants possess, this book encompasses more substantial topics. I would like to introduce the idea of the heirloom *kitchen* as a space that honors not just the best ingredients but also the techniques and wisdom of our ancestors.

Heirloom looks to the ancient methods of food preparation through the act of slow cooking and many, although not all, heirloom ingredients. Traditional foods, such as dairy, grains, meat, and, of course, vegetables all enjoy a place at my modern table. They are prepared using techniques of fermentation, soaking, and sometimes extended cooking to heighten and extract their most beneficial qualities. Alcohol is enjoyed in moderation with attention to its potential medicinal effects on the body, particularly when made with beneficial bitter and seasonal herbs. Although granulated sugar plays a part in some of the recipes of this book, they are celebratory indulgences, many with suggestions for alternative, more wholesome replacements.

Fermentation has played a strong role in my personal wellness regimen and the creativity of my culinary repertoire. It is an ancient technique of preservation for the scrupulous cook that has also proved to be remarkably beneficial to the human microbiome. (We are, after all, comprised of up to ten times more microbial

---

OPPOSITE *Heirloom tomatoes are prized in small-scale farming for their superior flavor and localized growing performance unlike the thick-skinned, mealy supermarket varieties bred to withstand industrial harvesting and a long shelf life. Due to concerted efforts to save heirloom seeds and a revitalization of farmers' markets, newer hybrid tomatoes are being developed for flavor and disease resistance rather than shelf life and mass production.*

cells than we are of human cells! This makes our genetic DNA a representation of more than just, well, us.) Simply put, the more fermented probiotic foods we consume, the stronger and healthier we may become.

This is the mind-set of this book. It is an investigation into preserving and baking techniques across cultures using whole and heirloom ingredients as a way to discover a healthy and more nourishing approach to food. It's also my act of peaceful resistance— a personal narrative progressing toward a more loving, gentle, and healthy society.

When I began studying ancient ways of preparing food, such as using sourdough, soaking methods, sprouting, and the inclusion of animal fats from healthy, mindfully tended animals, I was quite ill and anemically struggling to live a happy and functional life free of fatigue, candida overgrowth, and the interruption of diarrhea and vomiting. These symptoms are difficult to address or talk about in polite society, but I was not unlike many who suffer the effects of our industrialized food system—a system with the sole goal of growing and processing food in large quantities and with maximum efficiency and lowest cost. With the introduction of a few mindful kitchen techniques, eliminating processed foods, getting adequate sleep, and reducing my intake of refined sugar, I was on my way back to living a joyful, healthy lifestyle devoid of embarrassment. Although I can now tolerate unfermented or organically grown grains low in gluten in limited amounts without difficulty, I have implemented a way of cooking and eating that ensures the long-term stabilization of my gut flora within a modern context.

The techniques and recipes included in this book promote both healing and maintaining a healthy gut and enjoying foods that are part of a sustainable or regenerative agricultural system. That type of system harnesses the power of rotational crops and animal husbandry to support intensive vegetable cultivation. Using sourdough, soaking, and sprouting methods can mitigate the troublesome aspects of many grain- or seed-based foods important to these systems. These methods activate enzymes stored in most grains, seeds, nuts, and legumes that assist in breaking them down in the gut. Soaking, sprouting, and fermenting also mitigate phytates, compounds that can prove troublesome to diets high in plant-based foods. Our stomachs are not equipped to break down phytic acid in high amounts, and as a result, key vitamins and minerals in those foods are prevented from being absorbed.

If you make heirloom grains, flours, seeds, or beans a priority in your kitchen, you may at first be stumped for access to these specialty ingredients. Fortunately, the demand is growing as a reflection of interest in more delicious and nutritious alternatives to genetically engineered or commodity staples. With a little resourcefulness and some persistence, it is possible to source them through a local farmer or market or by mail order (see Resources, page 324). Some larger natural food stores are beginning to carry local small-batch flours and pulses, making them more affordable and accessible. If you are still having trouble, ask, and ask again. Farmers will not grow if they believe there is no market, and markets will not stock if they believe there are no customers.

This book encourages you to explore nourishing traditions, support better agricultural practices, and embrace heirloom ingredients

---

OPPOSITE *Using a combination of meaty paste and juicy, sweet beefsteak or salad tomatoes yields a rich tomato sauce with balanced flavor and moderate roasting times.*

in an attempt to restore long-term vigor for ourselves and generations to come. The following points will help you to make informed choices and incorporate techniques for a modern lifestyle of slow living.

HONORING INGREDIENTS

Heirloom plants introduced before the 1950s, landrace grains adapted to local environmental conditions, and modern hybridized plants hold sway in this book, and I will explore them all. We'll begin with heirloom plants, which by definition are stabilized hybrids grown from seeds that are open-pollinated but "come true," retaining the desirable traits of their parents. Heirloom seeds can be passed from one gardener or farmer to the next and are grown with relatively similar appearance and flavor characteristics expressed from parent to offspring. Cross-pollinated hybrids may occur either naturally or by the intervention of humans, who select for disease resistance, optimal yield, or, in the case of ornamental plants, superior morphological characteristics or even fragrance. Ephemeral and proprietary F1 hybrids (first-generation offspring of two different parent plants) must be bought or acquired with each successive planting, and its progeny, the F2 generation, will have an unstable lack of uniformity. And to be clear, both hybridized and open-pollinated seeds can be grown organically, unlike the seeds of genetically modified organisms (GMOs), which legally do not qualify for organic certification.

Although significantly more scientific study is needed to determine the long-term effects of genetically modified crops on our bodies and the environment, the chemicals associated with their usage are unacceptable. These include broad-spectrum systemic pesticides and herbicides with glyphosate that have been linked not only to lymphoma but also severe liver and kidney damage in those who apply it. In addition, these chemical products damage the microbiome of healthy soil. Microbial relationships between plants and their soil are essential for naturally providing the nutrients and water necessary for plants to thrive. Crops that are successively grown on land deadened by these chemicals are dependent upon synthetic fertilizers for the nutrients they need to be productive, resulting in decreased nutritional benefit from their harvests. It is a vicious cycle that is disrespectful to our land, the people who cultivate it, and the ancient wisdom of our ancestors.

We can usurp this system by supporting a community of accountable small farmers who offer transparency. These farmers have a rainbow of heirloom, landrace, and modern hybrid seeds that can be grown without the built-in requirement for chemical dependency. By reinstituting networks of farmers with small processors (millers or butchers) and cooks (home-based, chefs, or bakers), we can once again weave the fabric for robust communities and a more environmentally friendly footprint.

Please don't confuse my criticism of corporate agribusiness with the insistence that we should support only heirloom plants and animals or follow heirloom recipes exactly as they are passed down to us. We cannot move forward without honoring the past, and it is increasingly important that we preserve genetic accessibility when breeding for the challenges of our rapidly changing climate. Matching unique growing conditions with domesticated species that are developed by natural processes over time allows small farmers to grow landrace varieties well adapted to specific climate stresses and soil types. These plants can withstand extremes otherwise impossible without the genetic influence of resilient heritage selections.

I became acutely aware of the value of heirloom plants when I worked as the rosarian of the Brooklyn Botanic Garden. I was hired during a time when pest-resistant rose cultivars were becoming all the rage. Their trademarked marketability has meant the screaming bluish-red 'Knock Out' rose is now ubiquitous in popular landscaping. Although I find its pedestrian, stiff appearance offensive and its lack of fragrance an insult, I still credit this breeding advancement as a revolution in rose growing. The new rose kids on the suburban American block supplanted the notion that roses are finicky divas, need copious amounts of attention, and demand the use of harmful sprays to be healthy. But their lack of allure turned the attention of garden visitors once again to the multipetal, lusty pastel cushions of fragrance perched atop glossy, healthy green foliage of many heirloom roses that likewise require little care. If an ironically named cultivar is what was needed to bring the rose back into popular cultivation, then so be it!

I cannot help but make the analogy between the history of roses and the unfortunate fall from favor of certain foods. This includes a monoculture of hybrids bred for more versatile use in both food and nonfood by-products at the sacrifice of flavor and historical identity. Coupled with processing that eliminates the most nutritious and delicious aspects of these otherwise valuable ingredients and we have sabotaged the ability of so many foods to nourish our bodies. Genetic diversity, conversely, has the potential to bolster place-based economies where locally owned and operated businesses thrive, natural resources are used sustainably, and our unique cultural resources are leveraged.

Most people who have embraced eating whole, organic vegetables have ushered in a transition to embracing heirloom, organic grains. The staggering reality in the United States is that less than 1% of the acreage that is agriculturally cultivated or pastured is actually certified organic, whereas 60% of our farmland is dedicated to grains. And although it is important to support the cultivation of organic vegetables, to really make a difference in the way our soil, our climate, and our health is treated, it is paramount that we move to more sustainable practices that support small farmers bringing grains and pulses to market.

These practices include not only farming organically but also employing rotational and cover crops that regenerate the soil naturally, without heavy inputs of fertilizers. By using alternative grain and seed crops, such as millet, sorghum, amaranth, rye, and buckwheat in conjunction with the cultivation of legumes, farmers have the ability to work more sustainably, much in the way agriculture was practiced before the advent of synthetic fertilizers and pesticides. Studies have shown that regenerative practices in farming may even be able to sequester enough carbon to reverse the effects of climate change if done on a global scale.

Rotation simply means a change in some regular order, and in the case of certain crops, others should follow in a definite order. For example, to increase the yield of wheat or cotton, cowpeas or peanuts may be grown in rotation. These legumes take up inert nitrogen gas (N_2) from the air and, with the help of rhizobia bacteria that invade and live inside their root nodules, "fix" it into usable nitrogen for the plant. This is then stored in their vegetative parts and added to the soil once they are plowed under. This is an important technique for improving soil health, but the benefits of rotation crops may also include the suppression of weeds and the ability to avoid insect pests and diseases. For example,

when peanut yield declines under nematode damage, certain types of resistant pearl millet (*Pennisetum glaucum*) or corn may be sown as a rotational crop to alleviate this pest pressure. Rotational crops, such as millet, that can be left to go to seed may even provide a viable additional product for the farmer. The only catch to this system is that without a market or an audience for rotational crops, there is little economic incentive for farmers to employ these ancient techniques.

I often hear the complaint that heirloom grains and pulses grown or milled by small businesses are too expensive compared to supermarket brands. The reality is that we cannot afford to continue supporting commercial, subsidized agriculture in its current state, as it encourages the misuse of increasingly compromised resources. By supporting farmers and businesses that grow niche products, such as heirloom grains or hybrids that require fewer synthetic inputs and water, we may be spending a little more on our bread, but we are investing in our future.

Our insatiable hunger for meat and dairy has significant environmental implications, putting escalating pressure on the availability of water, land, feed, fertilizer, fuel, waste disposal capacity, and the other limited resources of our planet. Our per capita meat intake has more than doubled in the past half-century as the global population has continued to increase. This unchecked consumption has led to a greater depletion of resources through large-scale industrial facilities funneling animals with unnatural regard to their needs in order to satisfy our own. An unfortunate abundance

of toxic waste from these farms in the form of runoff has destroyed important waterways surrounding these factory farms, among other unfortunate consequences. This is not the only way to raise and consume meat and dairy.

In a closed loop agricultural system, animals are raised in a way that benefits the land, recycling all nutrients and organic matter back to the soil that supported them. This is a practice that preserves the nutrient and carbon levels within the soil and allows farming to be carried out on a more sustainable basis. Ruminants produce rich manure, which, when mixed with remnants of local crops, can become a seemingly endless supply of filtering material, fertilizer, and energy.

A sustainable agricultural model simply involves rotating animals on and off of land and using their manure to provide adequate fertility for the hungry and thirsty production of vegetables that when grown intensively uses these inputs to regenerate their soil. This model does not, however, support the consumption of animals that have been bred for industrial processing or that of one type of seemingly desirable cut of meat. Rather, it encourages a more mindful consumption of all of an animal's parts, a practice that supports the most economical use of resources. Ancient civilizations knew and practiced these methods, but I have not attempted to document recipes for offal in this book due to their limited accessibility. See the Resources section (page 324) for further guidance.

I grew up in the foothills of the Appalachian Mountains, barefoot and running free through valleys and hollers for most of my childhood. The rural customs of canning and preserving were a part of daily existence, and the annual planting of and tending to a large garden was only part of the plan to ensure we had the most delicious, nutritious, and economically

OPPOSITE *The chickpea, or* Cicer arietinum, *is an ancient legume sporting many colors. Soaking, draining, and sprouting grains as well as legumes before cooking leads to shortened cooking times and increased digestibility.*

prudent diet. My grandmothers and the elders of our community saved and shared seeds and kept culinary and farming traditions alive among themselves. It was commonplace to find wild foods, in particular game meats and seasonal greens, at the table. It wasn't unusual for one of my uncles to drag home a curious carcass of some sort, my grandmother sighing in anticipation of the work ahead. Wild mushrooms found their way into Thanksgiving dressing, mud turtle soup or barbecued squirrel occasionally made an exotic appearance, and to this day poke salat and eggs are my favorite way to enjoy a mess of the persistent perennial weed *Phytolacca americana* (common pokeweed). I now realize how lucky I was to be exposed to experiences that connected me to the natural world. They shaped my priorities as an adult and encouraged my return to some of their practices while living in a more urban location.

Foraging, preservation, and fermentation have been threaded through my culinary curiosity while traveling in search of knowledge that mirrors my Appalachian upbringing. No matter their location, most rural communities share similar themes of self-sufficiency based on climate and availability of ingredients. No-waste practices and scrupulous usage of each plant and animal have long been preserved in both my family and many of the places I have visited, knitting together communities and validating histories through food.

My exposure to various cultural recipes and customs began in Louisville, Kentucky, a city long established as a refugee resettlement destination. Restaurant work there taught me a more sophisticated understanding of flavor: how to balance sweet, sour, bitter, and savory with both cultivated and wild ingredients. The first time I tasted a lamb kofta meatball made with rice and aromatic fresh herbs swimming in a rich tomato sauce, I was delighted to bite

into a large, soft date hidden in the center. That revelation holds a dear place in my memory and accelerated a lifelong quest for exotic and complex aromas.

When I began developing digestive problems, my career in food became more focused on wholesome ingredients. As described in my first book, *Sourdough*, I wandered down a long and lonely road of investigation via Western medicine that led to few answers and little relief before discovering methods to properly prepare the foods I love. Fermentation has been my panacea, and through using it as one of several methods to bring whole grains and nutritious flours back into my daily diet, I have discovered other truths of ancient nutritional wisdom as well. This book is an ode to those truths, honoring the gifts from the plant and animal kingdoms. Properly preparing vegetables, fruits, grains, meats, and dairy and understanding their impact on my body made all the difference in my health. This may or may not ring true for you as well. I firmly believe that everyone should discover their own path by making informed decisions based on both science and the ancient knowledge of home cooks, preservationists, and administers of traditional medicine.

Although I have documented the practices shared in this book to the best of my knowledge and have given an explanation of the adjustments I've made, the recipes come together in a deeply rooted personal narrative rather than an encyclopedic effort to compile each country or region's traditional techniques. The following recipes are inspired by wanderlust, influenced by the multicultural eateries of New York City's outer boroughs,

OPPOSITE *Table Loaves (page 62) are excellent candidates for detailed scoring.*

shaped by the study of scientific journals and fragile old cookbooks, and informed by the generosity of friends and strangers eager to share the secrets of their families or diaspora. If your grandmother served you okroshka or kishk, juk, or æbleskiver, you will not find them in their purest representation here. I have adapted these traditional hallmarks of cultural identity, often decreasing sugar, adding or substituting ingredients for complexity or accessibility, and adjusting their cooking techniques and approaches to flavor to suit my preferences and digestive needs. This is all done with a simple understanding of how food is not only one of the most delightful carnal experiences but also potent medicine for the body and spirit.

This book is meant to be a gateway to healthier ingredients and techniques so you can welcome them into your kitchen. It explores cuisine through culture and fosters a relationship to our environment and the plant world in support of a more sustainable system of animal husbandry. Some recipes, such as Stone-Ground Grits/Polenta (page 55), are quite simple and almost rudimentary. My hope is that by the time you finish stirring that big pot of cornmeal porridge, you will appreciate how different it is from polenta in flavor, ingredient distinction, and cultural heritage. Others directly support integrated or regenerative farming with their use of alternative grains or whole animals for rendering fat or making broth. *Heirloom* commences the comfort and authenticity of generations past to create a deliciously meaningful menu for the future.

OPPOSITE From left to right: *Whey-Fermented Cipollini Onions (page 45), Sumac Vinegar, Pineapple Vinegar (page 8), Kumquat Liqueur (page 207), Fermented Green Tomatoes (page 287), Cranberry Marmalade (page 254), and Lacto-Fermented Mushrooms (page 11).*

PRESERVING TRADITIONS

Sumac Vi
Summer

Pinapple Hot Pepper Vin
Bottled 2/18 Started 1/23

Kumquats, gin
1/18
Sacramento

FRUITS AND VEGETABLES

OPPOSITE Brassica oleracea *is a species originally found in the Mediterranean from whence all cultivars of common vegetables, such as cabbages, kales, broccoli, and Brussel sprouts, were domesticated. Featured here is 'Red Express,' an excellent choice for northern climates and small gardens.*

ONE OF THE GREATEST REWARDS of seasonal market cooking is being able to stash preciously fleeting ingredients away to enjoy later. When you are blessed with abundance, knowing how to process and store this bounty ensures that nothing goes to waste. You will not only save money in the dormant season, but you will also have many options at hand in your freezer, refrigerator, and cabinets.

The following is an overview of the preservation methods used through the seasonal chapters in this book. Techniques range from fermenting and brining to canning and dehydrating. These methods will not only help you to prepare these particular recipes but will also teach you how to preserve other ingredients you have on hand.

Lacto-Fermentation (The Only Constant Is Change)

Fermentation is the validation of alchemy, and each time I successfully pickle, bake sourdough, drink coffee, eat chocolate, nibble on olives, or gorge on kimchi, I'm reminded that there is life in death, magic and mystery in the cycles of nature. We must celebrate the perpetual surging dance of the universe that brings about change regardless of—but sometimes in positive applause of—our participation. Honoring these truths challenges my consciousness to relinquish control over outcomes and entertain the growth of new ideas. It is empowering to change the chemical nature of anything, and by fermenting the foods we eat, we elevate them in a way that honors the potential of their ingredients.

Lacto-fermentation can be done in the home kitchen with little gadgetry and the most basic ingredients, including salt and/or a sweetening agent. With time and manipulation of temperature, you can create remarkably delicious foods with the added benefits of heightened nutrition and enhanced flavor. Some of the following recipes require only a few days, others a few months. By slowing our pace long enough to observe their progress, the evanescent knowledge of the seasons can be captured and preserved.

OPPOSITE *French tarragon (*Artemesia dracunculus*) originated in Russia and, like its larger Russian cousin (*Artemesia dracunculoides*), appreciates full sun but is picky about good drainage and prefers mild heat. It is versatile and can be used for garnishing Heirloom Melon Salad with Tarragon and Fig Leaf Powder (page 271) or paired with chicken, fish, or mushroom dishes.*

HOMEMADE VINEGARS

The first time I made vinegar, it was by happy accident. I had just moved to the Rockaway peninsula, a beach community in New York City with plenty of open space and wild plant communities both native and invasive. I began experimenting with various parts of botanicals I could harvest sustainably and in abundance, such as rose hips, honeysuckle flowers, and sumac. In exploring ways to preserve them, I began making yeast waters for both drinking and leavening bread. I gathered fruits or flowers and weighted them under a solution of sugar water, waiting patiently and with keen observance until it fizzed and gurgled with enthusiasm. I would then harvest this active solution and use it to create a sourdough culture (such as described in my first book, *Sourdough*) or mix it with liquor and soda water to make a refreshing probiotic cocktail. Both were novel ways to connect to a new environment in a rooted, earth-to-sea survey of plant allies.

But my curiosity got the best of me and I wound up with too many gurgling jars of pink, golden, and ruby-colored liquids—more than I could possibly use or consume. I gave many away to a courageous audience but found that after several months in the refrigerator (depending on how much sugar I had used initially) the yeast water started turning to vinegar. This is when I began to more deeply understand the metabolic biology of fermentation. I noticed the difference between the presence or absence of oxygen and the cycles that each substrate encouraged. I learned how to detect the presence of invisible life and how to identify the physical manifestations and various suspicious appearances of a fermentation culture. They all have unique characters, and each is endearing in its own way, subject to its creator, ingredients, and environment. I learned how to both manipulate and trust the dynamic laws of the microbial universe, and although some experiments didn't quite go as I had planned, there are few mistakes in fermentation but many opportunities to discover.

Apple Cider Vinegar
Makes about 2 quarts

Versatile and legendary for curing all manner of ailments, apple cider vinegar is one of the easiest and most cooperative ferments you can make at home, with a very simple set of equipment. There are a number of different ways you can make vinegar from scratch, including using pressed and unpasteurized cider, but I prefer to use apple skins and cores or whole apples themselves, chopped and weighted under a sweetened water. You are essentially fermenting fruit that is then converted to vinegar by the action of *Acetobacter*, microbes that thrive under the presence of oxygen, converting ethanol to acetic acid. This method can be applied to any fruit with sensitivity to its natural sugar content and trace minerals that assist with successful acidification of alcohol. Don't be afraid to use the knobby fruits from an old homestead you wouldn't normally eat out of hand in combination with a few other sweeter fruits, as the medley will provide a complex profile of flavors in the resulting vinegar. Occasionally I'll slip in a few sprigs of whatever pleases me from my porch garden or even the invasive mugwort plant (*Artemisia vulgaris*) for an unmistakably herbaceous identity with liver-cleansing and gastric benefits. After your initial batch of spontaneous fermentation and ensuing acidification, you will be left with your own mother that you can successively use in future batches of vinegar making to catalyze the process.

1120 g / 6 to 7 medium apples	2370 to 2845 g / 10 to 12 cups warm water
48 g / 6 tablespoons sugar	

Coarsely chop the apples including the cores and skins into 3- to 4-inch pieces (small enough to ferment fairly quickly but large enough not to float in between the fermentation weights). Place the apple pieces into a 1-gallon crock or other wide-mouthed, nonporous container with a wide surface exposed to air, as the *Acetobacter* responsible for converting ethanol to vinegar reproduces best under aerobic conditions. Dissolve the sugar in the water and pour it over the apples. Weigh the apples down with fermentation weights, a clean heavy plate, or a bowl or jar filled with water that will fit inside the crock to keep the apples from floating to the surface (to discourage mold). Cover with a cloth and rubber band or a loose-fitting noncorrosive lid to keep flying critters from establishing residence. Place the crock on a large plate to catch any spillover and allow to sit in a warm place.

In about 2 to 3 days, you will begin to notice activity in the form of bubbles breaking and foam possibly forming on the surface—this is the result of wild yeasts consuming the sugar and exhaling carbon dioxide as a by-product. After about a week of this exuberance, you will notice it will slow considerably as the yeasts become balanced with bacterial populations responsible for acidifying the ferment. A thin film may form on the surface of the liquid, but do not let this concern you too much. If it becomes so thick that it traps the liquid underneath from being exposed to air, pull it away with your fingers or a spatula and compost it, feed it to the chickens or pigs for a probiotic boost, give it away, or use it to kick-start another batch.

After about 4 weeks, you have several options depending on your availability, taste preference, and desired strength of acidity. You can strain out the apples and bottle the vinegar and allow it to age and mellow, or you can continue to let it ferment for another 4 to 6 weeks in pursuit of a vinegar stronger in acidity and flavor. Either way, try to remember to take a periodic peek under the cover during this 4- to 10-week period. It is simply fascinating to watch the vinegar develop over time. If you are lucky, a mother will form on the surface if you leave the apples to ferment for longer than 3 to 5 weeks. At first, this will look like a cobweb structure forming evenly over the surface. This could be easily mistaken for mold but will continue to thicken and solidify into a firm, almost slippery rubber disc if left to grow for another 2 to 3 weeks. This is the colony of cellulose and bacteria that have organized themselves into a physical culture and may be used to inoculate your next batch of vinegar.

When you are ready to bottle the vinegar, remove and reserve the mother if one has formed and strain the vinegar through a fine-mesh sieve into sterilized bottles with noncorrosive lids. If you have strained it after 4 weeks, you may need to "burp" the bottle every few days to relieve carbon dioxide pressure buildup from ongoing fermentation if the sugars have not been completely metabolized (resulting from using fruit that is already high in natural sugars or adding more than enough sugar to kick-start the process). After another month or two, you will notice a mother beginning to form as a circular disk at the top of the jar. If your mother already formed before you strained the vinegar, you can add it back to the bottled vinegar or use it to inoculate a new batch. Simply slip her into the sugar water in the crock after you've weighted a new batch of fruit. Over time, a new mother will form on the surface, pushing the older layers toward the bottom. Store in a cool, dark place until ready to use—it will keep indefinitely and will gain in flavor as it ages.

Pineapple Vinegar

Makes about 2 quarts

Pineapple has an abundance of natural sugars, making this one of the most vigorous mixtures you can create to achieve vinegar. The flavor is bright and slightly sweet, even after full fermentation, and is excellent used in marinades for grilling meats, especially chicken or fish. I love to add a dash or two of this complex vinegar to cocktails as well, especially those requiring a bit of acidity to balance flavors.

590 g / 3½ pounds / 1 large ripe pineapple

2 to 3 fresh or crushed dried hot chilies (optional)

2370 to 2610 g / 10 to 11 cups warm water

28 g / 3 tablespoons + 1 teaspoon sugar

Remove the crown of the pineapple and, using a knife, carefully shave off the thick, waxy rind from the outside of the fruit. Cut the flesh into 3-inch pieces and place into a clean crock or container along with the chilies, if using. Dissolve the sugar in the water and pour it over the pineapple. Weigh the pineapple down with weights, a clean heavy plate, or a bowl or jar filled with water that will fit inside the crock to keep the fruit from floating to the surface (to discourage mold). Cover with a cloth and a rubber band or a loose-fitting noncorrosive lid to keep flying critters from establishing residence. Place the crock on a large plate to catch any spillover and allow to sit in a warm place.

From here, follow the fermentation instructions for Apple Cider Vinegar (page 6).

Jujube Vinegar

Makes about 2½ cups

This uniquely tart and sweet ferment is an excellent drinking vinegar when the fermentation time is shortened and it is harvested young. Use to mix heirloom shrub recipes or allow to age for use in salads or to dress roasted fish with a splash of acidity. It is also a delicious candidate for making Agrodulce (page 196) to drizzle over Sweet Potato Tart with a Coconut Pecan Crust (page 112).

160 g / 16 large dried jujube dates

25 g / 3½ heaping teaspoons sugar

595 g / 2½ cups warm water

Pierce the jujube dates with a knife in several places. Place them in a sterile crock or other nonporous container. Dissolve the sugar in the warm water and pour over the jujubes. Weigh the fruit down with weights, a clean heavy plate, or a bowl or jar filled with water that will fit inside the crock to keep the jujubes from floating to the surface (to discourage mold). Cover with a cloth and a rubber band or a loose-fitting noncorrosive lid to keep flying critters from establishing residence. Place the crock on a large plate to catch any spillover and allow to sit in a warm place.

From here, follow the fermentation instructions for Apple Cider Vinegar (page 6).

JUJUBES

Jujubes are the olive-size fruit of a cold-hardy tree originally found growing throughout Central Asia and into the Levant with genetic studies more recently revealing its domestication into larger, sweeter versions in China as early as 7000 B.C. Its cultivation has since spread widely: it is an invasive species in Madagascar and is commonly found in the Caribbean, Korea, and Eastern Europe. When fresh, they resemble a small apple in both flavor and appearance— a crunchy balance of tart and mild sweetness—and they contain a little round pit much like a cherry. They are most often found dried as "dates" in Asian markets, although they have no botanical kinship with the fruit of date palms, or sold as prepared tea blends or syrup concentrates. I like to make Jujube, Ginger, and Turmeric Tea (page 203) with them. Jujubes are regarded with equal respect for both their flavor and medicinal properties, and in Eastern traditions they are used to treat digestive or sleep disorders, anxiety, and stress-related conditions. Dehydrated into dramatically shriveled, date-like treats, they are enjoyed with coffee or after-dinner in the Middle East.

Salt Preservation

Before the advent of refrigeration, salt was used throughout many cultures to cure and preserve vegetables and sometimes meat for lengthy periods of time. The salting process along with a good amount of time can also be used to transform otherwise bitter foods, such as olives, into a more delightful experience. Salt used in proper amounts encourages fermentation through the growth of friendly lactic acid–producing bacteria that are naturally found on food, in particular fruits and vegetables that have contact with the soil in which they are grown. These bacteria discourage spoilage microbes from taking hold by keeping acidity levels high.

This bacterial fermentation also encourages beneficial yeasts and molds to populate, leading to not only a longer shelf life but also increased nutritional content of the food in question. The action of the lacto-fermenting bacteria unlocks enzymes beneficial for digestion and produces vitamins that are nourishing to our bodies. Lacto-fermentation provides several benefits to us in addition to preservation. When anything is truly cultured, it is not only full of probiotics and enzymatic activity; the nutritional value is also more readily absorbed by our intestinal lining. The vitamin content of fermented foods is increased from their original, raw state and we can enjoy a greater bioavailability of mineral-rich foods, such as mushrooms.

Eating fermented foods for better health is nothing new. These traditions have been practiced for millennia not only to provide nourishment but also to treat or prevent illness. We now know the science behind how lactic acid bacteria prevent other pathogenic bacteria that cause sickness, but these foods were used long before lab studies proved as much: the

ancient Romans treated intestinal infections, the Greeks wrote of the benefits of fermented cabbage, and sauerkraut was eaten to prevent scurvy on long overseas sails.

Another fascinating benefit of fermented foods is the ability to intensify the production of acetylcholine in the body. This important neurotransmitter not only helps increase bowel movement; it also encourages the stomach, pancreas, and gallbladder to secrete digestive enzymes, making it a powerful aid to those with sluggish digestion. If this ticks a box on your wellness page, go easy initially on the amount of probiotic foods in your diet, increasing the frequency and amount as your body adjusts to this new suite of microflora. As you build up tolerance and an increased appetite for fermented foods, diversify what kinds you eat, as each will host a particular balance of microbes.

LACTO-FERMENTED MUSHROOMS

Makes about 1 pint

Preserved mushrooms are deeply embedded in classic Slavic cuisine in areas where mushrooms thrive in abundance and are revered for their culinary and medicinal value. In modern Western supermarkets, we often see preserved mushrooms in olive bars, pickled in a salty vinegar brine, buoyantly bobbing alongside garlic and other savory herbs. Although they are inarguably piquant, I prefer this method of preserving mushrooms, especially when I have a surplus that I have safely foraged (by

confirming their identity). Whether using foraged or cultivated varieties, I have found firm specimens such as *Pleurotus eryngii* ('King Trumpets' or their mini version seen here), *Boletus edulis* (porcini), or *Agaricus bisporus* (button or the more mature cremini mushroom) offer more success than their fragile counterparts. (Recipe also shown on pages 1 and 274.) Once fully fermented, it is best to cook these into savory dishes.

300 g / 1 to 2 cups (depending on variety) mushrooms	½ teaspoon black peppercorns
1 to 2 plump cloves garlic	9 g / 2 teaspoons sea salt
2 bay leaves	60 g / ¼ cup water

Bring a medium saucepan of water to a boil. Dunk the mushrooms in the boiling water for 30 seconds to slightly soften them. (This is optional, but I find it speeds along the brining process.) Drain through a sieve and transfer to a clean bowl. Add the garlic, bay leaves, and peppercorns and sprinkle in the salt. Toss to coat and allow to rest uncovered at room temperature for 20 to 25 minutes, until the mushrooms begin to release water. Pour the water over the mushrooms and gently stir. Transfer to a clean jar and submerge the mushrooms under the brine using fermentation weights. Allow to ferment at room temperature for about 3 days, until they begin to vigorously bubble and become somewhat foamy on the surface. Remove the weights, cover with a noncorrosive lid, and place in the refrigerator, occasionally burping the lid to relieve pressure. The mushrooms will keep for up to 6 months.

OPPOSITE *Firm, uniform specimens such as these baby* Pleurotus eryngii *'King Trumpet' mushrooms are excellent preserved with lacto-fermentation.*

LACTO-FERMENTATION BASICS

A basic understanding of influencing fermentation factors will help you to control the flavors, potential health benefits, and overall outcome of this magical process. The following are a few basic tenets to keep in mind when you are making a sourdough bread, natural pickle, dried meat, or lacto-fermented beverage.

Salt Types

There are many different sources for salt, including evaporations from both land and sea. For brine pickling or meat curing, choose a "dry" salt with low moisture content such as Himalayan pink or kosher salt. Sea salts that clump easily indicate higher moisture levels and will affect their weight and consequent brine solution. For baked goods, a fine sea salt is appropriate, as it will dissolve easier into the dough or batter.

Salt Ratios

Lacto-fermentation microbes need trace minerals found in salt to successfully perform their duties. Too much salt, however, will hinder not only the presence of mold but also desirable bacterial fermentation. The amount of salt necessary to encourage lacto-fermentation will depend on the type of vegetable you are trying to preserve. To create a brine, first weigh the amount of water in grams needed to cover the weighted vegetables. Multiply this by the appropriate percentage to calculate the amount of salt necessary to dissolve in the water. For firm vegetables, a basic 2% to 2.5% solution of salt to water is desirable (amount of water × .02 to .025). For vegetables with higher water content that are more prone to mold, such as mushrooms or green tomatoes, 3.5% is more appropriate, while whole or sliced cucumbers may require about 5% or more. For whole or sliced peppers, a more liberal use of salt (up to 10%) is desirable. If you are fermenting in a very hot and humid environment, leaning toward a more liberal use of salt is the safer option.

Temperature

For most types of fermentation mentioned in this book, an optimal temperature range of 70°F to 75°F is preferable. Lower temperatures are tolerable but will result in slower fermentation, especially for pickles. If you are attempting fermentation in a cold climate, the possibility of mold populations forming before your desired suite of microbes establishes is much higher. Higher temperatures (80°F or more), especially in the presence of high humidity, will encourage your pickles to go soft or your bread to taste curdled and sour from overproofing. Neither is harmful to your health, but they are not particularly appetizing.

Safety

Most fermentation methods culture lactic or acetic acid bacteria (*Lactobacillus or Acetobacter*) to not only increase the digestibility of grains and increase the probiotics of vegetables, but to also keep these foods safe. These incredible genera of microbes lower the pH of foods, making them inhospitable to the "bad guys" that cause spoilage. For this reason, use jars made of nonreactive materials, such as glass or ceramic.

Equipment

If you are culturing vegetables and fruits, you may want to invest in specialized equipment. Keep in mind your jar will need to accommodate your chosen method of weighting the vegetables or fruits underneath their brine as well as the exclusion of oxygen and the release of carbon dioxide as they ferment. If you do not accommodate these factors, you will end up with an explosive (and possibly even dangerous) mess.

One of the few rules of successful pickling is to keep the vegetables submerged in their brine while also allowing the opportunity for off-gassing. I fermented pickles safely and successfully for years without purchasing any specialized weighting equipment, simply using a plastic bag filled with water or a heavy plate or small jar that fits inside the container. If you like gadgetry and have space in your kitchen, refer to the Resources section (page 327) for a few alternative suggestions. These cleverly engineered crocks or jars will help to eliminate room for error, encourage the proper balance of lactic and acetic acids, and prevent mold from taking root on the surface of your ferments. You can also discourage this from happening in open-air crocks by using a large leaf to cover the mixture before weighting it. If a thin layer of mold appears, simply remove and discard this leaf layer.

SALTED KUMQUATS

Makes 1 pint

This recipe is based upon a traditional Cantonese preparation for preserving kumquats, a fleeting seasonal citrus fruit. The method here is to use salt to cure rather than ferment the citrus, which gives it a prolonged shelf life and unique flavor but a less bioactive result. With time and patience, the salt will draw out the oils and moisture from the fruit, creating a brine that can be used for cooking or making a medicinal tea (page 255) to soothe a sore throat. Once cured, they will keep at room temperature for an impressive amount of time; the longer these age, the more fragrant and complex their flavor becomes. You may incorporate additional spices such as cinnamon, star anise, cloves, sliced ginger, or bay leaf if you wish, but I prefer to keep these fairly simple to maintain their versatility in the kitchen. Use them in stir-fried greens, tagines, or salsa as you would preserved lemons, but with a more exotic and complex aroma.

260 to 390 g / 1 to 1½ cups kosher salt	345 g / 2 cups fresh kumquats

Sprinkle a ¼-inch layer of salt on the bottom of a pint jar. Arrange a layer of kumquats on top and sprinkle in spices, if using. Continue alternating layers until you reach the top of the jar, finishing with the kumquats completely covered in salt. Loosely position a noncorrosive lid and place in a cool, dark spot for at least one month. Over time the salt will dissolve into a brine and the kumquats will shrivel and turn brownish in color. Store in a cool, dark location for up to 2 years.

Quick Pickling

A quicker way to preserve fruits and vegetables is by preparing a brine of salt and sometimes a sweetener dissolved in equal parts warm water and vinegar, stirring in additional spices for a personalized outcome, and storing them in the refrigerator. This approach can turn an ordinary ingredient into flavorful condiments and culinary extras whose acidity will cut through fatty meats or creamy cheeses and brighten otherwise ho-hum porridges. When the brine is poured over fruits and vegetables, it also preserves the texture of those ingredients that would otherwise be lost in the lengthy exposure to heat of hot water canning. Most any vinegar can be used, including Homemade Vinegars (page 6), rice vinegar, red wine vinegar, or white wine vinegar.

A BASIC VINEGAR BRINE

A general approach to quick pickling is to warm one part vinegar to one part water in a saucepan. For every cup of each, add 1 tablespoon kosher salt and up to 1 tablespoon sweetener, such as pure cane sugar or honey, and stir to dissolve. If you wish to keep the bioactivity of a live vinegar such as those in this book, you may dissolve the salt and sugar in the warm water only and add the vinegar after the water has cooled. Add spices of your choice, such as black peppercorns, mustard seeds, cardamom, coriander, or cinnamon. When quick pickling, it is best to thinly slice dense vegetables, such as beets; you may leave others, such as green beans, whole. Pack them into a clean jar and pour over enough brine to completely cover the vegetables. Cover and place in the refrigerator for at least several

hours before enjoying. These will last up to 3 to 6 months in the refrigerator.

WHOLE PICKLING SPICE BLEND

The following is a suggested spice blend adapted from the Rodale Institute that works well for most fermented or quick pickled vegetables, giving them a well-rounded flavor with a touch of heat. You may adjust or simplify to your needs and preferences to include spices, such as caraway or dill seeds. Or place a few large sprigs of fresh herbs, such as dill or cilantro, a few peeled and crushed or sliced garlic cloves, and a fresh or split dried chili in each quart of pickles.

4 large whole bay leaves	1 tablespoon whole allspice
1 tablespoon green cardamom pods	1 tablespoon whole coriander seeds
1 tablespoon whole dried ginger pieces	1 tablespoon black peppercorns
2 dried chilies	One 4-inch stick cinnamon, broken or crushed into small pieces
1 tablespoon yellow mustard seeds	
1 tablespoon brown mustard seeds	

Break the bay leaves up and place them in a mortar along with the cardamom pods, ginger pieces, and chilies. Crush to a coarse texture using the pestle and place in a small container that has a lid. Add the remaining spices, cover, and shake to distribute. Cover and store in a cool, dry location for up to 6 months. Use 1 to 1½ tablespoons along with 1 or 2 plump sliced or whole garlic cloves per pint of pickles.

PICKLING TIPS

Quick pickling using a vinegar and water brine and your creative choice of spices is an easy way to brighten up a meal with crunch and acidity. The process is completely adaptable to the amount and type of vegetable you wish to preserve and requires little time and equipment to execute. And you save money by making use of produce that might otherwise go to waste!

Red beets (Beta vulgaris) add an attractive hue to the pickling pot.

- **Make it pink.** Bright, vibrant colors make any meal that much more festive, and pickles are excellent candidates to easily add a splash of color to the table. I look for ingredients such as fresh or dried hibiscus sepals or purple shiso leaves to stain the brine or take a nod from the Middle Eastern tradition of slipping a small beet into a jar of otherwise anemic-looking vegetables such as turnips, parsnips, or even sliced lotus root. The result is a natural but flashy fuchsia tinting with a slight influence of flavor.
- **Use soft water.** For the most attractive preserves, it is recommended you use soft water. Iron in hard water will darken pickles, and sulfur, calcium, or other salts can interfere with fermentation processes. Likewise, heavily chlorinated water has the potential to slow or halt friendly microbial growth necessary for both preserving and making sourdough. Although this is not always the case, you may need to experiment before determining if your tap water is appropriate for use in these recipes. When in doubt, you can leave water to sit uncovered at room temperature overnight for the chlorine to oxidize and evaporate or use filtered water instead. Bottled water is of course an option, but you may wish to avoid the use of unnecessary plastics.

Making Jams and Jellies

The naturally high acid and sugar content of most fruit combined with natural or added pectin make delicious cooked spreads for toast, desserts, or to use as a glaze for meat. Sugar and acid in proper amounts help to preserve fruits by discouraging pathogenic bacteria, such as botulism, from developing under anaerobic conditions, making it very important to follow both hygienic practices and appropriate methods for storage. These nasties at the very least lead to spoilage of jams and jellies and at the worst food poisoning or even death. Spreads made with low amounts of sugar and acid can be preserved in a hot water bath, in the refrigerator, or just as easily in the freezer. It is possible to use much less sweetener when storing in the refrigerator or freezer, as the possibility for bacteria to take hold is much lower under colder temperatures. When doing so, you may choose to use alternatives to cane sugar, such as honey or maple syrup.

A heavy, deep, and wide preserving pot is helpful for successful setting of jams, jellies, and preserves. This essential piece of equipment will not only conduct heat efficiently without the risk of scorching the bottom; its large surface area will also increase evaporation and aid in thickening your mixture. If processing for storage at a cool room temperature, you will want to purchase equipment for hot water canning (see page 17). Otherwise, you may store your jams and jellies in sterilized lidded jars in the refrigerator for up to 3 months.

Pectin

Many but not all fruits contain a natural source of pectin that when combined with the proper levels of acid and sugar will thicken preserves to a pleasing, spreadable texture. Although pectin is available commercially, the recipes in this book harness the natural processes and ingredients necessary to make preserves without this additional manufactured ingredient. When sourcing fruits for these recipes, try to choose a few that are slightly underripe, as they contain higher amounts of pectin.

There are several ways to make your own pectin, although this requires a certain acceptance of variable results. The easiest approach is to harvest citrus seeds and wrap them in a cheesecloth bundle to macerate and boil down with your fruit or juice. I have found that about 115 g (1 cup) of seeds works well with up to 6 cups of liquid or fruit. This may be your desired method if you do not wish to add additional liquid to your jam.

APPLE PECTIN STOCK

If you are blessed with an apple tree in your backyard or have one available to forage with permission, you can make your own pectin water to use immediately or for future preserving projects. It is best to do this early in the season when you may want to thin the set of your unripe apples, directing the tree's energy toward the fruit you wish to be larger and tastier.

454 g / 1 pound apples   950 g / 4 cups water

Coarsely chop the apples, including the cores. Place in a large saucepan, add 475 g / 2 cups of the water, and bring to a boil over medium-high heat. Boil for 15 minutes. Strain through a cheesecloth, jelly bag, or nut milk bag into a large bowl. Do not squeeze the pulp! Squeezing will lead to a cloudy liquid. Return the pulp to the pot and add the remaining 475 g / 2 cups water. Place over medium

CANNING BASICS

There are a few rules to keep in mind when preserving food in jars, and the following instructions are based on USDA guidelines for heat processing or canning food for long-term storage.

Home canning ensures that you have access to natural foods year-round without crowding your refrigerator or freezer. All you need is some basic equipment and a little time to perform a heat-processing step after your jams, jellies, or pickles are prepared. This type of processing works with foods that are acidic enough (a pH of 4.6 or lower) to inhibit the growth of botulism and have enough sugar to inhibit the growth of mold. Properly canned foods will keep in a cool, dry place for up to one year.

Equipment

Most kitchens are already equipped with the items necessary for heat processing, but you will need to purchase glass canning jars with noncorrosive two-piece metal lids. The recipes included in this book are for small-batch canning and require little more than a deep stockpot and a jar lifter (or salad tongs in a pinch). The pot should be large enough to immerse the jars completely in water by at least 1 inch, with ample room for the water to boil. A rack that fits into the bottom of the pot is a true asset, as it will protect the filled jars from direct heat, and canning funnels and magnetic lid wands can help with maneuvering the jars and lids in and out of the water bath. You can purchase a kit with these tools inexpensively (see Resources, page 327). Having the equipment on hand will streamline your production if you anticipate canning throughout the season.

A heavy, deep, and wide preserving pot, preferably made of copper, will contribute to the successful set of jams, jellies, and preserves. It will not only conduct heat efficiently without the risk of scorching the bottom, but it also exposes a large surface area to air, which aids in the evaporation and thickening of your mixture. If macerating fruit before processing, never do so in the preserving pot, as the fruit will oxidize.

Finally, although a sieve, large spoon, and bowl will suffice, a food mill will make processing many fruits easier, yielding a consistent and pleasing texture to some preserves.

Sterilizing Jars

Place the required number of clean jars on a rack in a large stockpot or boiling water canner. I often include at least one extra jar, as fruits and vegetables vary in volume and weight depending on the season, sometimes blessing you with a little extra.

Cover the jars with water, cover the pot, and bring the water to a simmer over medium heat. For ease of handling, place the lids (but not the screw rings) in a small saucepan, cover them with water, and heat until just under boiling. Sterilize the jars for 10 minutes, then turn off the heat. Leave the hot water–filled pot on the stovetop to heat-process the filled jars later.

Skimming Foam

Many fruits become viscous as you boil them into jam, trapping air as they cook, which results in a frothy foam. This foam has an unpleasant mouthfeel and compromises the keeping quality of the finished product.

continued

To avoid accumulating excessive amounts, simply skim and discard the foam with a spoon as the jam cooks.

The Set Test

It is not always clear when homemade jams, jellies, and preserves are ready to transfer into sterilized jars. Over time you will begin to notice subtle textures and even sounds that will cue jarring, but this simple test is an easy way to determine whether the mixture will set well upon cooling.

Place a clean, thin glass or ceramic plate in the freezer at least 10 minutes before you are ready to test your jam. When you are near the end of the suggested cooking time, remove the jam from the heat and place a small dollop onto the cold plate. Return the plate to the freezer for 2 to 3 minutes. Test for a set by nudging your fingertip into the dollop of jam. If a wrinkled skin has formed or your finger mark remains, your jam has reached a setting point and is ready to be ladled into jars. If the jam pools into a runny liquid, this is an indication that it is not ready and needs more cooking time or an adjustment of sugar, acid, and/or pectin.

Note: Depending on the fruit, whether it is fresh or previously frozen, the recipe, and the type of pectin you are using (if any), your jam, jelly, or preserves may take longer than others to set after processing. If the sealed jars have completely cooled and the mixture is still runny, try placing the jars in the refrigerator, as this rapid cooling will often encourage a better set. Once they have firmed up, remove from the refrigerator and allow to come to room temperature once again. If they return to a liquid state, you can reprocess your jam, altering the ingredients to get a better set. Otherwise, simply keep them stored in the refrigerator until you're ready to eat them.

Heat Processing for Long-Term Storage

When your jam, jelly, or pickle is ready to process, remove one jar at a time from the hot water bath, draining any residual water back into the pot. Place the jars on a clean baking sheet for ease of cleanup. Do not dry the jars with a towel; the extra water will evaporate from the heat. Ladle or pour the hot preserves or pickle into the hot jar, leaving about ⅓ to ½ inch of space from the top—do not be tempted to overfill your jars, as this will lead to an improper seal or the cracking of your jar. Slide a clean spatula down the inside of the jar to release any trapped air. Top off the contents if necessary and repeat until the jars are filled. Carefully wipe the rims with a clean, damp towel and position the hot lids before firmly screwing on the rings.

Place the filled jars back into the hot water bath, making sure they are covered by at least 1 inch of water, then position the lid on the pot and bring the water to a full boil over high heat. Process according to the recipe instructions, starting the timer when the water reaches a full boil. When the timer rings, turn off the heat, remove the lid from the pot, and allow the steam to clear for about 5 minutes. Remove the jars from the water bath without tilting them and place them upright on a towel to cool undisturbed.

After about 24 hours, check the lids for a seal by pressing down on the center of each one—they should show no movement. Lids that pop with movement when pressed have not sealed properly and must be refrigerated immediately. Label the sealed jars and store them in a cool, dry location, ideally between 50°F and 70°F.

heat and return to a simmer, then lower the heat to maintain a gentle simmer. Simmer for 15 minutes. Turn off the heat and allow to cool for at least 10 minutes, then strain the batch once more. Again, do not be tempted to squeeze the pulp! If you wish to extract all of the liquid, allow the bag to drip suspended over the bowl for several hours or overnight. You should end up with about 950 g / 1 quart of apple stock.

You can use this stock immediately for blending with other fruit to make jam or jelly; both work best if they include a high sugar and acid content. If not, you will need to add these in sufficient amounts to achieve a proper set. Alternatively, you can freeze apple pectin stock for future use. Cool the juice completely and pour into freezer-safe containers, leaving about 1 inch of headspace. Four cups of apple stock will replace approximately 3 ounces of commercial liquid pectin in most cases, but this is not a given, as the pectin content of any given apple will vary.

Using Agar-Agar

Agar-agar is a jelly-like substance that is obtained from algae and is often used in place of gelatin for those who don't eat animal products, but it can be a wonderful thickener for low-sugar jams or jellies as well. Dissolve a few grams (less than a teaspoon) in a ladle or two of warm liquid from your jam or jelly, stirring in toward the end of cooking. Return your preserves to a boil for 2 to 3 minutes before moving to sterilized jars.

Freezing

If you have space to accommodate summer's gift of produce, the freezer is an excellent place to store fresh vegetables at their peak of ripeness with little effort and maximum nutritive value. When harvested straight from the garden and moved to the freezer, foods contain more vitamins and minerals than if they were stored in the refrigerator before eating. Frozen foods are easy to use if preportioned and properly labeled indicating their identity and amount. They make meal prep a breeze, as the action of freezing and thawing deteriorates cell walls, encouraging faster cooking time. This is particularly helpful when making Quickie Congee (page 241), decreasing the cooking time from 1 to 2 hours to about 30 minutes. Frozen foods will keep well for a long period of time if stored properly, making sure that you freeze them quickly in well-sealed bags or containers to prevent freezer burn. Make sure your freezer is maintained at a temperature of 0°F or lower to avoid large ice crystals from forming in your foods.

Unfortunately, store-bought frozen foods can vary widely in their quality and additives used. For these reasons, it is best to prepare your own, especially if you have a garden, are a CSA member, or have access to a farmers' market. Some fruits and vegetables need little preparation before going into the freezer. Others require a quick blanch to stabilize them in colder temperatures. When vegetables are harvested, enzymes are at work that both break down vitamin C and turn sugars into starches. This process is slowed by cold temperatures but is not completely stopped; the only way to arrest or stop enzyme activity is through heat. A quick blanching will both help you achieve this and preserve the food's vibrant colors upon thawing.

To blanch vegetables, prepare an ice bath in a large bowl or pot with water and several

cups of ice cubes. Bring a large pot of water to a boil and drop your vegetables into the pot in small handfuls. For soft vegetables, such as leafy greens, fiddlehead ferns, and corn kernels, a quick 10- to 15-second blanch is sufficient. Other vegetables, such as cabbage, broccoli, and cauliflower, enjoy a 3- to 4-minute blanch. Harder vegetables, such as beets, are best fully cooked before frozen. When they're ready, use tongs or a sieve to transfer the vegetables to the ice bath to halt the cooking process.

Generally speaking, foods that are best suited for freezing are foods that you might cook before eating, such as beets, tomatoes, Brussels sprouts, rhubarb, or corn. Salad vegetables, such as radishes or cucumbers, that are normally eaten raw are better preserved using other methods, such as fermentation or quick pickling. The following are a few tips for preserving some of the ingredients most used in this book.

- **Greens.** Leafy greens (with the exception of lettuces), such as beet green tops, kale, Swiss chard, and spinach, are excellent quickly blanched and wrung of excess moisture. You may choose to coarsely chop them before storing.

- **Herbs.** Freezing herbs is an excellent way to preserve an end-of-season harvest. Try processing a large handful with ¼ cup water in a mini food processor, then freezing in ice cube trays. Alternatively, you can mix chopped herbs with softened butter or oil and freeze the herb butter in cubes. The cubes may be popped out, stored individually, and used to season soups, braises, and stir-fries.

- **Tomatoes.** My favorite way to freeze tomatoes is by placing them on a baking sheet, freezing them whole, and then storing them in large plastic bags to be pulled for later use. Once thawed, their skins slip easily from the flesh, avoiding the blanching and peeling step recommend for storing fresh tomatoes. They also keep wonderfully when cooked down into a coulis or thick sauce (see page 293) before being portioned into bags and frozen lying flat. This method saves space because you can stack them, or you can store them in freezer containers. Frozen tomatoes are best consumed cooked once thawed.

- **Corn.** Corn can be frozen on or off the cob but is best quickly blanched before heading to the freezer to avoid a starchy cardboard flavor upon thawing. Use in salads, soups, or Kale, Corn, and Fermented Mushroom and Onion Strata (page 275).

- **Green Beans.** Fresh beans are a delightful treat pulled from the freezer in the height of winter and prepared with Walnut and Cilantro Sauce (page 25). Pick when pods are of desired length but before the seeds fully form. Wash and drain before snapping any tough ends. Blanch in boiling water for 2 to 3 minutes or steam for 3 to 4 minutes before

OPPOSITE Clockwise from top left: Phaseolus vulgaris, *or the common bean, has Mesoamerican origins. The study of its genetic composition has led to a greater ability not only to preserve its diversity but to develop improved cultivars, such as the stringless French pole bean 'Fortex.' Blanching and then shocking green vegetables, such as these fiddlehead ferns (*Matteuccia struthiopertis) *in ice-cold water helps to preserve their vibrancy even after freezing and thawing. Swiss chard (*Beta vulgaris subsp. vulgaris) *is an ancient leafy green closely related to the beet (*Beta vulgaris) *and prefers a cool growing environment. Its vitamin-rich ornamental leaves can be harvested from the base of the rosette, leaving the plant to produce new leaves all season.*

packing in plastic bags and freezing flat to maximize storage space.

- **Peppers.** Harvest hot chilies or green, red, or yellow peppers when fully ripe with thick, glossy skin and firm flesh. Wash, halve, and remove the seeds. It is not necessary to blanch peppers before freezing, but you may wish to do so to relax their flesh and conserve space with easier packing. You may also roast or char peppers before freezing according to the directions on page 99.

Dehydrating and Drying

Drying is an easy and space-saving way to make seasonings, teas, delicious snacks, and convenience foods. By removing the water from fresh fruits or vegetables, you save space as well as preserve essential vitamins and minerals that are otherwise lost through heat processing or canning. Five pounds of produce can easily become half a pound for months to come. Drying is also a necessary technique if you wish to soak your nuts and seeds before eating them to eliminate phytates and other antinutrients from your diet.

Drying happens through evaporation and water loss, a process that requires sufficient air flow to achieve. The drier and sometimes warmer the air temperature, the faster evaporation will occur. This can be done by various means including your oven to make Fig Leaf Powder (page 23), dried rose hips, or dried tomatoes. The minimum temperature of a home oven can be too high for some applications, such as Kishk Powder (page 42), which is traditionally dried on trays and set out in the sun. The ideal drying temperature for most foods to preserve their optimal value is between 95°F and 145°F. Anything above may encourage a skin to form on the outside, trapping moisture on the inside and cooking instead of drying your food. In addition, vitamins and minerals normally preserved at lower temperatures may be lost. However, temperatures of 90°F or below may encourage mold and spoilage microbes, especially in humid environments.

When using an oven, avoid placing your food closer than 6 to 8 inches to either the top or bottom and consider propping the door open if the temperature cannot be adjusted below 175°F. Dehydrators are a preferred method and are more affordable and safer than ever, equipped with fan assists for increased air flow and adjustable temperature settings for better control of the evaporation process. They free up your oven as well, allowing you to keep the kitchen cooler in summer and the evaporation process going regardless of the weather. Whether you are using a dehydrator or your oven, check on your food frequently toward the end of the drying process to ensure chewy and succulent rather than brittle or tough results. You will need to dry herbs completely to avoid mold from forming in longer-term storage.

The cheapest and sometimes easiest way to dehydrate your food is to harness the power of the almighty sun, especially if you live in an arid environment with long, cloudless summer days. If this is your method, you will need to consider a few additional precautions, namely protecting your food with netting from opportunistic insects or animals. It is also advisable to secure a few drying racks by either pulling screening across stackable wooden frames or using baker's cooling racks positioned over baking sheets.

This will help to ensure adequate air flow around your food. In recipes for drying meat, such as Basturma (page 285), you will need to pay more attention to relative air humidity while the meat hangs and continues curing in a warm but not too hot environment out of the glaring sun.

Thin-skinned or dry-fleshed herbs and vegetables, such as mature peas and beans, small hot peppers, fava beans, and rosemary, air-dry fairly quickly, as do fruits such as apricots, persimmons, dates, and prunes that are naturally inclined to air-drying. Juicier, plump fruits, such as tomatoes, may need extra heat and ventilation to thoroughly dry if left whole. A dehydrator or your oven will speed along the process. Some vegetables may require steaming after slicing before you dry them to assist in the evaporation process. Pre-steaming also halts ripening, preserves color, and may prevent undesirable flavors from developing during storage. Place in a steam basket over 2 to 3 inches of water, cover, and steam until slightly softened and the color of the vegetable has just brightened. It is not necessary to cool before placing in a dehydrator or oven.

FIG LEAF POWDER

Makes ½ cup

I am often asked what my favorite fruit, vegetable, or flour is. The answer often reflects the season in which it is asked. And if it's fig season—a short space of time in the Northeast—it will no doubt be ambrosially flavored figs. Plants that possess more than one edible part will always win my favor, and the underappreciated flavor and aroma of fig leaves has sealed their place on my short list

of favorites. I have used them fresh to wrap and steam fish, dried whole to infuse ice cream custard or heavy cream for whipping, and toasted and powdered as a spice condiment for dressings or sprinkling over fresh fruits such as Heirloom Melon Salad with Tarragon and Fig Leaf Powder (page 271). You'll be surprised by the sweet, coconut-like aroma fig leaves impart to any dish, lending a complex and elusive flavor that will win over the palate of just about any skeptic.

To make fig leaf powder, you can either dehydrate or toast the leaves before grinding them into a powder. The flavor profile of the two are quite different: dehydrated leaves lend a bright, fresh green splash to a dish, while toasted leaves will have a nuttier character and brownish color. Fig leaves are best harvested from your own tree, as they weep sap and quickly wilt upon picking.

25 fresh fig leaves

TO DEHYDRATE FOR A GREEN POWDER

Wash and dry the fig leaves. If using a dehydrator, arrange the leaves in a single layer on each rack and dry overnight. If using your oven, preheat it as low as it will allow and arrange the leaves in a single layer on several baking sheets. Place in the oven and dehydrate for 6 to 8 hours, until dry and crispy to the touch.

TO BROIL FOR A TOASTED POWDER

Wash and dry the fig leaves. Turn the broiler to high and position a rack about 4 inches from the heat source. Place the fig leaves on a baking sheet and place under the broiler. With the oven door open, keep an eye on the leaves, watching for curling. Pay careful attention, as they will toast and then burn quickly. Most broilers will require only 30 to 45 seconds before the leaves are toasted brown and ready to be removed. Allow to cool.

Using your hands, roughly crush the dried leaves into a large bowl and discard any large or tough midribs. Then grind in batches in a coffee grinder or spice grinder to a powder. Sift through a fine-mesh sieve to remove any coarse bits. Store in a lidded container at room temperature for up to 1 year.

Pretreatment for Color Retention

Pretreating certain fruits will help them retain a vibrant color. This is done commercially most often using sulfur, a naturally occurring chemical element that some people with allergies may be sensitive to. As an alternative, you may slice and then dip your fruits in a bath of ascorbic acid, lemon juice, or honey water, each with their own effectiveness and contribution to flavor.

- **To use ascorbic acid:** Dissolve ¼ teaspoon ascorbic acid in 1 quart water.

- **To make a honey and lemon dip:** Whisk 1 cup honey into 1 cup water until dissolved and add the juice of 1 lemon.

- **To make a honey only dip:** Whisk at least ¼ cup or up to 2 cups honey into 2 cups water until dissolved.

FROM TOP TO BOTTOM *Ficus carica, or the common fig, is one of the first cultivated fruits. It has many cultivars including this prized 'Panache' tiger stripe whose superior candy-sweet flavor and raspberry red interior has earned it its position as a favorite heirloom variety. Fresh fig leaves infuse creams and custards with a flavor close to vanilla but when toasted add a nutty aroma reminiscent of coconut. Dried or toasted, they can be pulverized and sprinkled as a finishing spice.*

FRUIT FLOUR

If you have an abundance of ripe, sweet fruit, you can dehydrate it to make a fruit powder that you can substitute for granulated sugar or flour with added flavor and nutrition. Allow the fruit to dry longer than you would normally—to a brittle consistency—before running it through a food processor, high-powered blender, or spice grinder to a fine powder. Sift and store in a lidded container in a cool, dry location for up to 3 months.

Soaking and Dehydrating Nuts

Nuts contain a number of enzyme inhibitors that can unnecessarily tax the digestive system when consumed in large quantities. But they are incredibly nutritious when properly prepared. To ensure their nutrients are more readily available and your digestive system remains at ease, it is best to soak nuts before making milks or dehydrating them. Consider adding salt to the soaking water to further activate the enzymes that neutralize inhibitors. Use 1 tablespoon sea salt per quart of water.

Smaller nuts with high fat content, such as cashews and macadamia nuts, need a 4- to 6-hour soak. Larger nuts with protective outer skins, such as hazelnuts, pecans, walnuts, and Brazil nuts require a longer soaking time: 12 to 24 hours. For seeds such as pepitas (pumpkin seeds) or sunflower seeds, soaking time will be about 12 hours. If your kitchen is extremely warm during the summer months, consider moving extended soaks to the refrigerator. Always begin with raw nuts and cover them with at least 2 inches of water.

Drain and rinse the nuts in a colander and pat dry, then place in the oven at its lowest temperature or a dehydrator for 12 to 24 hours, until crispy and dry. If your oven's lowest temperature setting is above 175°F, consider propping the door or check periodically to ensure the nuts are done. Store as you would raw nuts and use them to make Sweet Potato Tart with a Coconut Pecan Crust (page 112).

WALNUT AND CILANTRO SAUCE

Makes about 1¾ cups

This bright, herbaceous sauce is commonly found in the canon of Eastern European, and in particular, Caucasian cuisine. It is a versatile accompaniment to grilled meat or roasted fish and is found in many variations depending on its creator and the dish it is served alongside. Although cilantro and parsley are the main herbs, you may alternate the others depending on availability—mint, summer savory, tarragon, dill, or basil all work well. Using freshly soaked walnuts makes for a smooth and creamy sauce without adding too much extra oil. If using soaked and dried walnuts instead, increase the amount of oil to 1 cup or supplement with tahini sauce instead to create a creamy effect. If you have the time and patience, this is wonderful made with a mortar and pestle, as the integrity of the herbs is preserved and the sauce retains a delightful texture. Serve stirred into Asparagus and Amaranth Soup (page 229) or toss with gently steamed green beans or the vegetable of your choice.

1 cup raw walnuts	1½ packed cups cilantro leaves
4 plump cloves garlic	1 packed cup fresh parsley leaves
¼ cup fresh lemon or lime juice	1½ cups additional herb leaves such as basil, dill, savory, or tarragon
1 teaspoon fine salt, or to taste	
½ cup walnut oil	
2 to 3 scallions, coarsely chopped	¼ teaspoon red pepper flakes, or to taste

At least 12 hours before making the sauce, place the walnuts in a medium bowl and add water to cover by at least 2 inches. Drain the water and lightly rinse the nuts. Place the garlic, lemon juice, and salt in a food processor and finely chop the garlic. Add the walnuts and oil and process to a thin paste, then pulse in the scallions and herbs until just combined. Adjust for salt and add red pepper flakes to taste. The sauce will keep tightly covered with plastic wrap over the surface (to avoid discoloration) in the refrigerator for up to 2 days.

SPICY MAPLE PECANS

Makes 4 cups

I developed this recipe after visiting southern Georgia, where the sweetest, richest pecans I have ever tasted are grown. Although they need little additional treatment to make them delicious, I wanted an extra crunchy texture for a salad of arugula, shaved fennel, and pickled strawberries. You may substitute any soaked and dried nut that you wish.

4½ cups soaked and dehydrated pecans (see page 25)	1 large egg white, at room temperature
2 tablespoons unsalted butter, melted	½ teaspoon cayenne pepper, or to taste
⅓ cup maple syrup	¼ teaspoon ground cinnamon
	¼ teaspoon fine sea salt

Preheat the oven to 250°F and line a baking sheet with parchment paper.

Spread the nuts onto the prepared sheet, pour the melted butter and maple syrup over the nuts, and toss to coat.

In the bowl of a stand mixer, combine the egg white, cayenne, cinnamon, and salt, and whip to soft peaks. Fold the coated nuts into the egg whites, then return them to the baking sheet and spread them out in a single layer.

Place in the oven and bake for 35 to 40 minutes, stirring three to four times to encourage even drying, until the nuts are fragrant and toasted. To test, pull a few from the oven and allow to cool completely. If the coating and nuts firm up to a crunchy texture, they are ready. Cool completely on the pan and store in a cool, dry location until ready to use, up to 1 week.

Making Vegetable Broths

Avoid waste by reserving your discarded ends and peels for making vegetable broth or stock. Many scraps, including the stems of herbs or the ribs of Swiss chard as well as the rinds of hard cheeses such as Parmesan-Reggiano, are excellent candidates for flavor. Feel free to substitute the greens of leeks or the tough ends of green garlic for the standard onion. You may save up your ends and peels, stuff them into a plastic bag, and store them in the freezer until you are ready to make your broth. Although I prefer to lightly salt broth after it has reduced, you may wish to omit the salt altogether, allowing for greater flexibility in use. Use these inspired vegetable broths to cook grains in place of water, for braising vegetables, or for building flavorful soups. If you have freezer space, keep a variety of broths on hand. Label their flavor profiles to match them to your recipes.

RUBY CHARD BROTH

Makes about 7 cups

If you aren't quick pickling your Swiss chard stems, using them to make a flavorful broth is a resourceful way to take advantage of this neglected ingredient. Just a few ruby-colored ribs will add a beautiful hue to your broth. This recipe is excellent for cooking a vegetarian borscht or preparing a savory porridge. For an easy lunch or dinner, I use this broth to prepare quick-cooking buckwheat soba noodles, whatever vegetables are found in the fridge, and a flurry of fresh herbs or sliced scallions.

1 pound Swiss chard stems (from about 3 bunches)

2 stalks celery, halved lengthwise

1 large carrot, cut into 2- to 3-inch chunks

1 medium onion, quartered

5 plump cloves garlic

3 large bay leaves

1 teaspoon black peppercorns

12 cups water

Salt, to taste

Combine all the ingredients in a large stockpot. Cover and bring to a boil over high heat. Reduce the heat to maintain a simmer and cook uncovered for 30 to 45 minutes. Adjust for salt, if using. Strain through a fine-mesh sieve and cool. The broth will keep covered for up to 1 week in the refrigerator or 1 year in the freezer.

GREEN BITS GINGER BROTH

Makes about 8 cups

Apple peels are excellent candidates for making apple cider vinegar, but if I have the ingredients for this recipe on hand, I will often throw them into a big pot for making broth. They add brightness and beg to be combined with fresh herb stems. This recipe is excellent for preparing a vegetarian Quickie Congee (page 241).

1½ pounds stalks and fronds from about 3 large fennel bulbs

1 medium onion

2 cups apple peels (from about 3 apples)

2½ ounces parsley stalks (from 1 to 2 bunches of parsley)

1 large knob fresh ginger

5 plump cloves garlic

3 bay leaves

1 teaspoon black peppercorns

16 cups water

Salt, to taste

Combine all the ingredients in a large stockpot. Cover and bring to a boil over high heat. Reduce the heat to maintain a simmer and cook uncovered for 30 to 45 minutes. Adjust for salt, if using. Strain through a fine-mesh sieve and cool. The broth will keep covered for up to 1 week in the refrigerator or 1 year in the freezer.

CORN COB BROTH

Makes about 6 cups

This is a versatile vegetarian broth that makes use of the humble corn cob, a bulky but flavorful scrap that typically sees little use in the kitchen. Make this in batches when fresh summer corn is in abundance, maximizing the whole ear by boiling the husks, stripped cobs, and silks in the pot. The flavor is remarkably sweet and excellent for stews, soups, porridge, or for making Lemony Vegetarian Cabbage Rolls (page 277).

6 corn cobs with their husks and silks, kernels removed

1 large carrot, cut into 2- to 3-inch chunks

Handful of fresh parsley and/or cilantro stems

3 sprigs fresh thyme

2 dried bay leaves

2 garlic scapes (or 1 clove garlic)

2 plump cloves garlic

12 cups water

Salt, to taste

Combine all the ingredients in a large stockpot. Cover and bring to a boil over high heat. Reduce the heat to maintain a simmer and cook uncovered for 30 to 45 minutes or until it has reduced by at least one third. (The longer you simmer, the more concentrated the corn flavor will become.) Adjust for salt, if using. Strain through a fine-mesh sieve and cool. The broth will keep covered for up to 1 week in the refrigerator or 1 year in the freezer.

OPPOSITE *Corn cobs add a delicate sweetness to an otherwise savory broth.*

2

MEAT AND ANIMAL PRODUCTS

OPPOSITE *Heritage poultry such as the Chilean Araucana have been used to develop improved breeds such as this Ameraucana prized for their beautiful powder blue eggs.*

Heritage Meat

Seeking out ethical and sustainably raised meat is an excellent way to engage in traceability and may save you money, especially if you purchase a whole or half animal from a local farmer or their processor (for suggestions on how to connect to small farmers, see Resources, page 324). Slower-growing heritage breeds are favored for their superior flavor and amenability to traditional farming methods best suited to a particular climate or region. You may, however, find yourself with a freezer of obscure cuts or bags of animal parts that you have no idea how to use.

I have had the great fortune to work with a number of talented farmers whose thoughtful approach has been a true inspiration. One such farmer who raises a small heritage breed of pigs called American Guinea Hog inspired the recipe for the Bacon-Wrapped Pork Loin with Charred Cabbage and Prune Sauce (page 179). I developed this recipe for a special fundraising dinner for the Red Hills Small Farm Alliance in north Florida. I wanted to honor the hard work, time, and resources that went into raising these animals but had never worked with or even tasted American Guinea Hog. Its sweet marbled meat and superior quality lard far surpassed my expectations, but I had not anticipated the difference in the cuts of this breed. In particular, the animal was so small that the loin was significantly thinner than a conventionally raised pig. Luckily, I had been paired with an up-and-coming chef who was not afraid to wield a hack saw to divvy up the loin that the butcher left attached to the thick spine and ribs. We seared and rendered the gorgeous lard, slow-cooked the portions with onions, prunes, and aromatics, and then carefully separated the meat from the bone. A few head-scratching moments of resourcefulness from the kitchen crew resulted in divinely delicious results.

I often use this story as an example of working with small farmers who raise or grow heritage breeds whose unfamiliar and sometimes inconsistent attributes can be challenging to the home cook. When trying to support a regional agricultural economy, we must adapt to these surprises, acknowledging the opportunities that are coupled with breeds that have not been developed for industrial processing. This especially applies to livestock and also wheat whose legacy may yield unparalleled flavor but needs to be cooked or fermented very differently than their conventional counterparts. Because the footprint of heirloom agricultural information is so specialized, it brings a community closer by sharing knowledge and enthusiasm for regional identity.

Rendering Animal Fat

Rendering animal fat is one way to avoid waste as well as honor the labor and resources that went into raising and butchering the animal. Rendering is the process of purifying fat and separating it from other parts including blood, connective tissue, and meat. The result is lard from pork, schmaltz from chicken, goose, or duck, tallow from beef or lamb, and ghee or clarified butter from milk fat. These are excellent alternatives to heavily processed and refined vegetable oils that have been bleached and filtered to remove minerals and enzymes that are volatile under high heat. Use rendered animal fat in the kitchen for searing, frying, or otherwise cooking at elevated temperatures.

Regardless of the animal or the resulting name, the process is relatively the same for rendering and clarifying. Separate the fat from the milk solids or the meat and bones and melt over low heat until the solids separate and the water in the fat evaporates. You will be left with a clear, clean fat that can then be used in cooking or to make soap, candles, or moisturizer.

It is of paramount importance to source fat from healthy, free-range or pastured animals that are free of antibiotics. Impurities are stored as toxins in animal fat and organs, and we are seeking to minimize or eliminate those from our diets! Small butchers are often happy and relieved to find a way to discard excess fat, so talk to them ahead of time and ask them to set some aside for you.

RENDERED ANIMAL FAT

Yield is variable

Although clarifying is most often done with pork fat, it works well with just about any animal, although at varying rates and yields. I like to begin on a morning when I know I'm spending the day in the kitchen, so I can keep a close eye on the rendering. Although you can follow this method beginning with any amount of fat, I suggest starting with at least 5 pounds to maximize your time and resources.

Properly rendered fat holds well at room temperature. I keep a small dish beside the stove and the remainder under cooler temperatures in the refrigerator for up to 1 year when covered. It will keep indefinitely in the freezer and is an excellent source for grating into piecrusts for flaky results. Once the fat has cooled completely, it will transform from a clear, sometimes golden liquid to a thick and creamy consistency.

5 pounds animal fat

When you have secured a good source for your fat, freeze it first. This will make it easier to handle, especially in warm temperatures. Remove any excess meat and chop the fat into small pieces. You can do this using a knife, scissors, or a food processor for large batches. If you are using a food processor, make sure the fat is fully frozen to avoid gumming up the blade.

Place the fat in a slow cooker or a large, heavy pot (ovenproof if placing in the oven). Cook in the slow cooker set to low, on the stovetop over very low heat, or in the oven at a very low setting. The goal

Clarified pork fat, commonly known as lard, is an excellent choice for making flaky piecrusts or for high-heat cooking such as frying.

is to keep the temperature hovering between 200°F and 212°F. If you are rendering pork, chicken, beef, or lamb fat, cook until you have browned cracklings swimming in a bath of clear fat. These are excellent drained and mixed into the batter for Herman's Heirloom Cornbread (page 220) or folded into Sweet Jane (page 82). Depending on the type and size of fat pieces, the clarifying process will likely take anywhere from 2 to 6 hours. Once the solids have separated from the fat, remove from the heat and allow to cool slightly, then pour through a sieve or funnel lined with cheesecloth to catch any fine particles. Filter the fat directly into a glass or ceramic container, cool completely, cover, and store as per the notes above.

CLARIFIED BUTTER AND BROWN BUTTER (BEURRE NOISETTE)

Yield is approximately 1½ cups

This recipe for creating clarified butter has the option of pushing it further to brown butter or beurre noisette, a deliciously nutty option for using in cakes such as Whey Caramel Upside-Down Fruitcake (page 49), porridges, pilafs such as Brown Butter Apricot Kasha (page 252), cookies, breads such as Brown Butter Sourdough Banana Bread (page 154), or for dressing roasted vegetables.

1 pound unsalted butter

Melt the butter in a large, wide saucepan over medium-low heat. As the butter melts and water begins to evaporate, it will separate into three

1 Begin with good quality, high fat butter. 2 Melt the butter slowly. 3 As the butter melts, foam will begin to appear on the surface. 4 Patience pays off when clarifying or browning butter. 5 Skim the foam from the top of the melted butter to clarify. 6 With more time, the butter will deepen in color and the bubbles will appear clear and effervescent with the solids sinking to the bottom. 7 When the solids have toasted to a deep golden brown and the aroma is noticeably nutty, remove from the heat.

layers: foam on top, golden clarified butter, and milk solids that will settle to the bottom. When you see these distinct layers appear, you have several options, including skimming away the foam and pouring off the clarified butter to use as a high-heat option for cooking or frying foods. Cool and store in a covered container at room temperature for up to 1 month or in the refrigerator for up to 1 year.

Continue cooking, and the milk solids will turn a toasty golden brown and the butter will become fragrant with hints of caramel. At this point, remove the pan from the heat and skim off the top foamy layer. You may then transfer the whole thing to a clean jar and store in the refrigerator for up to 3 weeks.

Making Broth, Bone Broth, and Stock

Rich in trace minerals, gelatin, collagen, and not to mention incredibly soothing, broths and stocks are traditional in many parts of the world that make use of the whole animal in their diets. Broths, bone broths, and stocks vary in ingredients and length of time they cook. The following explains the difference among the three.

- **Animal-based broths.** Animal-based broths are cooked with meat and often some bones, a mirepoix of vegetables, and seasonings including salt, pepper, and often bay leaves. After simmering for a short amount of time (usually between 30 minutes and 2½ hours depending on the meat), a thin and flavorful liquid is produced that is excellent for cooking whole grains or to use as a foundation to building soups and porridges. Broths are rich in protein.

- **Bone broths.** These are mostly bone with a small amount of meat attached. The bones can be roasted for deeper flavor and are seasoned with a mirepoix of vegetables. They are simmered longer than broths to extract the full nutrition from the bones, in particular trace minerals and collagen that gelatinizes when it cools. Bone broths are traditionally cooked on the stovetop for anywhere between 8 hours for chicken and up to 24 hours for denser bones such as lamb or beef. You may also use a slow cooker. If you sweat at the thought of a pot heating your kitchen for longer than an hour, you may want to invest in an Instant Pot or pressure cooker, which will cook the contents under pressure and cut cooking time immensely.

- **Stocks.** Stocks, like bone broths, include only trace amounts of meat (such as a chicken carcass or turkey or beef neck bone) and the bones are traditionally roasted to add flavor. Stocks differ in that they are simmered for less time, typically 3 to 4 hours.

CHICKEN STOCK/ BONE BROTH

Makes about 2 quarts

This recipe is an excellent follow-up to Butter-Roasted Sumac Chicken (page 245), as it makes use of its carcass to produce a flavorful, nourishing stock or bone broth. To keep the broth clear, do not let it cook higher than a simmer, as vigorous boiling will cloud the end result.

Carcass from a 4½- to 5-pound chicken	1 large carrot, cut into 3-inch pieces
1½ cups coarsely chopped fennel stems, cores, and fronds	3 plump cloves garlic
	Four to five 4-inch sprigs fresh thyme
1 small onion, quartered	3½ quarts water
1 stalk celery, cut into 3-inch pieces	1½ teaspoons kosher salt, or to taste

Combine all the ingredients in a large stockpot and bring to a boil over high heat. Lower the heat to maintain a gentle simmer and cook partially covered for about 2 hours to produce a flavorful stock, or up to 24 hours to reduce to a more concentrated bone broth. Strain into a heatproof bowl and taste for salt. Cool to room temperature, then cover and refrigerate. Skim the surface of excess fat before using (you can use it for cooking). Store in a lidded container in the refrigerator for up to 5 days or in the freezer for 6 months.

BEEF BROTH

Makes about 2 quarts

Butchers are often happy to set you aside their beef bones or will keep them stocked in the freezer section. I prefer to use oxtail in this recipe, as its flavorful meat is excellent for hearty stews such as Oxtail Borscht with Sour Cherries and Purple Barley (page 176). You may substitute lamb or pork bones in this recipe instead.

1½ to 2 tablespoons kosher salt, or to taste	1 stalk celery
	1 large carrot
2 pounds beef oxtail	2 plump cloves garlic
1 tablespoon extra-virgin olive oil	2 bay leaves
3½ quarts water	6 whole cloves
1 large onion, halved	1 teaspoon peppercorns, crushed

Place the oxtail on a plate or baking sheet and sprinkle 1½ teaspoons of the salt over it. Allow to come to room temperature for about 1 hour.

Heat the oil in a large stockpot over medium-high heat until hot, 1 to 2 minutes. Add the oxtail in a single layer and sear undisturbed for 3 to 4 minutes. Flip over and brown on the second side. Pour in the water and add the remaining salt, the onion, celery, carrot, garlic, bay leaves, cloves, and peppercorns. Bring just to a simmer over high heat, then reduce the heat to maintain a low simmer and skim the surface. Partially cover and cook for at least 2½ hours, until the meat is tender and falling off of the bone, making sure it doesn't start to boil (or it will turn the broth cloudy). Strain the stock into a heatproof bowl and taste for salt. Reserve the meat for making Oxtail Borscht with Sour Cherries and Purple Barley (page 176). Cool to room temperature, then cover and refrigerate. Skim the surface of excess fat before using (you can use it for cooking). Store in a lidded container in the refrigerator for up to 5 days or in the freezer for 6 months.

Fermenting Dairy

Cultured milk in the form of butter, yogurt, or cheese has many benefits beyond its irresistible complexity of flavor. As with most fermented foods, culturing not only improves the taste but also extends the shelf life of milk, exposes the gut to beneficial probiotics, and makes the raw ingredients more digestible. The following recipes attempt to explain some of the microbiology behind these beloved cultures and encourage you to use some, such as yogurt and milk kefir, as agents for further fermentation.

Yogurt and Milk Kefir

What do you do with milk if you don't have a refrigerator or you have too much of it? These are perhaps the questions that led the first herdsmen of cows, sheep, goats, and even camels not only to embrace the spontaneous fermentation of their raw milk but to propagate it indefinitely as an heirloom culture.

When I began making homemade yogurt, I was rewarded with success using an instant-read thermometer, some crude equipment, and very little understanding of the process. But over time, I found the yogurt would fade in potency several batches later. What I had failed to consider was that most commercial yogurts are made from a direct set culture of two isolated strains of thermophilic (heat-loving) bacteria: *Lactobacillus delbrueckii* subsp. *bulgaricus* and *Streptococcus thermophilus*. These are essentially isolated and reproduced in a lab before being introduced into milk. This milk is heated beforehand to denature its proteins and to allow for evaporation or thickening before being inoculated. The microbes then metabolize lactose (milk sugars) to produce tangy lactic acid, which lowers the pH of the milk, affecting its texture and extending its shelf life. This method produces a consistently reliable commercial product but is not a representation of a dynamic, undefined community of microbes that can keep a culture alive and thriving from one batch to another.

But since fermentation has increased in popularity, more commercial blends with a greater diversity of microbes are now available. Each culture, whether captured by clabbering raw milk or using a lab-fabricated powder, will prefer a different set of environmental circumstances to thrive and will produce wildly different end products. The advantage of a commercial starter is that you can select and regulate the taste and texture of your yogurt more easily, so you can decide how mild or sour, gelatinous, thick, or thin your yogurt will be. As with any homemade product, your power lies in your choice of ingredients, and you can tailor the method to your preferences.

You may, however, attempt to capture your own culture simply by leaving raw, unpasteurized milk to sit at room temperature until it clabbers, or clots and sours. Success varies based on the bacterial population in the milk: it needs to be high enough to bring on fermentation and acidification before the milk spoils. If you are successful, it is important to use that culture at the same temperature using the same method in successive batches. Thermophilic cultures require a culturing time of at least 5 hours or up to 24 hours at a sustained, warm temperature and yield a yogurt with a thick texture. Conversely, mesophilic cultures thrive at room temperature and yield yogurt that's much thinner in consistency. If you are using raw milk, choose a starter culture that reproduces at 110°F to maintain the enzymatic benefits of the raw milk.

If the temperature specifics of yogurt making sound intimidating or you have limited success at home, you may want to consider making your own milk kefir instead. Brain-shaped kefir granules, a fascinating symbiosis of bacteria and yeasts assembled into a physical manifestation, possess a greater variety of beneficial microbes than yogurt and culture milk at room temperature.

Making kefir requires only a strainer, a few clean jars, and a healthy appetite. The grains need to be fed every few days to keep them thriving, making a milk kefir practice a commitment. Kefir, like yogurt, is an incredibly versatile ingredient and is used throughout this book as both a condiment and an agent of fermentation for bread porridges.

FRESH YOGURT

Makes about 8¼ cups

The following recipe requires about 15 minutes of preparation time using a thermophilic culture that prefers a warm temperature. You can use an heirloom starter that has been passed on to you or you can purchase a commercial starter (see Resources, page 324). If using a commercial starter, follow the directions on the package closely, as those microbes may have a very specific window of temperature preference. Be sure to have an instant-read thermometer on hand as well as a way to regulate and keep the inoculated milk warm while it ferments. A dehydrator with a temperature control setting, an Instant Pot, or a specialized yogurt maker all work well. Use the best milk you can source, and if, like me, you love the cream top, choose an unhomogenized brand or substitute heavy cream for ½ cup of the milk.

8 cups whole milk	4 tablespoons whole milk yogurt

Pour the milk into a large double boiler or heavy-bottomed pot and place over low heat. Heat as slowly as possible to avoid a granular or clumpy texture, stirring and scraping the bottom of the pot until the milk reaches 180°F on an instant-read thermometer. The edges will begin bubbling and the milk will lightly steam. Do not boil or scorch the milk. Turn off the heat and allow to cool for 5 to 10 minutes, until the temperature comes down to 110°F and it feels warm but not hot when dabbed on your wrist.

Ladle a cup or so of milk from the pot into a small bowl and whisk in the yogurt. Pour the mixture back into the pot or combine with the remaining milk in a large container. Cover with a cloth and leave to sit in a consistently warm location for at least 6 hours or up to 24 hours, checking periodically to gauge flavor and thickness. The longer it ferments, the tangier the yogurt will become. Store covered in the refrigerator for up to 3 weeks.

MILK KEFIR

This delicious and nutritive fermented milk beverage likely originated in the Caucasus Mountains, where it has long been regarded as an elixir of life. Its anti-inflammatory probiotic benefits and increased vitamin profile have won it a coveted position in both my daily diet and baking repertoire. It is easily reproduced using a SCOBY (symbiotic culture of bacteria and yeast) that may be purchased or given to you by a friend. If you are purchasing your SCOBY, follow the instructions on the package to rehydrate the culture before making the recipe. All you need is about a tablespoon of milk kefir grains to get started and a source of good-quality pasteurized milk or raw milk that is preferably no more than a day old.

The amount of milk you use will vary depending on the culture and how much you want to drink. At the minimum you will need to feed the grains 2 cups or up to 1 quart if you anticipate drinking that much. You may also double the recipe in a jar that will accommodate if you have a large family to feed! Just make sure you have 1 to 2 inches of headspace at the top to account for any increase from the gases the fermentation produces.

FOR THE INITIAL FERMENTATION

1 tablespoon milk kefir grains	2 cups to 1 quart whole milk

Labneh balls make an impressive table presentation when rolled in chopped, fresh herbs.

Fruit of your choosing

Place the kefir grains in a large jar, pour in the milk, and stir well to combine. Cover with a loose-fitting noncorrosive lid and allow to ferment at room temperature for 12 to 48 hours. As fermentation progresses, the bacteria will digest the lactose in the milk and lower the pH. The longer the kefir ferments, the thicker and more effervescent and tangy it will become.

Decant the kefir through a strainer into a clean jar and place the grains back into the bottom of your original jar, repeating the process. Over time, the grains will multiply or increase in size. When this happens, you may choose to scale up your recipe or give some to a friend.

If you wish to flavor the kefir to make a beverage, you may simply add spices such as ground cardamom or cinnamon and a little honey to taste. Or you may consider a second fermentation using fruit to flavor your kefir. For about every cup of kefir, add about half the volume of fruit, cover loosely, and leave at room temperature for up to 1 day. Strain and refrigerate.

LABNEH BALLS

Makes one 1-pint jar

I was a labneh enthusiast for years before experiencing eye-catching spheres of preserved labneh. Initially I assumed there was a significance behind the shape of the labneh balls, much in the same way other cultures celebrate the implied meaning of oranges for Chinese New Year or challah for Rosh Hashanah. We define not only events but ourselves through eating, and I have come to associate round foods with wholeness, unity, and respect for the lunar cycles that govern certain agricultural practices and religious holidays. Although labneh balls have no association with a particular event, they are ritually created in Lebanon at a specific time of year in large batches in response to summer milk production. This is when milk is sweetest and most abundant, both good reasons to preserve it for the months ahead.

Attractively rolled in herbs and spices and then set in olive oil, labneh balls can be made with many different flavor combinations. I prefer nigella seed, sometimes referred to as black cumin, for its distinctive flavor that compliments a Mediterranean-style meal. Use the following method to explore ingredients you love that are most readily available to you. I prefer these made with goat's milk yogurt, but cow's milk yogurt will work equally well. Either way, be sure to strain out as much moisture as possible before shaping the balls to keep them from cracking in the oil. You can also skip the dried herbs or spices and roll the balls in chopped fresh herbs such as mint, cilantro, and/or parsley moments before serving them alongside fresh pita or Nomad Flatbread (page 224) as part of a larger mezze spread.

FOR THE LABNEH

1 quart goat's or cow's milk yogurt

1¼ teaspoons kosher salt

1 large clove garlic, grated on a Microplane (optional)

1¼ teaspoons nigella seeds, toasted (optional)

1 cup extra-virgin olive oil, plus more for dipping your fingers

2 or 3 dried bay leaves

¼ teaspoon black peppercorns

FOR THE GARNISH (OPTIONAL)

2 tablespoons crushed dried mint

2 tablespoons crushed dried savory

1 tablespoon crushed dried oregano

1 tablespoon crushed dried thyme

PREPARE THE LABNEH

Stir together the yogurt, salt, and garlic and/or nigella seeds, if using, in a medium bowl. Transfer the yogurt to a nut milk bag or cheesecloth and place in a sieve or colander positioned over a bowl. Squeeze gently and tie off the loose end. Weight the bundle with a heavy jar, stone, or bowl to encourage as much moisture as possible to drip from the yogurt. Place in the refrigerator for 3 days, allowing the whey to drain completely from the yogurt to create a thick, cream cheese–like consistency. The yield will be about 380 g, or a scant 1¾ cup labneh, and about 440 g / 1¾ cups whey depending on the yogurt. You may use either of these products in recipes elsewhere in this book, such as Kishk Powder (on right) or Whey Caramel Upside-Down Fruitcake (page 49).

MAKE THE BALLS

Remove the strained yogurt from the bag or cloth and place it into a small bowl. Pour half of the oil into a sterilized jar and pour a few tablespoons oil into a small bowl. In a separate bowl, mix together all the herbs, if using. Slip the bay leaves and peppercorns into the jar. Dip your fingers into the oil bowl to keep them from sticking and form the labneh into balls about 1½ inches in diameter. If the balls are particularly sticky, place them on a parchment-lined baking tray in the refrigerator, uncovered, for an additional day to allow them to dry out. Roll each ball in the dried herbs, if using, and gently slip them into the jar. Fill the jar with balls to about 1½ inches from the rim and top off with the remaining oil. Store in the refrigerator for up to 3 weeks. Bring to room temperature before serving.

KISHK POWDER

Makes about 2¼ cups

When I began researching methods of making grains more digestible, I stumbled across literature on an obscure fermented powder called *kishk*. I was intrigued by its promised savory but sour quality and how the process of fermentation would decrease the troublesome aspects of wheat. Recipes for kishk vary greatly from the Middle East to the Caucasus and even into Central Asia and Mongolia. Although often referred to by the same name, they differ by both ingredients and methods based on the particular herding culture, cultural preferences, and the necessity to preserve animal milk into the winter months. Daunted by what seemed like specific environmental conditions, ingredients, and tools, I wrote it off as a technique I would never be able to replicate let alone enjoy properly prepared at the table. Brooklyn, after all, wasn't exactly teeming with flocks of sheep or goats.

Years later, I finally met the charismatic flavor of kishk in Lebanon. Lebanese home cooks are devoted preservationists, and any urban or remote kitchen or provisional storefront will proudly display a bountiful collection of brightly colored *mouneh*, the Arabic word for preserves. Kishk is considered more of a rural preservation tradition, found in places where goats, sheep, and cattle roam in abundance.

While I was in Lebanon, I visited a goat farm where they preserved kishk as a powder through a lengthy fermentation and dehydration process. It is first made into a salted, strained yogurt called labneh, then combined with bulghur wheat into a paste. The paste is then spread into thin layers on trays, covered with protective netting, and left to dehydrate on roofs in the scorching summer sun. Once completely dried into cake-like chunks, it is then ground into kishk powder by using specialized mills that are often shared collectively. I first enjoyed it in Beirut slathered on griddled flatbread manoushe, but it wasn't until it was prepared as a steaming morning porridge that I truly appreciated its unique attributes. I pleaded for a tutorial from my hosts, and as their method was translated, I scribbled it into my notebook. A year later, when I had stirred the last of my coveted stash into a steaming bowl back home, I mustered the bravery to replicate making kishk in my own kitchen.

The following is a relatively simple approach adapted from my Lebanese hosts and the iconic handbook *Nourishing Traditions*, a strong influence on my own recipes. I prefer to begin by making my own labneh (see page 41), or you may purchase labneh from a Middle Eastern grocer. If you wish to simplify, you can substitute Greek cow's milk yogurt, although it contains more water than its cheesy counterpart and will take longer to dehydrate. Although making it from commercial cow's milk yogurt doesn't yield the same funkiness as using homemade goat's milk labneh, it certainly delivers the digestive benefits of soaking and fermentation in a delicious presentation. A high-powered blender can be used with impressive results, but if you have an electric home mill, you can mill the kishk on the finest setting.

1 cup medium grind (#2) bulghur wheat	3 cups labneh, or strained yogurt, salted to taste

Combine the bulghur and labneh in a small bowl and stir until a thick paste forms. Line a large baking sheet with parchment or wax paper and spread the paste in a thin, even layer. Place in a warm, dry location, such as the oven with the pilot light on, lightly covered on your roof or patio in the dry summer sun, in a dehydrator on its lowest setting, or in a proofing box set to 85°F to 90°F. Once fully dried, transfer to a high-powered blender and blend, starting at low speed and gradually increasing the speed, making sure the powder does not become hot. If it begins to get warm, take a break for 10 to 15 minutes or place it in the freezer to cool before resuming. When it has been ground to a fine powder, place in an airtight container and store in the freezer for up to 1 year.

KEFIR SALAD DRESSING

Makes about 1 cup

This creamy ranch-style dressing is delicious drizzled over fresh spring lettuces and gently tossed right before serving. Straining the kefir through a cheesecloth-lined fine-mesh sieve for about an hour will help improve the consistency. The seasonings are flexible, but powdered onion and garlic will greatly boost its flavor.

1 cup Milk Kefir (page 39), strained (see headnote)	½ teaspoon onion powder
½ tablespoon fresh lemon juice	¾ teaspoon fine sea salt
½ tablespoon extra-virgin olive oil	1½ tablespoons fresh chopped herbs (dill, parsley, cilantro, basil, or chervil all work well)
½ of a small clove garlic, grated using a Microplane	

Combine the kefir, lemon juice, oil, garlic, onion powder, and salt in a large jar and secure the lid. Shake vigorously to combine, then stir in the herbs. Serve the day it is made.

CULTURED BUTTER

Makes about 1 pound

Nothing is more nourishing and decadent than a warm piece of homemade bread slathered with naturally sweet and salty cultured butter. Although I've used both mesophilic and thermophilic yogurt in this recipe with equal success, there are several ways to culture cream before agitating it to make butter. If you have milk kefir grains on hand, follow the recipe for Milk Kefir (page 39) to culture the cream before putting it in the food processor. Each culture produces a slightly different flavor, but either way your butter will be remarkably more delicious than anything you can purchase at most grocery stores, especially if you are starting with raw milk. If you balk at the idea of using a food processor to make butter, you may use an heirloom churner as my family collectively did, passing it around from one to the other on rainy afternoons. But if you don't have a porch and a banjo picker somewhere nearby to entertain you, your arms may give out before the butter is ready.

3 cups heavy cream

⅓ cup plain whole milk yogurt

¼ to ½ teaspoon flaked sea salt

Pour the cream into a large bowl and whisk in the yogurt to completely combine (alternatively, shake the ingredients in a large lidded jar). Cover and leave to culture at room temperature for at least 12 hours or up to 36 hours. When the cream has reached your desired flavor of sourness balanced with enhanced sweetness, transfer it to the refrigerator to chill and thicken for at least 2 hours or up to 3 days, then remove it from the refrigerator a few minutes before processing to let it warm slightly.

Pour the cultured cream into the bowl of a food processor and add the salt. Process on high speed for 3 to 4 minutes, until you see the curds separating from the buttermilk liquid in a clumping fashion. Line a sieve with cheesecloth and place it over a bowl. Slowly pour the buttermilk through the sieve, then transfer the curds to the sieve. When the buttermilk has drained mostly free from the curds, gather the cheesecloth and gently squeeze the butter ball to release any last liquid into the bowl. Using a clean cloth or paper towel, pat the butter ball free of any excess moisture.

Optional: To give your butter a smooth and light consistency, wipe the bowl of the food processor dry and return the butter ball to the food processor. Whip the butter on high speed until it is smooth and creamy. Transfer to a clean cheesecloth or a container and serve immediately or store in the refrigerator for up to 2 weeks. Let come to room temperature before serving.

Yes Whey!

One of the most delightful home fermentation practices is creating your own yogurt or even straining store-bought yogurt into labneh, a thick and creamy spreadable cheese (page 41). The by-product of this process is a yellowish liquid called whey (whey can also be a by-product of cheese making). It is often discarded, but it is in fact a versatile, probiotic-rich ingredient that can jump-start fermentation.

The term *lacto-fermentation* can be somewhat misleading, as it does not necessarily refer to milk products or ferments using whey. It simply refers to the lactic acid bacteria that are a member of a suite of microbes responsible for most fermentation processes. When subjected to an anaerobic environment with an abundance of bioavailable food, *Lactobacillus* sp. will eagerly convert sugars into lactic acid. This lowers the pH of the ferment, which in return acts as a preservative by inhibiting other harmful microbes from thriving.

Vegetables already house the microbes necessary to initiate fermentation from the soil they are grown in. Under the right set of circumstances, these microbes will proliferate: the yeasts will bubble away, and the bacteria will contribute to acetic acids responsible for the characteristic sour flavor of ferments.

So why use whey? If you love making strained yogurt or labneh, you will be looking for clever ways to repurpose whey. In the heirloom kitchen, nothing is left to waste, and we often sneak whey into all kinds of recipes. Because of its high calcium content, whey is an excellent meat tenderizer and can replace water in a brine for leaner cuts of turkey or pork. When soaking grains overnight, stir in a few tablespoons to help eliminate phytic acid, as I do in my Golden Oats (page 105). Try it as a replacement liquid in hearth breads or flatbreads such as Whey Kaak/Pita (page 215), porridge, smoothies, soups, or stews, or use it in select ferments such as the one that follows. The result is a distinctively funky flavor that I adore.

WHEY-FERMENTED CIPOLLINI ONIONS

Makes 2 quarts

I source many ingredients from nearby farms, often relying on weekly pick lists to inform my menus. This recipe came about one July after I had mistakenly ordered five pounds of fresh cipollini onions and was looking for a way to preserve them beyond their two- to three-month life in the fridge. I created a whey-activated brine, added some herbs, and after two days of fermentation moved them into cold dormancy. They sat quietly in the back of the fridge until I gasped one winter morning at the realization that I was out of onions. I reached for that long-forgotten jar and transformed the simple dish I was making into one with an extraordinary savory quality from the briny, lactic flavor of the fermented cipollini onions.

Cipollini onions (*Allium cepa*) are an Italian heirloom variety of onions that are oval or squat in appearance and one to three inches in diameter. Their higher sugar content and firm flesh make them excellent candidates for pickling. Roasted or skewered on the grill, they are a delightfully simple side dish to meat served swimming in a bath of sweet and sour Agrodolce (page 196). They sport a thin, hard-to-peel outer skin that is easily removed by quickly blanching in boiling water then immersing in an ice bath.

As with most lacto-preserved recipes, the following is more of a method than a rigid set of instructions. You may use a different type of onion or even another vegetable while keeping more or less the same proportion of ingredients. Don't be tempted to add more whey in an effort to speed up fermentation, as you may end up with a slimy or mushy ferment. Do feel free to add more spices, such as yellow or brown mustard seeds, or use rosemary or tarragon instead of sage.

I love to sear these onions in a pan of Clarified Butter (page 34) or Rendered Animal Fat (page 33) to caramelize their flavor. Use in place of raw onions in a mirepoix for soups and stews or sauté with spring or autumn mushrooms for an umami-packed toast topper. They are a key ingredient in Kishk and Mushroom Porridge (page 169), where they playfully complement the sour notes of the dish.

4 cups warm water	1½ teaspoons black peppercorns, lightly crushed in a mortar and pestle
2 tablespoons yogurt whey	
1 tablespoon + 1 teaspoon fine sea salt	8 to 10 fresh sage leaves
2 pounds (about 80) cipollini onions, peeled	2 bay leaves

Place the warm water and whey in a large crock or nonreactive container and stir in the salt to dissolve. Stir in the cipollini onions, spices, and herbs. Secure the onions under the brine using fermentation weights. Loosely cover with the lid or secure a cloth with a rubber band or tie over the top to protect it from fruit flies. Ferment for 2 days at room temperature, checking periodically. Once the brine has progressed to a milky cloudiness, transfer

to a nonreactive container, cover, and move to the refrigerator, periodically burping the lid to release pressure. The onions will keep and continue to deepen in flavor for up to 1 year.

WHEY-MARINATED SHRIMP CEVICHE

Serves 3 to 4

This easily assembled dish is lush and colorful, and it maximizes the benefits of whey to create a flavorful but unorthodox ceviche. It is important to steam the shrimp first, as the whey will not quite "cook" the shrimp like a more concentrated citrus-only marinade. I prefer to peel, devein, and then slice the shrimp lengthwise, which encourages them to curl playfully as they are steamed.

½ cup yogurt whey	Scant 1 cup (3 large) tomatillos, sliced
¾ cup fresh lime juice (from about 5 limes)	1 small sweet mango, chopped
1½ teaspoons fine salt	1 to 2 tablespoons minced fresh chilies, such as jalapeño, to taste
¾ cup sliced mild radish such as daikon radish or watermelon radish	
½ cup (2 to 3) scallions, sliced or slivered	1¾ cups peeled and halved (lengthwise) shrimp

FOR THE GARNISH

Fresh cilantro leaves	A few pinches of red pepper flakes

Combine the whey and lime juice in a large bowl and stir in the salt. Stir in the radish, scallions, tomatillos, mango, and chilies and leave to marinate while you cook the shrimp.

Fill a medium saucepan with 3 to 4 inches of water and bring to a boil. Place the shrimp in a steamer basket and steam until they just begin to turn a blush pink and curl, 2 to 3 minutes. Rinse the shrimp under cool water and shake dry. Stir the shrimp into the ceviche and marinate in the refrigerator for at least 30 minutes or up to 2 hours before serving. Garnish with fresh cilantro leaves and crushed red pepper flakes.

OPPOSITE *Yogurt whey is a versatile ingredient that can even be used to make a delicious, probiotic ceviche!*

WHEY CARAMEL UPSIDE-DOWN FRUITCAKE

Makes one 10-inch cake

The flavor of whey is subtly present in this sweet but wholesome moist cake made with einkorn flour. The recipe calls for plums but is flexible to the season. Apricots or even fresh cranberries also play well against the sticky caramel. This cake is excellent slightly warm from the oven but holds well for several days of snacking. The recipe calls for discarded sourdough starter, but if you don't possess a culture, you may omit it.

240 g / 1 cup whey

100 g / ½ cup granulated sugar

310 g / 3 large plums, pitted and quartered

165 g / 1½ cups whole einkorn flour

1½ teaspoons baking powder

¼ teaspoon baking soda

¼ teaspoon fine sea salt

1 teaspoon ground cardamom

½ teaspoon ground cinnamon

114 g / ½ cup Brown Butter (page 34), softened

125 g / ½ cup + 1 tablespoon light brown sugar

2 large eggs, at room temperature

1 teaspoon pure vanilla extract

50 g / about ¼ cup 100% sourdough starter

100 g / ⅓ cup + 1 tablespoon whole milk or buttermilk

Preheat the oven to 350°F.

Combine the whey and granulated sugar in a 10-inch cast-iron skillet, place over medium-high heat, and stir to dissolve the sugar. Bring to a low boil, then lower the heat to medium and cook uncovered for about 10 minutes without stirring, until the mixture reduces to a thick syrup. Watch the syrup closely and continue cooking for another 2 to 3 minutes, until it begins to brown and emits a toasty aroma. Turn off the heat and arrange the plums in the caramel. Set aside.

Combine the flour, baking powder, baking soda, salt, cardamom, and cinnamon in a medium bowl and whisk to blend. Combine the brown butter and brown sugar in a separate bowl and beat with a handheld electric mixer until fluffy and light in color, 4 to 5 minutes. Add the eggs one at a time and beat until smooth. Add the vanilla and sourdough starter, if using, and mix until just incorporated. Add the dry ingredients, alternating with the milk in two or three additions, mixing until the flour is hydrated and the mixture is smooth.

Spread the cake batter over the caramel and fruit in the pan and smooth the top. Bake for 25 to 27 minutes, until a toothpick inserted into the center of the cake comes out clean. Remove from the oven and cool for 20 to 30 minutes, then loosen the edges with a knife and invert onto a serving plate. Serve immediately, or keep covered at room temperature for up to 3 days.

HEIRLOOM GRAINS AND FLOURS

OPPOSITE *Seeds that can be cooked as porridges, pilafs, or ground into flour have many appearances and flavors. Featured from top to bottom are* Triticum monococcum *(einkorn),* Sorghum *sp. (sorghum),* Triticum aestivum *'Frederick' wheat,* Secale cereale *(rye),* Amaranthus *sp. (amaranth),* Fagopyrum esculentum *(buckwheat) and* Hordeum vulgare *'Purple Egyptian' (purple barley).*

HERITAGE GRAINS ARE DEFINED as varieties or cultivars that existed pre-1950s. Seeking out heirloom grains and seeds farmed with integrity is a big part of the heirloom kitchen's goals of reintroducing flavor and digestibility to basic food staples such as bread and porridge. Many heritage grains have been abandoned by commercial agriculture in search of higher yields and more consistent harvests but at the expense of aroma and complexity. By supporting agricultural systems that use heirlooms as part of an integrated system of regenerative farming, we are investing in a future of traceable food with character. Our challenge isn't to dismantle large commercial enterprises or criticize dietary habits but to transform them by promoting appreciation for values of flavor, digestibility, and strong localized communities. Home and commercial bakers are in the best position to steer change by supporting farmers who grow heirloom grains.

There are more heirloom grains than there is space to honor here, and I encourage you to experiment with many of them to experience their distinct flavors, learn about their unique histories, and use them in both old and new ways. Using heirloom grains is not a fashionable culinary trend but an enduring matter of realism. Sustainable farming economies seek to respectfully feed the body and nourish the spirit while honoring the societal assets of kinship.

Heirlooms are increasing in popularity not only for their superior complexity of flavor but for their role in the conservation of land and water. An increasing number of rural communities are seeing a revival in local food economies as a result of the revitalization of heirloom grains reflecting regional identity and climate.

Heirlooms are not without their challenges in terms of sourcing (see Resources, page 324), storage, and usage. Storing these flours in cool to freezing temperatures, particularly in the summer months, is essential to maintaining their vitality and nutritional benefits. You may also consider purchasing a small home mill and whole grains in bulk to mill small amounts of flour at a time. If you are new to baking or cooking with heirloom grains, look for community on social media or in local cooking classes.

OPPOSITE *Breads featured here include Smoked Paprika and Cheese Sourdough Bread, Sweet Jane, Table Loaves, Benne Sourdough, and Sprouted Buckwheat and Cranberry Porridge Bread.*

Cooking with Whole Heirloom Grains and Seeds (Pseudocereals)

Heirloom grains and seeds that are considered staple cereals or pseudocereals provide a deliciously diverse canvas of textures and flavors for any number of nutritious meals. Soaking grains before cooking brings many benefits, including easier digestion, proper absorption of nutrients, a more tender bite, and decreased cooking time. Below are general directions for measuring, soaking, and cooking whole heirloom grains along with a quick reference chart for preparing some of my favorites. You may cook your grains in water or a homemade broth (pages 36 to 37) for additional flavor. When looking for whole wheat, rye, or spelt berries or barley, be sure to choose varieties that have not been pearled or stripped of their nutritious bran. These will cook faster but do not offer the same fiber or flavor as whole berries.

Measure the grain into a bowl and cover with water by at least 2 inches. Add an acidifier such as lemon juice, vinegar, or whey to help eliminate antinutrients such as phytates and make the grain more digestible. Use a ratio of 1 tablespoon per cup of water. Soak according to the directions on the chart, drain, and rinse, then place in a pot large enough to accommodate the amount you're making, noting that grains will increase in size while cooking. Measure in the liquid and add a dash of oil or butter (and in most cases, a generous pinch of salt toward the end of cooking). Bring to a boil over medium-high heat, then reduce the heat to maintain a simmer. Cooking grains at temperatures that are too high will cause them to burst and scorch the pan. Low and slow is best, as is leaving the grains to steam for 10 to 15 minutes in the pot after you turn the heat off. Whole grains can vary considerably in cooking time depending on their age when purchased, the variety, the size of your pot, the relative air humidity, and the length of time you soaked them. For example, the name *farro* can be used to describe several different species of wheat, each of which has a different cooking time. Black or red varieties of quinoa can take longer to cook than their tan cousins.

GRAIN	MEASUREMENT	SOAKING TIME	COOKING WATER	COOKING TIME	YIELD
Hard wheat, spelt, farro, or rye berries	175 g / 1 cup	12–24 hours	3 cups	35–55 minutes	2–3 cups
Freekeh	175 g / 1 cup	8–12 hours	3 cups	35–45 minutes	3 cups
Short-grain brown rice	225 g / 1 cup	12–24 hours	2 cups	50 minutes	3 cups
Raw (untoasted) buckwheat	170 g / 1 cup	6–8 hours	1¼ cups	25 minutes	1½ cups
Millet	200 g / 1 cup	6–8 hours	1½ cups	10–15 minutes	3½ cups
Sorghum	185 g / 1 cup	8 hours	3 cups	45–50 minutes	3 cups
Amaranth	210 g / 1 cup	6–8 hours	1 cup	12–15 minutes	2½ cups
Quinoa	185 g / 1 cup	6–8 hours	1 cup	12–15 minutes	3 cups

STONE-GROUND GRITS/POLENTA

Serves 4

Cornmeal labels in the United States can be confusing, and people often ask me what the difference between grits and polenta is. Both are cooked on the stovetop in the same way, but their botanical identities are somewhat different. Grits hail from the Southern states and have a reputation for being soft and white in appearance and a bit mushy after they are cooked. Grits are ground from *Zea mays* var. *indentata*, a type of dent corn named after the indentations at the crown of each kernel resembling the teeth of an animal. Classic Italian polenta can be prepared as a porridge or baked into squares and is ground from flint corn, or *Zea mays* var. *indurata*, a variety of common corn that most often has a yellow appearance. Both are sold in varying grinds, and you may not know the style of the product until you get it home and cook with it. Like many other whole or stone-ground grains, cooking times will vary greatly depending on how coarse it is ground, how long it has been sitting on the shelf, and the climate in which it was grown.

Whether you prefer grits or polenta, they can be prepared here in the same manner.

5 to 6 cups water, or as needed

1 cup coarse grits or polenta

1 teaspoon fine sea salt

3 to 4 tablespoons unsalted butter or Clarified Butter (page 34)

Combine 5 cups of water, the grits, salt, and butter in a large saucepan and bring to a boil over medium-high heat. Turn the heat down to as low as possible and continue cooking, stirring occasionally. After about 20 minutes, you will need to attend to the mixture more frequently to prevent the bottom from scorching, so plan your other tasks accordingly. The mixture will stick to the bottom no matter how much you stir, but don't worry, this is normal. Continue stirring, scraping both the bottom and sides for another 1 to 3 hours depending on the corn and its grind, until it is soft and easy to chew but not mushy, with the textural integrity of the distinct individual grits intact. Add more water as needed. To test for doneness, gather a spoonful and let it fully cool before tasting. If you can chew it with your back teeth, it's not yet done.

Baking with Heirloom Flours

Though much is still being learned about working with heirloom flours, an increasing number of chefs are recognizing their unparalleled flavors, colors, and textures and are honoring their unique history through modern interpretations of otherwise familiar recipes. In order to make the right choices for our pantries, it is important to first understand the mechanics of making flour as well as the different types of grains used to make flour. Consider the following when incorporating these ingredients into your kitchen repertoire.

Flour starts as a whole grain that possesses three different components: the bran (outer coating that protects the seed), the endosperm (the starchy inside with protein also present that feeds the germinating embryo), and the germ (the oils and proteins that are responsible for flavor and their short shelf life). Flour can be milled using either a roller mill, a hammer mill, or a stone mill. Roller milling is used most often for industrialized flour. During this process, both the germ and the bran (where most of the flavor and nutrition are stored) are crushed in a fast, high-heat motion that destroys the integrity of the germ. With roller milling, the bran is sifted, milled again, and added back to the endosperm for what is erroneously labeled *whole wheat flour*. Unfortunately, there is nothing whole about this process, as the most delicious part of the grain, the germ, is left out of the end result. According to Food and Drug Administration guidelines, flour can be called whole grain if a meager 51% of all those components are added back to the endosperm.

With stone milling, both the bran and germ remain in the flour. The bran may be sifted out for a finer product, but the germ oils will always be present in stone-milled flour. This is why the shelf life of stone-milled flour is so short but the flavor is so exceptional. Store in cool to freezing temperatures, especially in the summer months.

Whole-grain flour should contain the entire seed, including bran particles, germ oils, and endosperm. This gives us the opportunity to taste the profile of the grain and the influencing factors of where it is grown. Industrially grown wheat varieties are selected for superior yield and disease resistance, often at the expense of flavor, and then are tested and blended to produce a product with consistent performance. Industrial roller milling of whole wheat flour destroys the delicious but non-shelf-stable germ oils, with the resulting flour often tasting bitter. Thankfully, there are now dozens of heirloom grains being revived through stone milling that bring not only superior nutrition and digestibility but excellent baking properties for artisan-style breads.

The challenge of working with stone-ground heirloom flours is that they have not been standardized to achieve consistency. How these flours perform is a result of many variables, namely the variety as well as the weather, soil, and the hands and machine of the miller. To taste and to use them is an experience that requires the same deliberation as sampling a wine. Familiarizing ourselves with the characteristics of each individual heirloom flour will enable us to fully appreciate its unique attributes.

1 *A spike of wheat with multiple mature spikelets (kernels) before they are threshed of their glumes (papery husks) for milling flour. Hulled heirloom species and landrace varieties of wheat often have thick, difficult-to-remove husks, making processing more challenging than modern wheats.* **2** *The inset features the outer and inner bran layers and outer aleurone layer (protein stored as granules in the endosperm).* **3** *This cross-section represents the three main parts of the kernel: the nutrient-dense germ concentrated with precious oils that become oxidized upon milling, E and B vitamins, and trace minerals; the endosperm made up of starch and protein and contains iron and B vitamins; and the hard outer and inner protective bran layers of the seed rich in fiber, essential fatty acids, starch, protein, vitamins, and minerals.*

Depending on how finely the flour was ground, how hard the berry is, or the bran that is present in whole grains, whole-grain or high-extraction flours will tend to be a bit sharp and thirsty. This means if a whole-grain dough is overworked, especially in the beginning of the mixing process, its gluten potential will be compromised. Working with higher-hydration formulas is preferred for achieving a pleasing crumb and crust and will allow the dough to build strength over bulk fermentation time (see Table Loaf variations, page 62).

There are a number of different ways the baking properties of flour can be described, and the language sometimes can be confusing. Common labels in the United States such as *bread*, *all-purpose*, or *whole wheat* are familiar terms, and others such as *high-extraction* can be puzzling. These labels are mostly based on protein percentages, how they are sifted, and potential for gluten development. When making bread, we look for a higher protein (between 11% and 14.5%) that generally (but not always) reflects greater gluten potential necessary for trapping fermentation gases that go into leavening dough. With cakes, cookies, and most pastries, a lower protein flour (3% to 11%) with less gluten potential produces a softer, more tender crumb.

Flour can also be referred to by names of cultivars, such as 'Red Fife,' or 'Marquis' wheat, or 'Danko' or 'Abruzzi' rye. This is simply a way to identify a particular heritage, a selection that was made on the basis of preferred attributes of that cultivar or variety. Much like their botanical Latin species names, cultivar names sometimes can give you clues as to their performance in a recipe.

Here are some points to remember when using stone-ground heirloom flours:

- Depending on where the grain was grown and milled, you will most likely need to use either more or less water to make dough than if you were using commercial flour.

- If you have purchased flour that was dry-farmed, get ready for thirsty flour! Conversely, if you live in a humid area, you may need to decrease the amount of water to achieve a workable dough.

- Always talk to your miller about the character of the flour you are buying and how you intend to use it. Remember that climate can drastically alter the performance of a grain regardless of its cultivar name.

- Einkorn is one heirloom wheat for which you will most likely need to *reserve* moisture rather than add it, in particular for making biscuits and cakes.

- Many heirloom wheat varieties (but not all!) have weaker gluten potential than flours you may be used to, resulting in squatter breads. If lower-profile breads bother you, you may want to consider using heirloom flours in conjunction with an organic strong bread flour with a higher gluten content. These weaker (but tasty!) flours include einkorn, emmer, and spelt, to name a few.

- Other types of heirloom wheat will be very strong in character and will hold their shape better as a dough. These cultivars include 'Turkey Red,' 'Red Fife,' 'Oland,' 'Rouge de Bordeaux,' 'Charcoal' Wheat, and 'Marquis.'

- If you are looking for a very open and light crumb, consider sifting out the bran (*whoa, time-consuming!*) and soaking it first before mixing it back into the dough. This will allow time for it to soften before being mixed.

- If you are making whole-grain bread, you can mix the flour with water first, cover, and autolyze (rest) it for a few hours before adding the leaven and salt. This allows the bran to hydrate and the gluten proteins to assemble before fermentation begins.

FERMENTED WHOLE-GRAIN PIECRUST

Makes one 9-inch double crust pie, two 9-inch single piecrusts, or six 5-inch mini pies

This is my no-fail all-purpose whole-grain heirloom flour piecrust. You can use whole spelt flour and whole wheat pastry flour interchangeably. 'Maris Widgeon,' 'Sonora,' and 'Frederick' are excellent heirloom wheat selections, but a more generic whole wheat pastry flour will work well here too. For a malty, fruity quality, try substituting in one-third whole rye flour for the spelt or pastry flour, being aware that this will both alter the texture as well as increase the rate of fermentation. Your choice of flour will influence the color of the crust and will determine how much water you need to add. I prefer using a combination of butter and homemade leaf lard (see Rendered Animal Fat, page 33) for added flakiness, but all butter is also a perfect choice.

300 g / 2½ cups whole-grain spelt or pastry flour	90 g / 6 tablespoons frozen leaf lard (or more butter)
30 g / 2 tablespoons sugar	50 g / 2 tablespoons sourdough starter
½ teaspoon fine sea salt	80 to 120 g / 8 to 12 tablespoons ice-cold water
113 g / ½ cup frozen unsalted butter	1 egg yolk, beaten

Combine the flour, sugar, and salt in a large bowl and whisk to blend. Cut in the butter and lard with your fingers or a pastry cutter or pulse in a food processor until pea-size crumbles are formed. Alternatively, you may freeze the butter as a block ahead of time, grate it directly into the flour mixture, and toss to coat. Work swiftly to avoid warming the butter. If you are using the sourdough starter, place it in a small bowl and whisk it with 80 g / 8 tablespoons of the ice-cold water to form a slurry. Add the slurry or plain ice-cold water 30 to 40 g / 3 to 4 tablespoons at a time, tossing lightly with your fingers or pulsing in the food processor until just combined. Test by squeezing together a handful. If it crumbles, add up to 40 g / 4 tablespoons more water. When it forms a cohesive lump, divide it in half, wrap in plastic wrap, and place in the refrigerator for at least 1 hour or up to 2 days for maximum fermentation benefits before rolling. Or keep in the freezer for up to 3 months.

Remove the dough from the refrigerator and roll it out to ¼ inch thick. Fold it into thirds like a letter (top down, bottom up, and overlapping) and rotate the dough. Roll and fold again, wrap in plastic wrap, and place in the refrigerator for at least another 30 minutes. Doing this encourages flaky layers in your finished piecrust.

If you are par-baking a single crust, preheat the oven to 375°F. If you intend to use the crust to make Shaker Lemon and Sage Pie (page 187); Sorghum, Vanilla, and Rosemary Apple Pie (page 118); or Mini Fruit Galettes (page 306), refrigerate until ready to use.

(recipe continues on page 61)

OPPOSITE *Whole-grain piecrust can be made with a mild and creamy white wheat such as* Triticum aestivum *'Sonora,' featured here, or more robust flours such as spelt (*Triticum spelta*).*

UNDERSTANDING HEIRLOOM FLOURS

Here are a few helpful terms when buying flour:

Red Wheat vs. White Wheat

These colors indicate the color of the wheat kernel bran layer. Red wheat varieties possess small amounts of tannins in their bran, much as grape skins or red wine do. White wheat varieties do not contain these tannins, making them less bitter with a creamier aftertaste.

Hard Spring Wheat vs. Soft Winter Wheat

Bread flour most often comes from high-protein hard spring wheat, and pastry flour is usually classified as lower-protein soft winter wheat, according to the texture of the starch in the grain's endosperm. Spring wheat is sown after the last frost and harvested in mid-to-late summer depending on the climate, whereas winter wheat requires a vernalization period to flower. It is sown in the fall so it may germinate before a necessary cold period ensues. It continues to grow and is harvested in late spring. Dry climates are best for producing high-protein wheat.

Bread Flour

Bread flour is strong flour that's milled and sifted to a 75% extraction or lower with the ability to produce an elastic matrix for trapping fermentation gases. This means at least 25% of the bran has been removed. In the case of stone-ground flour, most of the germ will remain present, whereas roller-milled bread flour contains little to no remaining germ oils. Bread flour can be combined with lower-gluten or gluten-free whole-grain flours for a light texture and pleasing loft.

High-Extraction Wheat

Usually a strong flour (11% to 14.5% protein) but sometimes a lower-protein flour that has been stone-ground or roller-milled with integrity (lower temperatures and slower milling) and then sifted of 15% or less of its bran. You may see it labeled simply as 85%, and you must be careful to determine the gluten potential. When stone milled, it is a highly nutritious and flavorful alternative to industrial bread flour, but it perishes easily. Use right after purchasing or store in the freezer.

Whole Wheat

Contains 100% of the original wheat kernel. It can be purchased as high- or low-protein flour. For pastries and cookies, I use spelt flour or a whole wheat flour ground from soft white or red wheat that has some bran sifted and then reground. For breads, I use a higher-protein heirloom variety of red wheat for the deep caramelization that results in the crust. White wheat varieties are also available with a milder, creamier flavor from their lack of color and tannic flavor compounds in the bran. These may be desirable when allowing other flavors to come through that may compete with red wheat. Like high-extraction flour, the germ oils in this stone-ground flour spoil quickly, so use right after purchasing or store in the freezer.

All-Purpose

Available in both sifted and whole versions milled with none or, in the case of stone-ground, all of its germ. It contains anywhere from 3% to 11% protein depending on your supplier. It is a finer texture than most flours and can be used in biscuits, quick breads, cookies, and cakes. Sonoran or Frederick wheat are excellent all-purpose choices.

On a lightly floured surface, roll the dough into a 10½-inch circle that's ⅛ to ¼ inch thick. Using a rolling pin or your forearm for support, swiftly transfer the dough to a 9-inch pie pan and encourage it to sink into its form by adjusting the edges inward. Using kitchen shears, trim the edge to a ½- to ¾-inch overhang. Gently turn the overhang under the circumference of the pie. Use a fork to press a pattern into the outside crust or use your fingers to crimp the edges. Prick the bottom generously with a fork and line the bottom with parchment paper. Fill with pie weights or dry beans and chill for 30 minutes in the refrigerator.

Par-bake for 15 to 17 minutes, until the edges are firm. Carefully remove the pie weights and parchment and brush with the egg yolk. Bake for another 5 minutes for a partially prebaked crust or 15 to 20 minutes for a fully blind baked crust. Remove from the oven and follow the instructions for your choice of filling before continuing to bake.

Using Sourdough as Natural Leavening

In my first two books, *Sourdough* and *Toast and Jam*, I describe in detail how to create and maintain a wheat- or rye-based sourdough starter. The following recipe assumes you already have this important resource in your kitchen and wish to use it to make delicious baked goods and other recipes using non-commodity flours. (See Appendix for Bread Baking Basics and page 67 for a beginner starter recipe.) The basic loaf below is the foundation for the bread recipes in this book and includes a few suggestions for changing it up.

Wheat or Rye Starters

Use the flour of your choice to maintain your starter, and be consistent with it for the most reliable performance. Remember that you are culturing not only the microbes all around you but those on the particular flour. You may find that you prefer a whole rye starter for its sour, honeyed perfume over a whole wheat or spelt flour starter. If using rye, be aware of its

A starter can be made and maintained with many different types of flour, including rye, whole wheat, or rice, featured here.

particular enzymatic profile that will increase the fermentation activity of both your starter and dough. These are nuanced details of your bread practice that develop with time and experience.

Maintenance for a 100% Hydration Sourdough Starter

If you keep your starter in the refrigerator, it is important to refresh it before using it to make your leaven, the intermediate step between the starter and making bread dough. To simplify starter maintenance and to maintain the 100% hydration starter used in this book, refresh your starter in a one-to-one ratio using equal parts water and whole-grain flour *at least* to the weight of the starter 8 to 12 hours before you make your leaven or use it directly in a recipe such as Cornmeal Flatbread (page 266). For example, if you have 50 g of starter, add *at least* 50 g of water and 50 g of flour to feed it. You may add more than these amounts in an equal ratio, but never add less than the amount of starter in your jar. When performing a feed, make sure you have enough for the leaven recipe as well as some left over to maintain your starter.

TABLE LOAF

Makes 2 loaves

This basic, everyday bread harnesses the microbial power of sourdough as natural leavening. It is a gateway recipe with modest hydration that's perfect for learning to make sourdough using locally sourced stone-ground flours. Although commercial flours will work in this recipe, they contain fewer flavor and nutritional benefits. As you make your loaf, it is important to engage all of your senses to discover and master the subtle cues of sourdough fermentation. I suggest you practice this recipe until you feel comfortable with each step, the flours you have sourced, and the outcome before moving on to more advanced recipes.

This formula contains only about 20% whole grain with the remainder of the recipe using high-extraction stone-ground hard wheat bread flour, which you can purchase or mail-order from specialty millers (see Resources, page 324). You will often see these flours referred to by percentages, with the standard for high-extraction 85% or above. These extractions include all of the precious germ and a maximum of 15% of the bran sifted out. This leads to a lighter crumb with almost all of the flavor and nutritional benefits of whole grain. But feel free to tweak the flour and fermentation to your personal preferences of flavor, texture, nutrition, and aesthetics (see notes below). If using commercial flour, you may need to decrease the water content by 5% to 10% (40 to 80 g).

FOR THE LEAVEN

25 g / 1 heaping tablespoon 100% hydration active starter, refreshed (fed)

55 g / about ¼ cup tepid water (70°F to 75°F)

55 g / ½ cup whole-grain flour (rye, spelt, or whole wheat work well)

FOR THE DOUGH

135 g / ⅔ cup leaven (see left)

610 g / 2½ cups + 3 tablespoons tepid water (75°F)

620 g / 4¼ cups + 2 tablespoons high-extraction bread flour

120 g / 1 cup + 1 tablespoon whole wheat bread flour

40 g / 2½ tablespoons whole rye flour

16 g / 1 tablespoon fine sea salt

Cornmeal, for sprinkling

PREPARE THE LEAVEN

Place the starter and tepid water in a large bowl and stir to form a slurry. Add the flour and mix with a spoon until no dry lumps remain. Cover with an inverted bowl or plastic wrap and ferment at room temperature for about 8 hours, until the leaven shows bubbles breaking the surface and has swelled considerably in size.

MIX THE DOUGH

When the leaven shows bubbles breaking the surface and has swelled considerably in size, add the water and stir to combine. Add the flours and, using your hands, mix and squeeze the dough in a circular motion until no dry lumps remain. Cover and autolyze (rest) the dough for about 20 minutes, until the flour is fully hydrated. Sprinkle the salt evenly over the surface of the dough and squeeze to combine. This is an excellent time to feel how the flour is performing in the recipe. The dough should feel sticky and be easy to mix with your hands. If the dough resists or feels too stiff, add more water in 20- to 25-gram increments, thoroughly mixing it in until the dough is no longer slick or shiny on the surface.

At this point, you may slap-and-fold the dough on a clean work surface to encourage further gluten development. (Note: this technique doesn't work with the 100% whole-grain version below, as the increased bran content will encourage more tearing than is desired at this point.) To slap-and-fold, remove the dough from the bowl using a bowl scraper and slap it against a clean surface, dragging the dough to stretch and then fold it over itself. Repeat this step in a rhythmic fashion until the dough transforms from a shaggy mass into a more cohesive, smooth form, about 5 minutes. If the dough begins to tear, cover with an inverted bowl or plastic wrap and allow to rest for a few minutes before starting again.

Table Loaves made with stone-ground high-extraction bread flour, whole wheat, and rye flours have all of the delicious germ oils present and only some of the bran removed, giving the flavor of 100% whole grain without the heaviness.

PERFORM BULK FERMENTATION

Return the dough to the bowl and cover once more. Set the bowl aside in a warm location (ideally 75°F) to bulk ferment for 3½ to 4 hours, possibly a bit longer in winter or a tad shorter on a hot summer day. As it ferments, stretch-and-fold the dough in the bowl every 30 to 45 minutes to help develop the gluten network essential for trapping fermentation gases. To do this, wet your hands to prevent the dough from sticking and gently slide the fingers of both hands under the dough mass. Release the dough from the side of the bowl and gently fold it to the center. Rotate the bowl and repeat 3 or 4 times, until you have worked your way around the dough mass. Toward the end of bulk fermentation, take care not to overhandle or deflate the dough. The dough will start as a shaggy mass and as it ferments become cohesive and smooth. It's ready to be shaped when the dough has increased by at least one third and you see fermentation bubbles breaking the surface.

SHAPE THE DOUGH

Shaping the dough is done in two stages: a pre-shape with a short bench resting period, followed by a tighter final shaping. Using a bowl scraper, swiftly remove the dough from the bowl and place it on a lightly floured surface. Use a bench scraper to divide the dough in half. Using your hands, bring the top of the dough to the center, followed by the bottom and two sides in a north, south, east, west motion. Tuck the resulting four corners to the middle to make a slightly rounded form. Using your bench scraper, release the dough from the work surface and flip it over so it's seam-side down. Cover with a kitchen towel or plastic wrap if the air is dry and allow to rest for 10 to 30 minutes until it has visibly relaxed.

To final shape moderate- to high-hydration doughs, I use a "stitching" method: Use the bench scraper to flip the dough over onto a lightly floured surface so it's seam-side up. Starting from the top, tuck the right side to the center, holding it in place while you bring the left side to the center, overlapping with the first. Repeat this side-to-side stitching until you reach the bottom of the dough. Roll the bottom to the center and then all the way over so the seam is facing down, tucking as you go to create tension. Flour the top of the loaf generously. Use your bench scraper to pick up the dough and flip it over into one hand so it's seam-side up. Cradle it into an 8- to 8½-inch proofing basket, then cover with a cloth. Cover that with plastic wrap and place in the refrigerator to retard for at least 8 hours or up to 24 hours before baking.

BAKE THE LOAF

Remove your loaf from the refrigerator and allow to come to room temperature for about 1 hour. When it is ready to bake, it should feel like an inflated water balloon when gently poked with a finger. The impression should linger in the dough rather than immediately bounce back, signaling that the bacteria and yeast have done their work.

Place a 5- to 7-quart Dutch oven in the middle rack of the oven and preheat the oven to 480°F for 20 minutes.

Sprinkle a touch of cornmeal on a piece of parchment paper cut to fit the Dutch oven and carefully flip your loaf onto it seam-side down, gently releasing it from the liner if it sticks. Sprinkle a little flour onto the surface of the loaf before scoring for a more graphic contrast (but be sure to dust off any excess, as a mouthful of raw flour is rather unappetizing!). Score the top of the loaf with a sharp, thin razor blade about ⅓ inch deep (this allows the loaf to fully expand in a controlled manner as it bakes). For the characteristic "ear" that also sports a delicious crunch, cut about two thirds across the loaf lengthwise at a 45-degree angle. For more complicated designs with multiple cuts, cut at a 90-degree angle with shallower pressure. Regardless of your approach, swift confidence will give you the cleanest lines. With time and practice, you'll know how much pressure to apply to achieve the designs you want. If you add decorative scoring flourishes to the first score, be aware that this will cause the loaf to spread and flatten before going into the oven. Carefully lower the loaf into the preheated Dutch oven, cover, and return it to the oven. Bake with the lid on for 20 minutes. Remove the lid and decrease the oven temperature by 10°F to 15°F (more for doughs with higher hydration). Bake for another 15 to 20 minutes, until the crust is a deep, rusty brown or the color of your liking. Remove using a spatula and cool on a wire rack for at least 2 hours before slicing to allow the crumb to fully set.

Kitchen notes: Home ovens vary widely in their heat source and distribution. I suggest using an oven thermometer to gauge the proper temperature, making minor adjustments to the oven temperature and baking time if necessary. If your oven is equipped with a fan assist, turn it off as your loaf bakes if possible to prevent the crust from setting before the loaf has fully expanded.

If you are using a cast-iron pan, you may need to remove the loaf from the Dutch oven after about 25 minutes of total baking time to keep the bottom from burning before the crumb is set. Do this carefully to avoid burning yourself. Finish baking on the middle rack for an additional 12 to 20 minutes.

Variations on the Table Loaf

When making adjustments, ingredients are calculated in percentages measured against the total flour weight of the dough.

USING 100% WHOLE-GRAIN FLOUR

If you are fortunate enough to have access to low-temperature, slowly and finely milled whole wheat bread flour, you may use this instead of high-extraction bread flour with an additional 8% to 15% (60 to 115 g) water in the final dough. I also suggest holding back the leaven from the initial mix of flour and water and adding it along with the salt at least an hour (or up to 3 hours) after the dough has been mixed. This will allow the flour to become fully hydrated and gain gluten strength necessary for proper leavening before fermentation begins. Once the leaven and salt have been added, continue with bulk fermentation at room temperature for 3½ to 4 hours before moving on to shaping, retarding, and baking. Be aware that using a higher percentage of freshly milled whole-grain flour will yield a faster fermentation from greater enzyme activity in the flour, increased microbial populations on the flour, and more bioavailable food for those microbes. Shorter bulk and refrigerated fermentation times will likely be necessary. If you find overproofing to be an issue, decrease the leaven to about 10% to 12% (78 to 94 g).

USING HOME-MILLED OR HOMEMADE HIGH-EXTRACTION FLOUR

If you cannot source high-extraction flour (see Resources, page 324) or you have a home mill, you can use a screen or sieve to sift out bran particles of stone-milled whole wheat bread flour to achieve a high-extraction flour. If, however, you wish to make this bread 100% whole grain using coarsely ground flour but want a lighter result, simply use this sifted bran to help feed your starters. This will soften its sharp nature by soaking and fermenting it for an extended period before incorporating it into the dough.

This mitigates the potential of the bran cutting through the gluten network that captures the carbon dioxide gases responsible for leavening your bread, with less dense results. Toast the bran before fermenting for a robust flavor boost.

FOLDING IN ADDITIONAL INGREDIENTS

This loaf is incredibly versatile, welcoming other ingredients to make versions such as Black Garlic, Fig, and Walnut Levain (page 263) or Smoked Paprika and Cheese Sourdough Bread (page 80) or using your own imagination to create a personalized variation. Fold in nuts after the dough is mixed and the salt is added. Calculate 20% to 25% of the total flour weight of the dough to figure out the appropriate amount. You may also use this formula to add dried fruit, but remember that thirsty ingredients will rob your dough of moisture. Tossing the fruit in a small amount of liquid such as water, whey, buttermilk, or a liqueur several hours prior will avoid this, or you can add 3% to 5% (25 to 40 g) more liquid to the dough to counter the fruit.

ACCOUNTING FOR CLIMATE FLUCTUATIONS

When I teach basic sourdough classes, this is the recipe I suggest bakers new to using natural leavening follow throughout the seasons. Along with keeping a detailed journal of notes, using one formula time and again will allow you to compare differences in variables including fluctuating seasonal temperatures and humidity. If your summers are hot and you find the dough is overproofing, try using less leaven, taking the percentage of this formula (17% or about 135 g) down to 12% to 15% of the total flour weight (94 to 117 g) to slow the fermentation process while maintaining the same timing for each step. In the winter, when dough moves considerably slower, you may wish to increase the leaven by another 2% to 7% of the total flour weight (156 to 195 g leaven).

Whether you are following this recipe to the letter or any of its suggested variations, remember that using regional flours may require more or less water in the final dough. There will be some trial and error depending on your familiarity with the flour. If you live in or are using flours sourced from a humid climate, you will need anywhere from 5% to 10% less water to achieve a workable dough. Conversely, if you live in or are using flour grown and milled in an arid environment, you may need 10% to 15% more water to properly hydrate your flours. The goal is to find a happy median that you are comfortable handling and that yields a pleasing loaf. There is no right or wrong in how this is done, but if you understand the methods and reasoning behind each step, you can make the necessary adjustments.

SOURDOUGH BREAD CRUMBS

Makes about 1 cup

Learning to make homemade sourdough bread is one of the most rewarding steps you can take toward both self-sufficiency and increasing digestible grains in your diet. It takes a dedicated amount of time and effort to master and inevitably produces mishaps, especially in the beginning. This bread crumb recipe recycles your efforts in a most delicious way, but of course you can make bread crumbs from a perfect loaf as well.

Once you have homemade bread crumbs on hand, you'll find yourself slipping them into just about everything. Pan-fry them with butter and minced garlic to top Fermented Pasta (page 70) or a roasted vegetable dish. Dredge chicken cutlets or fish fillets in egg, then dip into bread crumbs and pan-fry to a crispy finish. Use them to add textural interest to Kale, Corn, and Fermented Mushroom and Onion Strata (page 275). Apple Charlotte (page 115) wouldn't be the same without this homemade pantry staple flavored with cinnamon. Or use it to fortify meatballs or crab cakes. Really, their uses are endless!

Most sourdough bread will hold a considerable amount of moisture even after it is considered stale. Toasting the croutons first eliminates any lingering moisture.

3 cups stale bread, torn or sliced into 2-inch croutons

Preheat the oven to 350°F.

Spread the croutons onto a baking sheet and toast for 15 minutes, stirring halfway through until the pieces feel dry and hard with no moisture remaining. Remove from the oven and cool completely on the baking sheet. Transfer to a food processor and pulse until the pieces break down to the size and consistency of your liking. Store in a covered container in a cool, dry location for up to 6 months.

Alternative Starters

Although the microbial power of sourdough can make gluten-containing flours more digestible for the intolerant, people who have celiac disease or are allergic to wheat must avoid it altogether. It is completely possible to achieve natural leavening using gluten-free flours, as many of them contain the sugars necessary to feed wild yeasts and *Lactobacillus* bacteria found in a sourdough culture. The following are a few methods for creating your own; choose the

method that speaks to your dietary needs. These approaches can be applied to making a wheat-based sourdough starter as well. Note that non-wheat starters take less time to create and will often ferment much faster.

CREATING A LOW-GLUTEN OR NO-GLUTEN STARTER FROM SCRATCH

Creating a sourdough starter using just flour and water is fairly easy and requires anywhere from 3 to 7 days depending on the season and the flours you choose. Be aware that flours with low or no gluten and high sugar content, such as rice and sorghum, will ferment very quickly.

Combine equal parts flour and water by weight in a small bowl. Cover with a damp cloth and allow to sit in a warm location for one day, then check to see if any bubbles have broken the surface. This is an indication that fermentation has begun and it is time to feed your starter. If this is not visibly obvious, continue to the next step anyway. Add an additional amount of flour and water in equal parts weight to the weight of your initial mix (a 1:1:1 ratio). Transfer the starter to a lidded glass or ceramic container at this time. Position the lid loosely and allow to sit at room temperature until it shows bubbles and signs of fermentation. Feed your starter again, being aware that it will most likely double in size after this feeding. If you need to make room in your jar to do so, discard or compost enough to allow for this activity. Continue feeding your starter water and flour in equal parts weight to the weight of the starter for the duration of its life (hopefully a long time!), allowing 6 to 12 hours between feedings. This will ensure you are providing enough food to the growing population of microbes.

It will take about a week after it gains full strength to reach a balance of microbial activity, during which time it may smell a bit funky. Give it time and be patient. When you want to test your starter to see if it is ready to leaven bread, you can perform the float test 6 to 12 hours after a feeding: without stirring or disturbing the starter, grab a dollop using a spoon and drop it into a glass of water. If it floats, it has trapped enough carbon dioxide gas as a by-product of yeast activity to be able to leaven your bread. If it sinks, continue performing feedings at 6- to 12-hour intervals.

Once the starter passes the float test, use it immediately, feed it again, or store it in the refrigerator until ready to use. When you wish to make bread, remove it from the refrigerator and refresh it at least once, allowing it to feed for 6 to 12 hours (or until passing the float test once more) before creating leaven for dough.

CREATING A LOW-GLUTEN OR NO-GLUTEN STARTER FROM INOCULATION

A faster way to create a starter using a low-gluten or no-gluten flour is to begin by inoculating it with a small amount of a wheat- or rye-based starter combined with water. If doing this, follow the steps described above but add a pinky nail amount of wheat or rye starter to the first mix—this is all the activity you need to spawn your new starter! Although this method is acceptable for those who are gluten intolerant, those with allergies or celiac disease will need to create theirs from scratch or using a yeast water.

USING A YEAST WATER TO CREATE A STARTER

In my first book, *Sourdough*, I described a method of creating a culture by harvesting the yeast from raisins to inoculate the flour. This can also be done to create a starter using alternative flours. First create a yeast water such as Rose Hip Fizz (page 140). When it is active and bubbly, use this in place of water for the initial mix and successive two or three feedings following the steps described above.

A WHEAT-FREE SANDWICH LOAF

Makes two 9 × 5 × 3-inch loaves

Although I prefer the toothsome texture and flavor of properly fermented gluten-containing breads, alternative flours also play an important role in sustainable and regenerative agricultural systems (see Amaranth, Millet, and Sorghum Bread, page 213). These systems employ drought-resistant crops that tolerate poor soils or those that are used to build or rehabilitate soil without the use of chemical fertilizers. Candidates for these non-gluten-containing crops are most notably amaranth, sorghum, buckwheat, teff, millet, and oats. Feel free to play with them in this recipe. My favorite combination is a mixture of brown rice, teff, buckwheat, and oat.

If you are used to baking with a wheat- or rye-based starter, keep a close eye on your first dough to make sure it does not overproof. The advantage of using these flours is that, depending on the amount of leaven, you can mix and bake a fully fermented loaf in a single day, as opposed to the two- to three-day process required to bake wheat-based breads. The following recipe, however, uses a slower schedule to overnight the dough in the refrigerator for increased flavor, digestibility, and rise. If you wish to speed along this process, simply triple the total amount of leaven in the dough.

FOR THE LEAVEN

60 g / 1 heaping tablespoon brown rice starter, refreshed	60 g / a generous 4 tablespoons tepid water (70 to 75°F)
	60 g / ⅓ cup brown rice flour

FOR THE DOUGH

810 g / 3⅓ cups + 1½ tablespoons water, tepid (70 to 75°F)

60 g / 3 tablespoons mild-tasting honey

48 g / 4 tablespoons psyllium husk powder

24 g / scant 2½ teaspoons salt

180 g leaven (see previous page)

140 g / 1 cup brown rice and/or buckwheat or teff flour

660 g / 5¾ cups sorghum, millet, oat flour, or a combination

FOR THE TOPPING (OPTIONAL)

30 g / 3 tablespoons pre-soaked and drained whole amaranth, or an equal volume of seeds of your choice (sesame, poppy, or flax work well)

MAKE THE LEAVEN

In a large bowl, combine the brown rice starter, water, and rice flour. Cover with a plate or plastic wrap and allow to ferment at room temperature for 4 to 6 hours.

MAKE THE DOUGH

Line two 9 × 5 × 3-inch baking pans with parchment paper overlapping the sides lengthwise and butter it generously. Add the water, honey, psyllium husk powder, and salt to the bowl with the leaven and whisk vigorously to combine. Stir in the flours until completely incorporated. The result will be somewhere between a thick batter and cookie dough. Divide evenly and transfer in large chunks to the baking pans, pressing evenly into the corners. Wet your hands well and smooth the surface of the dough. Sprinkle your choice of seeds on top and spread to evenly coat. Cover with plastic wrap and allow to rise at room temperature for 6 hours.

Cover the loaf with a kitchen towel and then plastic wrap and place in the refrigerator for at least 6 hours or up to 12 hours. Remove from the refrigerator 2 hours before baking. You will notice a barely discernible rise when removing from the refrigerator. The loaves will be ready to bake when the batter dough appears puffy and there are shallow cracks on the surface.

BAKE THE LOAF

Place a roasting pan in the bottom of your oven and preheat to 480°F. Pour ½ cup water into the roasting pan and place the loaf into the oven. Bake for 15 minutes, checking to see if any remaining water is in the pan. Remove the pan if so and lower the oven temperature to 450°F. Continue baking for another 45 minutes, or until the internal temperature reaches 210°F as measured on an instant-read thermometer. Remove from the oven, cool in the pan for 10 minutes, then remove from the pan. Cool completely on a wire rack before slicing.

Using Sourdough to Improve Digestibility

We are all familiar with sourdough starter as a leavening agent for flavorful, crusty breads, but it is a versatile ambassador of digestion that can be used in less conventional ways as well. I sneak it into most baked goods I make, including batters that are flexible enough to receive extra moisture and an added volume of flour. If you are not following a recipe, a general rule is to use anywhere between 50 and 150 g of starter after the eggs have been incorporated into the creamed butter and sugar, being mindful of how much batter your chosen baking pan can accommodate. Recipes that include sourdough starter in the batter include Whey Caramel Upside-Down Fruitcake (page 49), Brown Butter Sourdough Banana Bread (page 154), Millet Sourdough Pancakes (page 108), and Æbleskiver (page 111). The flavor is typically just slightly more acidic, and the crumb is more moist and sometimes pleasantly dense and spongy.

For stiff doughs such as Fermented Pasta (page 70) and Fermented Whole-Grain Piecrust (58), the object is not only to improve digestibility but to use sourdough's natural acidity to make the dough easier to work. More is definitely not better in this case, however, as a little starter can go a long way. Using sourdough starter in cookies can be tricky, as added moisture will encourage a cake-like rather than a chewy or crispy texture. Use a teaspoon of a stiffer starter for cookies, using less water to refresh the starter before incorporating it into the cookie dough. Allow the cookie dough to ferment in the refrigerator overnight, but no longer than 2 days is advised.

Sourdough starter can also be added to your whole-grain soaking liquid (see page 54) instead of vinegar or lemon juice. If you are simply looking to use up a little extra starter, you can use it as a thickening agent for soups or stews, as in the Chicken and Fennel Sourdough Dumplings (page 249), where it is used both to make the dumplings more digestible and thicken the liquid.

Note that your starter need not be active (refreshed) for you to use it as a digestive aid, although this will lead to more acidic flavor in the final outcome.

FERMENTED PASTA

Serves 4

Although this pasta requires few ingredients, it can teach us a great deal about how various flours perform. It is important to understand the qualities that each ingredient brings to the final pasta dough. For the purposes of this book, we are aiming for a toothsome but tender noodle with rich, distinctive whole-grain flavor to pair with rustic sauces. Once you understand the influence of hydration, protein, and bran in dough, you can adjust this recipe to make it your own using different types of flour and ratios of water, oil, and eggs if you so choose.

Making fresh pasta is a gateway to mastering different types of flour, whether they are stone-ground heirloom selections or commodity-grown and blended industrial brands. With a little time and very simple equipment—mainly your hands, a clean surface, and a rolling pin—the delight of fresh pasta is easily within reach.

Flour is the most important ingredient in fresh pasta. I prefer using fresh stone-ground, whole-grain options not only for their increased nutritional value but also for their superior flavor. Pasta made with the germ oils and finely milled bran of stone-ground wheat invite rich, rustic sauces made with roasted tomatoes (page 293) or anchovies (page 97). As with most dough, pasta made with whole wheat will be thirstier and will require more hydration than dough made with sifted flour. The amount of protein in a flour will also influence the final outcome of the pasta: a soft wheat with lower protein will yield a more malleable dough, and a higher-protein, coarser-textured flour such as

OPPOSITE *Although pasta is not traditionally fermented, doing so by adding a touch of sourdough starter leads to a more digestible result.*

durum or Khorasan wheat will result in a more fortified, sturdy mouthfeel.

Protein will not always tell you everything about a wheat flour's potential performance, especially if it is a stone-ground seasonal product. How and where the flour was grown (dry farmed or irrigated), how it was milled (stone-ground or roller-milled), and if it has been sifted are just a few factors influencing the characteristics of wheat. Consider the weather during the time of harvest, as one variety of wheat may have a very different performance from the same one grown and harvested in a different season in the same location. The nuances of fresh small-lot flours require you to become more intuitive with your ingredients. Commodity, industrial flour that has been blended from a number of different sources has been engineered to perform exactly the same way and sit on the shelf for up to one year. Today's commodity flours are a direct casualty of the industry's focus on mass production. Choosing heirloom grain varieties invites culinary experiences rich in both history and flavor.

When we consider the gluten potential of wheat, a higher-protein flour typically will reflect a stronger gluten network, but we have to dig a little deeper and look at gluten's specific components. Gluten is made up of two proteins: glutenin, which governs the elasticity, stretching ability, or strength of a flour, and gliadin, which reflects the extensibility or plasticity of dough. For bread we want an elastic dough encouraged by kneading or stretching and folding to form a strong network for trapping fermentation gases. When dough made with strong bread flour is worked, it organizes the glutenin molecules into an elastic network. This balanced with extensibility, or the ability for the dough to hold its shape, allows us to form a loaf with excellent potential for oven spring. For cakes, cookies, and other tender baked goods, flour that is low in protein and is mixed in a way that develops little gluten in the crumb is ideal.

Most pastas occupy a space somewhere in between bread and tender baked goods with the flour you choose reflecting the style of pasta you are creating. When purchasing flour to make pasta, you will often see it labeled with the Italian terms Tipo 00, 0, 1, or 2 with the degree of coarseness increasing as the numbers increase. Tipo 00 is typically ground from soft wheat and is used for fresh pastas. Tipos 1 and 2 are made from higher-protein wheats and are suitable for pizza or bread dough. When in doubt, or when purchasing American flour from a small stone-ground mill, look for the protein content of the flour to help inform you of its performance. This recipe is versatile and can utilize flour with moderate protein content such as spelt or a whole wheat bread flour with around 11% to 12% protein. You could use a flour with a lower protein, but you may need to adjust the amount of egg to strengthen the dough slightly without making it too tough.

Flour needs to be hydrated to become pasta and can be done so using water, oil, egg yolks, egg whites, or any combination of them in various proportions. Each ingredient has its own influence: water catalyzes gluten development, helping it to become elastic; conversely, the fat in oil coats gluten proteins and softens the dough; and the protein in egg yolks strengthens the dough. This recipe unconventionally uses sourdough starter both as a flavoring agent and to increase the digestibility of the flour. The acidity of a sourdough starter also helps to condition the dough, making it easy to roll out once it has fully hydrated. If you do not keep a starter, you can omit it or add 1 teaspoon vinegar instead.

This dough is excellent for hand rolling or for using with a hand-cranked machine and can be adapted using different flours. If you use a refined flour, simply decrease the water content a dash or use two egg yolks instead of three. Once mixed, the dough will be fairly stiff but should knead easily without tearing. My favorite flours to use in this recipe are higher-protein high-extraction emmer, Sonora whole wheat, and Rouge de Bordeaux whole wheat (see Resources, page 324), and a little durum semolina will add a coarser, more toothsome texture. Because most semolina flours have the bran and germ oils removed, I use semolina in small amounts to add texture without losing too much flavor. If using a lower-protein soft wheat, you may wish to decrease the water or oil and increase the amount of egg yolks.

220 g / 2 cups whole wheat flour	15 g / 1 tablespoon 100% hydration sourdough starter
½ teaspoon fine sea salt	60 to 75 g / 4 to 5 tablespoons water, plus more if needed
3 large egg yolks	
2 teaspoons extra-virgin olive oil	40 to 50 g / 4 to 5 tablespoons semolina flour for dusting

Whisk the flour and salt in a medium bowl. In a separate bowl, whisk the egg yolks, oil, starter, and 3 tablespoons of the water until a thick slurry is formed. Make a well in the center of the flour and pour in the slurry. Using a fork, bring the flour into the center to toss it with the yolk mixture. As the dough begins to come together, add the remaining 1 to 2 tablespoons water (or more if needed) until the mixture feels quite stiff but is not crumbly.

Turn the dough out onto a clean work surface and knead gently for 1 to 2 minutes, until the dough feels smooth. Wrap in plastic wrap and place in the refrigerator for at least 1 hour or up to 1 day.

Remove the dough from the refrigerator and allow to come to room temperature for about 10 minutes. Divide the dough into 4 parts. Using a rolling pin on a lightly floured surface, roll out two pieces at a time. When one piece begins to resist rolling out further, set it aside and allow it to rest while working with the second piece. When you have rolled them to the thinness directed by your intended noodle style, cut them to size. If you are making lasagna, leave it as is. Alternatively, use a pasta machine to roll the dough, adjusting from the thickest to thinnest setting as you go. Do not be tempted to roll the dough too thin, as this may cause the noodles to disintegrate when you boil them. Lightly dust with flour and set aside uncovered until ready to boil. If rolling in advance of boiling, consider storing between lightly dampened cloth or paper towels in an airtight container or plastic bag in the refrigerator for up to 8 hours.

Part
TWO

SEASONAL RECIPES

4

AUTUMN

From left to right: *apples (Malus 'Black Twig' and 'Rhode Island Greening'), 'Fuyu' persimmon (Diospyros kaki), dried roselle (Hibiscus sabdariffa), hazelnuts (Corylus sp.), rose (Rosa 'Louis Philippe'), and hong gochu (Capsicum annuum).*

Harvesting Abundance

BREADS

Smoked Paprika and Cheese
Sourdough Bread / 80

Sweet Jane
(Anadama Bread) / 82

SAVORY DISHES

Fresh Jujube Waldorf
Salad / 85

Spicy Boiled Peanuts / 86

Sweet Potato Peanut
Hummus / 90

Baked Root Chips with
Avocado Lime Crema / 92

Lasagna with Hazelnut
Béchamel / 94

Preserved Lemon, Caper,
and Anchovy Pasta / 97

Charred Peppers / 99

Muhammara with
Hazelnuts / 100

Beef Liver Pâté / 103

SWEETS AND DRINKS

Golden Oats / 105

Morning Kasha Porridge / 107

Millet Sourdough
Pancakes / 108

Æbleskiver / 111

Sweet Potato Tart with a
Coconut Pecan Crust / 112

Apple Charlotte / 115

Candied Persimmons / 117

Sorghum, Vanilla, and
Rosemary Apple Pie / 118

Orange and Vanilla
Rose Hip Sauce / 121

Brown Butter Corn Cake / 123

Pomegranate Paste (Seven
Months of Longing) / 124

Scuppernong Jelly / 128

Quince Preserves / 130

Hibiscus Poached Quince / 132

Spicebush Custard Cream / 135

Hazelnut Milk / 137

Rose Hip Tea / 138

Rose Hip Fizz / 140

Roselle and Rose Spritz / 142

Sweet Meadow Vermouth / 145

A Stranger's Door
Cocktail / 147

OPPOSITE *Be sure to properly identify the small oblong berries of spicebush (*Lindera benzoin)*, as it may be confused with the poisonous bush honeysuckle (*Lonicera tatarica*) that fruits at the same time of year.*

SMOKED PAPRIKA *and* CHEESE SOURDOUGH BREAD

Makes 2 loaves

Everyone loves a cheesy bread, and this one is my favorite. I like to make mine with flavorful, small-batch Tomme-style cheeses, such as Griffin from Sweet Grass Dairy in Thomasville, Georgia, or alpine favorites, such as Kaltbach from Emmi Cheese in Switzerland. It makes an impressive spread served with Sweet Potato Peanut Hummus (page 90), Fermented Green Tomatoes (page 287), and Basturma (page 285). I sprinkle the paprika in with the cheese to give the bread pockets of intense flavor upon baking, but you may add it to the initial mixing of the dough to evenly distribute it. (The recipe is also shown on page 91.)

1 recipe Table Loaf (page 62), made with the adjustments below

FOR THE FOLD-INS
140 g / 1 generous cup cubed or flaked (½- to 1-inch pieces) sharp cheese, at room temperature
1½ tablespoons smoked paprika

After you mix the salt into the Table Loaf, sprinkle one third of the cheese and paprika over the surface of the dough. Gently lift the dough from the bottom of the bowl and stretch to the middle, folding it over the add-ins. Rotate the bowl and fold two or three more times, until you have worked your way completely around the dough. Continue lifting, stretching, and folding every 30 to 45 minutes for the remainder of bulk fermentation at room temperature, about 4 hours, adding the cheese and paprika divided into thirds for the first three folds. This will both strengthen the dough and evenly distribute the fold-ins. When the dough has increased in size by at least one third, continue to the shaping, retarding, and baking steps as instructed for the Table Loaf (page 62).

SWEET JANE (ANADAMA BREAD)

Makes 2 loaves

There are more than a few competing narratives circulating as to the origin of Anadama bread, the inspiration behind this recipe. We know that it existed pre-1850 and enjoyed popularity in Rockport and Gloucester, Massachusetts, where it circulated from bakeries to the greater Northeast until the 1970s. It recycles a cornmeal and molasses mush (no doubt leftovers from many an early American meal) into a sweet and darkly baked loaf. I'm not particularly fond of the prevailing legend behind the origin of this bread: chastising a wife named Anna for her reputed laziness in preparing her husband's dinner. Exhausted of the same cornmeal mush, he is said to have returned home from fishing (or perhaps stacking stones) to throw together some wheat flour, a pinch of yeast, and molasses before declaring "Anna damn her!" and tossing it into the oven.

When I was testing this recipe, the Cowboy Junkies' version of Lou Reed's "Sweet Jane" kept me company on more than a few occasions, which inspired me to consider a new, more affectionate name for this recipe. I suggest you queue up that song and set to work making this loaf using ingredients that reflect your sense of place or availability. My Southern background and love for sugar cane syrup and buttermilk shine in this recipe, giving the crumb a robust, moist keeping quality, while the crust deeply caramelizes into a slightly bitter but nut-fragrant shell. You may substitute maple syrup, sorghum, or even carob, date, or grape molasses for the sweetener, and milk kefir or unstrained yogurt can be substituted for the buttermilk for a double fermentation of the soaker. I prefer to use a 100% hydration whole rye or whole wheat leaven for this bread, but a refreshed starter or leaven made with a more refined flour will work fine as well.

When you are ready to bake the prepared loaves, do not rush it. This is a very moist dough and will need a long and slow bake and a complete cooling before slicing to allow the crumb to set. (Recipe shown on page 52.)

FOR THE SOAKER
115 g / 1 cup coarse cornmeal
115 g / ½ cup boiling water
120 g / ½ cup whole buttermilk

FOR THE LEAVEN
25 g / 1 heaping tablespoon 100% hydration starter, refreshed (fed)
55 g / about ¼ cup tepid water (70°F to 75°F)
55 g / ½ cup whole-grain flour (rye, spelt, or whole wheat works well)

FOR THE DOUGH

135 g / ½ cup + 1 heaping tablespoon whole-grain leaven (see left)

300 g / 1⅓ cups water

160 g / scant ½ cup sugar cane syrup or maple syrup

450 g / 3¼ cups high-extraction bread flour

150 g / 1¼ cups whole wheat bread flour

25 g / ¼ cup rye flour

30 g / 2 tablespoons unsalted butter, softened

15 g / scant 1 tablespoon fine sea salt

PREPARE THE SOAKER

Place the cornmeal in a small bowl, pour the boiling water over it, and stir vigorously to combine. Allow to cool to at least 130°F, then stir in the buttermilk. Cover and leave to ferment at room temperature for about 8 hours or until the leaven is ready.

PREPARE THE LEAVEN

Place the starter and tepid water in a large bowl and stir to make a slurry. Add the flour and mix with a spoon until no dry lumps remain. Cover with plastic wrap and allow to ferment at room temperature for about 8 hours, until it has become active and bubbly.

MIX THE DOUGH

When the leaven is active and bubbly, add the water and sugar cane syrup. Stir to form a slurry, then add the flours and mix with your hands until no dry lumps remain. Cover with a kitchen towel or plastic wrap and allow to autolyze (rest) for about 20 minutes.

Distribute the butter and salt evenly over the dough and work it in as best as you can. Spread the soaker over the dough and gently incorporate by repeatedly folding the dough over it and rotating the bowl 4 or 5 times. The dough will feel overhydrated and mushy, but don't be too concerned; it will change texture during bulk fermentation. Cover with an inverted bowl or plastic wrap and set in a warm spot, ideally 70°F to 75°F. Bulk ferment for 3 to 4 hours depending on the temperature of the room.

To help develop the dough, stretch-and-fold it every 30 to 45 minutes until you are ready to shape it.

When the dough has increased in size by at least one third and it feels puffy and alive, divide it in half and follow the instructions for shaping the Table Loaf (page 62). Refrigerate for at least 8 hours or up to 12 hours.

BAKE THE LOAVES

Remove the dough from the refrigerator and allow it to come to room temperature for about 1 hour, until it feels like a water balloon and when gently poked with your index finger retains the impression. Place one of the loaves back into the refrigerator after it has fully proofed.

Place a 5- to 7-quart Dutch oven in the oven and preheat for 20 minutes at 470°F. Sprinkle a touch of cornmeal on a piece of parchment paper cut to fit the Dutch oven and carefully flip your dough onto it seam-side down. Score the top of the loaf with a razor blade ¼ to ½ inch deep. Carefully lower it into the preheated Dutch oven, cover, and bake for 20 minutes. Remove the lid, decrease the oven temperature to 450°F, and bake for another 25 to 30 minutes, removing about halfway through if your oven runs hot or if you are baking in unenameled cast iron. You're looking for the crust to be a deep, dark brown—do not be tempted to pull it before an instant-read thermometer registers an internal temperature of 200°F. Cool on a wire rack completely before slicing. Repeat with the second proof.

FRESH JUJUBE WALDORF SALAD

Serves 4 to 6

The first Waldorf salad was served in the late 1800s at the historic Waldorf Astoria Hotel in Manhattan. The original recipe is described by the maître d'hôtel, Oscar Tschirky, in *The Cook Book by "Oscar" of the Waldorf*. This ubiquitous salad has been reimagined over the last century in countless ways. My playful twist swaps fresh jujube for the apples and adds poppy seeds and tangy, chewy dried barberries. A visit to a Chinese market in early autumn will reveal mounds of burnished brown and green fresh jujube piled high. Ask for a sample and choose fruits that are firm and crisp with a pleasant acidity. If you cannot find barberries, substitute dried cranberries.

3 large stalks celery

1 tablespoon mayonnaise

2 tablespoons sour cream

2 tablespoons fresh lemon juice

1 teaspoon poppy seeds

2 generous pinches of salt

3 tablespoons chopped fresh flat-leaf parsley

1½ cups fresh jujube, pitted and coarsely chopped

⅓ cup toasted walnuts

¼ cup dried barberries

1 tablespoon extra-virgin olive oil

1 head chopped or torn romaine lettuce

3 cups arugula

FOR THE GARNISH

1 tablespoon fresh flat-leaf parsley leaves

1 tablespoon chopped fresh chives

Sprinkling of poppy seeds

Cracked black pepper

Use a vegetable peeler to peel the celery into ribbons, running it along the length of the back of the stalk. Place the ribbons into a bowl of ice water for 30 to 45 minutes to encourage them to curl.

In a medium bowl, whisk together the mayonnaise, sour cream, lemon juice, poppy seeds, and a pinch of salt. Stir in the chopped parsley, jujubes, walnuts, and barberries and set aside. In a small bowl, whisk together the remaining 1 tablespoon lemon juice, the oil, and the remaining pinch of salt.

Drain the celery ribbons and return them to the bowl. Toss with the lemon juice and oil mixture to coat. Toss in the lettuce. Arrange the celery and lettuce on individual plates or a large serving platter and top with the jujube mixture. Garnish with the parsley leaves, chives, poppy seeds, and black pepper. Serve immediately.

SPICY BOILED PEANUTS

Serves 2

You'll find boiled peanuts at makeshift roadside stands and gas stations littered across the South. I recently learned from a friend from South India that they are also popular in Asia. With my curiosity piqued, I came up with this boldly spiced version that's perfect as an afternoon snack with a cold glass of beer. It takes a few days of soaking then boiling them to make them deliciously edible, so you'll need to plan this snack food ahead. Instead of boiling them, you can combine all the ingredients in a slow cooker, add water to cover by at least 2 inches, and cook on high for 5 to 6 hours, scaling up if feeding a crowd. Once fully cooked, they will keep for three days in the refrigerator, or shell and use in Sweet Potato Peanut Hummus (page 90).

1 pound raw peanuts in their shells

1 stick cinnamon

3 whole star anise

1 fresh or dried chili

2 or 3 plump cloves garlic

3 tablespoons fine sea salt

Place the peanuts in a bowl, cover with warm water by at least 2 inches, and leave to soak overnight.

Drain the peanuts, place them in a large saucepan, and add the cinnamon, star anise, chili, garlic, and salt. Add water to cover by at least 2 inches. Bring to a boil, then reduce the heat to low. If the peanuts float to the surface, place a stoneware plate into the pot to weigh them down. Cook with the lid on for 3 to 4 hours, until the shelled peanut has a soft texture and yields to the bite. Drain and serve.

PEANUTS

The humble peanut, also known as the goober pea, has had a long history in the American diet. In the early days of our country, it was considered more appropriate for livestock than human consumption. It was not widely cultivated in the Southern colonies outside the hands of slaves and was made into a coffee-like beverage in the kitchens of the poor rather than eaten out of hand. It wasn't until the Civil War, when Confederate soldiers were desperate for food, that this protein- and oil-rich legume rose above its status as animal fodder.

Peanuts are not a nut at all but rather a legume. They were brought to the American colonies from their original native South American lands as an indirect result of the Atlantic slave trade. Although Europe and the colonies were less than enthusiastic for its cultivation, the peanut gained status as a productive and resilient staple crop in West and Central Africa. The etymology of the words *goober* and *pindar*, early terms for the peanut, are most likely derivatives of the languages of these regions. Despite the horticultural and nomenclature confusion, peanuts rose to a popular position in the early twentieth century when Dr. George Washington Carver began his research on their potential as a rotational crop with cotton and developed more than three hundred different uses for the once unassuming legume.

Using peanuts as a rotation crop resulted in a dramatic shift in soil nutrition. Cotton zaps the soil of nitrogen, which is essential to plant growth, while the peanut pulls nitrogen gas from the air and with the help of symbiotic rhizobial bacteria, fixes it in clever little root nodules before giving it back to the soil. Peanut production rose even more rapidly around 1900 when equipment was invented to better harvest and process them. After World War II, the popularity of the peanut rose as Allied troops would enjoy peanuts as a tasty snack. Peanuts are now a multibillion-dollar industry, and while the United States continues to grow and process most of what we consume as a commodity crop, Africa and China are now the biggest producers.

OPPOSITE *Peanuts* (Arachis hypogaea) *are formed on the roots of a leguminous plant and are not actually a true nut. They are related to beans and peas such as the pigeon pea (*Cajanus cajan)*, seen here.*

SWEET POTATO PEANUT HUMMUS

Makes about 1 cup

This sweet and spicy dip combines two hallmarks of Southern cuisine: sweet potatoes and peanuts. If you do not have boiled peanuts, you can substitute an equal volume of cooked chickpeas or another mild cooked dry bean of your choice. Green peanut oil is a regional specialty oil that is worth seeking out (see Resources, page 324) for its earthy, vibrant flavor, but you can also use a good-quality extra-virgin olive oil.

1 medium sweet potato (about 11 ounces), roasted, peeled, and chopped

1½ cups (about 12 ounces) Spicy Boiled Peanuts (page 86)

2 tablespoons fresh lime juice

2 tablespoons unsweetened smooth or chunky peanut butter

1½ teaspoons harissa or hot sauce, or to taste

1 teaspoon ground cumin

¾ teaspoon fine sea salt, or to taste

2 small cloves garlic

3 tablespoons green peanut oil, plus more as needed

Small handful of fresh cilantro leaves

FOR THE GARNISH

Drizzle of green peanut oil

Handful of fresh cilantro leaves

½ teaspoon nigella seeds

¼ teaspoon smoked paprika

1 tablespoon crushed toasted peanuts

Combine the sweet potato, peanuts, lime juice, peanut butter, harissa, cumin, and salt in a food processor. Using a Microplane, grate the garlic into the bowl of the machine. Process on high speed until smooth. With the motor running, drizzle in the oil through the hole in the lid until emulsified, adding a little more if needed for a smooth consistency. Check for salt, then add a handful of cilantro leaves and pulse to combine. Transfer to a serving dish, drizzle with oil, and decorate with the second handful of cilantro leaves, the nigella seeds, paprika, and crushed toasted peanuts.

OPPOSITE *This delicious spread can be made with either peanuts or chickpeas and is a spicy-sweet companion to Smoked Paprika and Cheese Sourdough Bread (page 80).*

BAKED ROOT CHIPS *with* AVOCADO LIME CREMA

Serves 2 to 3

If you've ever perused the root vegetables of an Asian or Hispanic market, you may be overwhelmed by the collection of unfamiliar purple, brown, and red-skinned root vegetables on display. Without a firm understanding of their labeling language or previous cooking experience with them, you may find yourself scurrying past to more familiar territory. But don't let the culinary possibilities for flavor, texture, and nutrition pass you by, as the dry-fleshed, starchy taro and ube are two excellent candidates for these addictively crunchy chips. Although I prefer mine simply seasoned with salt, you could sprinkle with cumin, chili powder, or lime juice before baking them. Enjoy them with persimmons, jicama spears, and avocado lime crema for dunking.

FOR THE CREMA
8 ounces sour cream
1 ripe avocado, flesh
    scooped out
2 tablespoons fresh lime juice
Zest of 1 lime
3 tablespoons chopped cilantro,
    mint, or a combination

2 tablespoons chopped fresh
    sorrel or flat-leaf parsley
½ teaspoon ground cumin
Few dashes of hot sauce
Generous pinch of salt,
    or to taste

FOR THE CHIPS
340 g / 12 ounces taro root
    or ube
1½ tablespoons Clarified Butter
    (page 34), coconut oil, or
    extra-virgin olive oil
¾ teaspoon fine salt

PREPARE THE CREMA
Combine all the ingredients in a food processor and process on high speed until smooth and creamy. Check for salt.

MAKE THE CHIPS
Preheat the oven to 375°F and line a baking sheet with parchment paper.

Use a vegetable peeler to remove the outer skin of the taro or ube and slice the flesh using a mandoline or sharp knife as thinly as possible for crisp chips. Place in a bowl and toss with the butter and salt. Place the slices on two prepared pans in a single layer. Bake for 10 minutes, then turn them over and bake for an additional 8 to 10 minutes. Taro chips are done when a toasted brown halo forms around the edges, and ube will darken considerably to a deep purple color. Remove from the oven and cool (they will crisp up as they sit). If any of the chips remain soft, return them to the oven for a few more minutes before serving. These chips can be prepared up to 2 days in advance; store in a paper bag in a cool, dry place.

OPPOSITE *Baked roots chips are a cravable addition to an autumn crudité spread of persimmons, jicama, and avocado sprinkled with salt and a pinch of sumac.*

TARO AND UBE

Taro, or *Colocasia esculenta*, is a large-leaved ornamental herbaceous tropical plant of the Araceae family that produces heavy tubers with dry flesh. It is a staple crop throughout Southeast Asia, South America, and much of the Caribbean where it is referred to as *dasheen*, *malanga coco*, *yautia*, or *eddo*. It can be fermented into starchy Polynesian poi, baked into puddings or breads, or stewed like yucca. When tossed with oil and salt, it bakes into a crunchy chip.

The flesh of ube is also dry, but it is much sweeter than taro. It has been cultivated in China since the 1600s and holds a significant place in Filipino cuisine. Ube has enjoyed recent popularity in ice cream, cake, and pudding for its surprisingly vivid purple color and complex flavor slightly reminiscent of raw almonds.

LASAGNA *with* HAZELNUT BÉCHAMEL

Serves 4 to 6 (makes one 8 × 12-inch casserole)

Americanized versions of Italian dishes are often meat and red sauce heavy with lots of cheese and just a whispered suggestion of vegetables. Much like Tex-Mex cuisine, lasagna has never wavered far from landing as a rock in your stomach. It wasn't until I was away from my family one Christmas that I learned the secret of using béchamel sauce rather than heaps of cheese to lighten up lasagna. Using only a sprinkling of Parmesan meant that I could go back for seconds without remorse! Béchamel sauce is one of the quintessential French mother sauces. Once you master it, you can tweak it to your satisfaction, using more or less flour and butter to adjust the thickness of the sauce. This version uses hazelnut milk rather than cow's milk for a rich but lighter option, but you may also use another nut milk of your choosing or whole cow's milk. This dish is now an annual tradition with the group of friends I gather with for Christmas to create our own sense of family closer to home.

Lasagna takes some work, especially if you're using handmade pasta, but thankfully it can be prepared in advance. If you're making it the day you plan to serve it, call a friend and ask them to come early to help while you catch up. You can assemble the layers and refrigerate the lasagna a few hours ahead while you prepare the dessert, or you can make it several weeks in advance, stash it in the freezer, and thaw overnight in the refrigerator before baking. Have it lustily bubbling in the oven while you arrange the appetizers and make the salad.

Like all casseroles, lasagna is a quintessential comfort food and lends itself to any number of fillings according to the season. Here I've offered an option for romanesco and fennel sausage and a vegetarian butternut squash version, although buttercup is a suitable substitute or even delicata squash, seeded, thinly sliced, and roasted until tender.

FOR THE HAZELNUT BÉCHAMEL

6 tablespoons unsalted butter, cubed

6 tablespoons all-purpose flour

2 cups Hazelnut Milk (page 137)

½ teaspoon fine sea salt, or to taste

¼ to ½ teaspoon freshly grated nutmeg

¼ teaspoon freshly ground black pepper

FOR THE ROMANESCO AND SAUSAGE FILLING (IF USING)

1½ teaspoons extra-virgin olive oil

8 ounces loose fennel sausage

3 cups (1-inch) romanesco florets (about 1 small head)

2 plump cloves garlic, minced

FOR THE BUTTERNUT SQUASH AND KALE FILLING (IF USING)

One 2½-pound butternut squash

1 to 2 tablespoons extra-virgin olive oil

½ teaspoon ground cinnamon

1½ teaspoons kosher salt

2 tablespoons Clarified Butter (page 34) or extra-virgin olive oil

1 medium onion

3 plump cloves garlic, sliced

8 cups shredded lacinato kale leaves (from 2 large bunches)

FOR THE NOODLES

½ recipe Fermented Pasta dough (page 70)

Semolina flour for dusting

Salt

Dash of extra-virgin olive oil

FOR THE SAUCES AND CHEESE

2 cups Tomato Sauce (page 293)

1 recipe Béchamel Sauce (see previous page)

½ cup grated Parmesan cheese

MAKE THE BÉCHAMEL

In a medium heavy-bottomed saucepan, melt the butter over low heat. Whisk in the flour 1 tablespoon at a time until a thick paste is formed. Continue to cook for about 1 minute, until the mixture begins to bubble and smells delightfully nutty. Slowly whisk in the milk 3 to 4 tablespoons at a time, allowing the mixture to come together before adding more. Initially it will seize and get very thick but will begin to loosen as you add more milk. Increase the heat to medium-low and cook for 3 to 4 minutes, until the sauce comes to a simmer. Remove from the heat, stir in the salt, nutmeg, and pepper, and let cool (it will thicken as it cools). Use immediately, or place plastic wrap directly over the surface to prevent a skin from forming.

MAKE THE SAUSAGE AND ROMANESCO FILLING (IF USING)

Heat the oil in a large skillet over medium-low heat. Add the sausage and cook, stirring to break it up, until it begins to brown, 6 to 7 minutes. Add the romanesco and garlic and continue cooking until the romanesco is just fork tender but still quite firm, 6 to 7 minutes. Remove from the heat and allow to cool.

MAKE THE BUTTERNUT SQUASH AND KALE FILLING (IF USING)

Preheat the oven to 400°F.

Cut the squash in half and remove the seeds. Rub the cut side with the oil, sprinkle with the cinnamon and ¾ teaspoon of the salt, and place cut-side down onto the prepared baking sheet. Roast for about 1 hour, until the squash is fork tender. Remove from the oven and cool. Peel the skin from the squash and slice about 2½ cups of the squash into 2- to 3-inch pieces and set aside.

Heat the clarified butter in a large skillet over medium heat. Add the onions and cook, stirring occasionally, until translucent and soft, about 7 minutes. Add the garlic and cook until fragrant, about 30 seconds. Add the kale and the remaining ¾ teaspoon salt, toss to coat, and cook until the kale is wilted, 3 to 4 minutes more. You may need to work the kale in batches depending on the size of your skillet, allowing it to wilt slightly before adding more. Stir in the squash pieces and cool.

(recipe continues)

**COOK THE NOODLES AND ASSEMBLE
THE LASAGNA**

Divide the pasta dough into four parts. Using a
rolling pin, roll two portions of dough at a time on
a lightly floured surface. When one piece begins to
resist rolling out further, set it aside and allow it to
rest while working with the second piece. Roll the
dough thin enough to just see your hand through
the noodle—too thin and it will disintegrate once
baked; too thick and it will be tough and rubbery.
Lightly dust with semolina flour. Cut into noodles
to fit your dish by slightly overlapping enough
noodles to create three layers of filling, using
scraps to fill any corners. Set aside uncovered on
the work surface until they feel leathery in texture,
about 10 minutes.

Fill a large bowl with ice and water to create an ice-
water bath. Fill a large pot with water, lightly salt it,
and bring to a boil over high heat. Gently slip a few
noodles into the pot and boil for 30 to 45 seconds,
until they are al dente. Remove each noodle gently
with tongs and transfer to the ice bath to cool.
Pull the noodles from the ice bath and lay flat on
a clean kitchen towel to drain. Repeat with the
remaining noodles.

Preheat the oven to 350°F.

Spread 1 cup of the tomato sauce over the bottom
of an 8 × 12 × 3-inch casserole dish. Arrange the
noodles over the sauce, slightly overlapping to
form a single layer. Add half of your chosen filling
and spread half of the béchamel over the top.
Add another layer of noodles and the remaining
filling. Spoon the remaining 1 cup tomato sauce
on top. Add a final layer of noodles and spread the
remaining béchamel over the noodles. Sprinkle the
cheese on top and cover with aluminum foil. Bake
for 30 minutes, then remove the foil. Increase the
oven temperature to 400°F and bake for another
15 to 18 minutes, until the top is toasty brown and
the edges are slightly crisp. Cool for at least
30 minutes or up to 1 hour before serving warm.

PRESERVED LEMON, CAPER, *and* ANCHOVY PASTA

Serves 3 to 4

This salty, umami-packed anchovy sauce is an easily executed reward for the work of handmade noodles. For an extra hit of veggies, toss in steamed broccoli or spinach after the anchovies have dissolved in the oil. Preserved lemons are easy to make at home with a little time and patience, or you can purchase them at Middle Eastern grocery stores.

1 recipe Fermented Pasta (page 70), cut into fettuccine noodles, or packaged fettuccine

¼ cup extra-virgin olive oil

One 2-ounce can flat anchovies in oil

¼ cup drained capers

3 or 4 plump cloves garlic, thinly sliced

¼ cup minced preserved lemon rind

Salt

½ cup chopped fresh herbs (fennel fronds, dill, or parsley work well)

Heat the oil in a large saucepan over medium heat. Add the anchovies, capers, and garlic and cook until the anchovies start to dissolve, 3 to 4 minutes. Turn off the heat and stir in the preserved lemon.

Bring a large pot of water to a boil and salt it before slipping the fresh pasta into the water. Cook for 1 to 2 minutes, until al dente. Drain the noodles, reserving 3 to 4 tablespoons of the cooking water. Transfer the noodles to the anchovy sauce and toss to coat, adding pasta water 1 tablespoon at a time until the sauce coats the noodles. Toss with the fresh herbs and serve immediately.

CHARRED PEPPERS

Charring the skins of peppers over an open flame brings a primal identity to any number of dishes, such as Muhammara with Hazelnuts (page 100). If you don't have an outdoor grill, you can use the broiler or even your stovetop burners to mimic that campfire flavor. My favorite candidates for charring include heirloom Hungarian wax peppers, which range from mild to quite spicy, poblanos, and smaller varieties such as jalapeños and habaneros. Use kitchen gloves when handling hot peppers. You may save and dehydrate the charred bits of flavor from the skins to make a smoky spread out of softened Cultured Butter (page 44).

Peppers of your choice

High-heat oil such as grapeseed, coconut, or avocado oil, if broiling

---

IF GRILLING

Place the peppers over the grate of a gas or charcoal grill over medium flame. Grill, turning frequently with tongs, until all sides are evenly charred and blistered black.

IF BROILING

Position a rack 4 to 6 inches under the heat source and preheat the broiler to high. Lightly oil a baking sheet.

Cut the peppers in half lengthwise. Place cut-side down on the prepared baking sheet. Broil for 6 to 10 minutes, until the skin of the peppers is evenly charred and blistered black.

IF USING A GAS RANGE STOVETOP

Position the peppers on the burners and turn on the exhaust fan. Turn the heat to medium-low and watch carefully as the skin blisters and turns black, rotating the peppers with tongs until the peppers are evenly charred and blistered black.

TO STEAM AND PEEL THE PEPPERS

Place the charred peppers in a paper bag and close it, or place in a bowl and cover with a plate. Allow to rest for at least 10 minutes, until cool enough to handle and the captured steam sweats the skins loose. Then peel away the charred skin and remove the stem, core, and seeds. (To retain some heat from the hot peppers, leave behind some of the seeds.)

Slice the peppers into thin strips and use immediately, or place in a jar, add oil to cover, a splash of vinegar, some minced garlic, and salt. Cover and store in the refrigerator for up to 3 weeks. Include in spreads, or serve as a condiment for crostini or a garnish for soups.

MUHAMMARA *with* HAZELNUTS

Serves 6 to 8

This recipe takes the best of two of my favorite red pepper condiments—muhammara and romesco sauce (muhammara is traditionally made with walnuts, and romesco sauce is based on hazelnuts)—and combines them into a tart, nutty, slightly bitter but mildly sweet dip. You may prepare this in a food processor, but I prefer the chunky results achieved with a mortar and pestle. If you can source green coriander in season, it will add a fresh and piquant flavor. Skip the toasting step for green coriander.

To simplify, you can substitute store-bought pomegranate molasses, which you can find at Middle Eastern markets or online (see Resources, page 324), for the pomegranate paste.

¾ cup hazelnuts

1 teaspoon cumin seeds

½ teaspoon coriander seeds

1 plump clove garlic

1½ teaspoons Aleppo or Urfa Biber pepper flakes

1 teaspoon fine salt

1¼ cups (about 6 large) sweet red Charred Peppers (page 99)

¼ cup (about 2) long and hot red Charred Peppers (page 99)

1 tablespoon fresh lemon juice

2 tablespoons Pomegranate Paste (page 124)

1 tablespoon extra-virgin olive oil

1½ tablespoons Sourdough Bread Crumbs (page 66)

2 tablespoons mint cut into chiffonade

Preheat the oven to 400°F.

Spread the hazelnuts onto a baking sheet in a single layer. Toast until they are fragrant and the skins begin to curl and pull away from the meat, 10 to 12 minutes. Remove from the oven and cool. Rub the nuts in a dry towel or between your hands to remove the skins.

Place the cumin and coriander seeds in a heavy skillet and toast over medium-high heat until fragrant, about 2 minutes. Transfer to a mortar and crush with the pestle to a powder. Add the garlic, Aleppo pepper, and salt and mash to a paste. Add the hazelnuts and crush to a coarse consistency. Add the charred peppers and continue working until a coarse paste forms. Transfer to a bowl and stir in the lemon juice, pomegranate paste, oil, and bread crumbs. This is best made several hours before serving. Top with the mint at the end. The spread will keep stored in a covered container in the refrigerator for up to 5 days.

OPPOSITE *Nothing compares to using a mortar and pestle when preparing Muhammara with Hazelnuts.*

BEEF LIVER PÂTÉ

Makes about six 4-inch ramekins

When sourced from healthy, happy grass-fed cows, beef liver provides a wide spectrum of benefits including protein, fat, vitamins, and minerals in easily absorbable forms. The strong, sometimes unpleasant flavor of beef liver can be tamed by soaking it in a bath of buttermilk, an old trick my mother taught me when she prepared liver from our cows. The result is a tender texture and milder flavor that blends into this smooth and delicious pâté. It is delicious served with fresh passion fruit pulp or Orange and Vanilla Rose Hip Sauce (page 121), thinly sliced fennel, and pomegranate arils as canapés. The color of the pâté is rather unfortunate, so I suggest packing it into ramekins and disguising it with tart and sweet Scuppernong Jelly (page 128) or another jelly to finish. The ramekins keep well this way, so you can easily prepare them in advance.

1½ pounds beef liver

2¼ teaspoons kosher salt

2 cups buttermilk

5 tablespoons Clarified Butter (page 34)

2 medium onions, sliced

1 large stalk green garlic, chopped, or 2 scallions, chopped

3 tablespoons port wine

½ head garlic, peeled and sliced

One 5-inch sprig rosemary, leaves finely chopped

1½ cups (3 sticks) unsalted butter, softened

8 ounces cooked smoked bacon, cut into ½-inch pieces

About ¾ pint Scuppernong Jelly (page 128) or another jelly

Line a baking sheet with parchment paper. Lay the liver onto the sheet and pat dry with paper towels. Sprinkle both sides with 1½ teaspoons of the salt and leave at room temperature for 20 minutes. Place the liver in a large bowl, pour in the buttermilk, and toss to coat. Cover and marinate in the refrigerator for 8 hours or overnight.

Drain off the buttermilk from the liver. Heat 3 tablespoons of the clarified butter in a large skillet over medium heat. Add the onions and green garlic and cook until the onions are softened and beginning to caramelize, about 15 minutes. Add the port and cook until it is absorbed, about 3 minutes. Add the garlic and rosemary and cook until fragrant, about 1 minute. Remove from the skillet to a bowl and set aside to cool. Wipe the pan with a paper towel and add the remaining 2 tablespoons clarified butter to the pan. Heat over medium heat until hot. Lay the liver flat into the skillet and sear on one side for 2 to 3 minutes, then flip and continue to cook for an additional 3 to 4 minutes, until the liver is tender but still slightly pink in the middle. Do not overcook. Transfer to a plate to cool.

(recipe continues)

OPPOSITE *This rich liver spread benefits from the sweetness of Scuppernong Jelly (page 128) and fresh passion fruit pulp.*

Coarsely chop the liver and place it in the bowl of a food processor. Add the softened butter and process on high speed until the mixture is smooth and pasty. Pass through a food mill or sieve into a large bowl. Return to the food processor, add the remaining salt and cooked onions and garlic, and process until smooth. Pulse in the cooked bacon and transfer to a serving bowl or small ramekins. Alternatively, you may reserve the bacon for garnishing if preparing canapés.

If using the jelly to cover ramekins of pâté, place it in a small saucepan and heat gently over low heat until it softens to a pourable texture. Pour in the jelly until it covers the ramekins by ¼ to ½ inch. Cool fully (it will set as it cools). Cover and store in the refrigerator for up to 5 days or in the freezer for up to 3 months. Serve at room temperature.

GOLDEN OATS

Serves 2

Precious saffron elevates this humble morning porridge into a nourishing feast for the senses. I call for adding whey to the soaking liquid to increase the digestibility of the oats, but you may substitute lemon juice or a small thimble-full of sourdough starter. My favorite way to make my oats is with coconut milk, cranberries, and toasted coconut and almonds.

1 cup thick rolled oats

1 cup water

2 tablespoons yogurt whey (see page 45)

2 generous pinches of saffron

1½ teaspoons sugar

1 cup whole milk, full-fat coconut milk (canned or fresh) or nut milk of choice

¼ cup dried fruit (cranberries, strawberries, or raisins work well)

1 to 2 tablespoons honey, to taste

FOR THE GARNISH (OPTIONAL)

2 to 3 tablespoons yogurt or Milk Kefir (page 39)

¼ cup toasted almonds and/or coconut flakes

1 tablespoon toasted sesame seeds

Place the oats in a medium nonreactive saucepan and cover with the water and whey. In a small mortar and pestle, grind the saffron with the sugar to a fine powder. Stir it into the oats, cover loosely, and leave to soak overnight.

The next morning, add the milk and dried fruit and bring to a gentle simmer over medium-low heat. Cook for 10 to 12 minutes, stirring often, until the oats are to the consistency you like. Stir in the honey and serve with the garnishes of your choice.

MORNING KASHA PORRIDGE

Makes 1 large or 2 small servings

This hearty, sweet recipe is a basic morning gruel that you can enrich with the milk of your choice, fruits, nuts, and warming spices. The garnishes are a delightful autumn blend of pears and persimmons, but feel free to substitute other seasonal fruits such as apricots, peaches, plums, or apples. This porridge is a canvas—you can barely sweeten it and top it with a simple sprinkle of hemp seeds or chia seeds, you can finish with a decadent dollop of Spicebush Custard Cream (page 135), or you can meet somewhere in between like I do.

½ cup whole kasha (toasted buckwheat groats)

1¼ cups whole cow's milk or nondairy milk of your choice (coconut works well)

2 tablespoons maple syrup

¼ cup dried cherries or golden raisins

¼ teaspoon ground cardamom

¼ teaspoon ground allspice

¼ teaspoon ground cinnamon

Pinch of salt

¼ to ½ cup water

2 tablespoons Clarified Butter (page 34), coconut oil, or a nut oil

1 large pear, or a handful of small Seckel pears or prune plums, cored and sliced ½ inch thick

FOR THE GARNISH (OPTIONAL)
2 to 3 tablespoons Spicebush Custard Cream (page 135), fresh cream, or Milk Kefir (page 39), to taste

1 to 2 tablespoons maple syrup, honey, or brown sugar, to taste

Generous spoonful of Candied Persimmons (page 117) with their syrup

1 to 2 tablespoons chopped toasted nuts (walnuts, pecans, or hazelnuts work well) and/or 2 teaspoons hemp seeds or chia seeds

In a small saucepan, toast the kasha over medium-high heat until fragrant, 2 to 3 minutes. Add the milk, 1 tablespoon maple syrup, dried cherries, cardamom, allspice, ¼ teaspoon cinnamon, and salt and cover. Bring to a gentle boil, then reduce the heat to low and simmer for 5 to 8 minutes until the mixture thickens, stirring occasionally. Add the water and continue cooking until the groats have begun to break down and become thick and creamy, 10 to 12 minutes more.

In a small bowl, toss together the sliced fruit, 1 tablespoon maple syrup, and ¼ teaspoon cinnamon. While the porridge is cooking, heat the clarified butter in a medium heavy skillet over medium-high heat. Place the sliced fruit into the skillet in a single layer and leave to sizzle until golden brown. Flip the fruit and cook until both sides are golden brown.

Spoon the porridge into bowls and drizzle with cream and maple syrup. Top with the caramelized fruit, the candied persimmons, and toasted nuts and/or seeds.

OPPOSITE *Porridge made with earthy buckwheat pairs naturally well with autumn flavors such as pears, Candied Persimmons (page 117), Spicebush Custard Cream (page 135), and pomegranate.*

MILLET SOURDOUGH PANCAKES

Makes 10 to 12 pancakes

It was difficult to settle on a recipe for sourdough pancakes, as I have so many versions with varying techniques, ingredients, and time commitments. Pancakes aren't usually a planned meal in my household, so when I make them, I end up mixing the batter the morning of using whatever flour I have on hand. Millet is an excellent choice, but sorghum, spelt, or einkorn will work as well. For a more digestible outcome, mix the batter at least two hours before making your pancakes. Bring all the ingredients to room temperature before mixing your batter.

2 large eggs, beaten

150 g / ¾ cup 100% hydration sourdough starter

40 g / 2 tablespoons maple syrup or honey

70 g / 3½ tablespoons unsalted butter, melted and cooled

245 g / 1 cup whole milk yogurt

1 teaspoon orange zest

240 g / 2 cups + 2 tablespoons whole millet flour

1 teaspoon ground cinnamon

1 teaspoon baking soda

Generous pinch of salt

165 g / ⅔ cup whole milk

FOR THE GARNISH
Butter

¼ cup Orange and Vanilla Rose Hip Sauce (page 121) or maple syrup, heated

1 tablespoon pistachios or pepitas, toasted and crushed (optional)

Beat the eggs, starter, maple syrup, 2 tablespoons of the melted butter, the yogurt, and orange zest in a large bowl until well combined. In a medium bowl, whisk together the flour, cinnamon, baking soda, and salt. Stir the dry ingredients into the wet ingredients, then add the milk 4 to 5 tablespoons at a time until you have a thick but pourable batter. If you wish to ferment the batter, cover with a dish towel and allow to sit at room temperature for 2 to 3 hours.

Heat a cast-iron or other heavy skillet over medium-low heat for 2 to 3 minutes. Add the remaining 1½ teaspoons butter and let it melt. Decrease the heat to low and pour in the batter to form a 5- to 6-inch pancake, using a scant ½ cup of batter. Cook for 2 to 3 minutes on each side until bubbles visibly and consistently break the surface, flipping to cook, until golden brown and fluffy. Repeat with the remaining batter. Serve with pats of butter, Orange and Vanilla Rose Hip Sauce (page 121), and toasted nuts, if using.

Æbelskiver are excellent served with preserves such as Cranberry Marmalade (page 254).

ÆBLESKIVER

Makes about 24 pancake puffs

I had been lugging around an authentic Danish æbleskiver pan for about four years before I finally gave these special little puffs a try. It takes practice to get them just right: you need to make sure the pan is well heated and know when to roll them over to complete their round shape. But once you get the hang of it, you will be happy you did! I like to use a stone-ground whole wheat pastry, spelt, or kamut flour for flavor and nutrition, but you may use all-purpose flour for a lighter texture (hold back 1 tablespoon milk and use it only if the batter isn't quite pourable). Serve with cups of strong tea or coffee.

110 g / 1 cup whole wheat pastry, spelt, or kamut flour

30 g / 2 tablespoons granulated sugar

2 teaspoons baking powder

1 teaspoon ground cardamom

½ teaspoon ground ginger

¼ teaspoon ground allspice

¼ teaspoon fine sea salt

175 g / ¾ cup whole milk

55 g / ¼ cup whole milk yogurt or Milk Kefir (page 39), plus more as needed

1 large egg

25 g / 1 tablespoon 100% hydration sourdough starter

90 g / 6 tablespoons unsalted butter, melted and cooled (3 tablespoons unsalted, melted and cooled + 2 to 3 tablespoons for the pan)

FOR THE GARNISH

30 g / ¼ cup powdered sugar

Orange and Vanilla Rose Hip Sauce (page 121) or your choice of jam

---

Whisk together the flour, sugar, baking powder, cardamom, ginger, allspice, and salt in a small bowl. In a large bowl, beat the milk, yogurt, egg, and starter by hand or with a handheld or stand mixer until smooth. Fold the dry ingredients into the wet ingredients, drizzling in 3 tablespoons of the butter as you fold. Mix the batter until it is relatively smooth. If it feels thick and holds its shape on the spoon, add more milk or kefir 1 tablespoon at a time until the batter is loose enough to pour. Allow to rest at room temperature for at least 1 hour or up to 4 hours.

Heat a well-seasoned æbleskiver pan over medium-low heat until lightly smoking. Turn the heat to the lowest setting and generously coat melted butter into each depression using a pastry brush. Add about 1 tablespoon batter to each depression to fill it halfway—do not be tempted to overfill, as the æbleskivers will not cook through in the middle. Cook until a noticeable skin is created around the outside rim of each æbleskiver. Using a skewer to pierce one side, lift the æbleskivers and tip the uncooked contents into the depression. When this batter forms a skin, flip them all the way over to create an enclosed ball. Cook for another 4 minutes, or until the middle is completely cooked through. Repeat with the remaining butter and batter. Dust with powdered sugar and serve immediately with Orange and Vanilla Rose Hip Sauce (page 121) or Cranberry Marmalade (shown in photo) (page 254).

SWEET POTATO TART
with a COCONUT PECAN CRUST

Makes one 10-inch tart

This naturally gluten- and dairy-free tart's rich, creamy filling is a delightful contrast to the nutty-sweet pecans, dates, and coconut that go into the crust. Milk kefir can be substituted for the coconut milk if you like. Coconut sugar and light brown sugar may also be exchanged freely in both the crust and the filling. You can make this tart a day ahead and serve it cold or at room temperature.

FOR THE FILLING
615 g / 2 medium (about
    1½ pounds) sweet potatoes
170 g / 3 large eggs
80 g / ½ cup brown sugar
220 g / 1 cup canned full-fat
    unsweetened coconut milk
2 teaspoons ground ginger
1 teaspoon ground coriander
1 teaspoon ground allspice
½ teaspoon freshly grated
    nutmeg
¼ teaspoon fine sea salt

FOR THE CRUST
210 g / 2 cups pecan halves
60 g / 1 cup shredded
    unsweetened coconut
55 g / 5 tablespoons coconut
    sugar
110 g / 6 to 8 large dried dates
    (4 ounces), pitted
1 teaspoon ground cinnamon
½ teaspoon fine sea salt
55 g / scant ¼ cup coconut oil
1 large egg white

**FOR THE SALTED MAPLE
WHIPPED CREAM**
255 g / 1 cup heavy cream
40 g / 2 tablespoons maple
    syrup, or to taste
½ teaspoon kosher salt

FOR THE GARNISH
Agrodulce (page 196)

ROAST THE SWEET POTATOES

Preheat the oven to 400°F and line a baking sheet with aluminum foil or parchment paper.

Wrap the sweet potatoes in aluminum foil and place on the prepared baking sheet. Bake for 45 to 60 minutes, until fork tender. You may roast the sweet potatoes up to 3 days ahead; store in the refrigerator until ready to use.

PREPARE THE CRUST

Reduce the oven temperature to 350°F.

Combine the pecans, coconut, coconut sugar, dates, cinnamon, and salt in the bowl of a food processor. Process until a coarse, sticky meal is formed. Add the oil and egg white and pulse to combine. Transfer the sticky-wet mixture into a

(recipe continues)

OPPOSITE *Sweet potato, coconut, dates, and pecans are a cravable combination in this tart, especially when served with salted maple whipped cream and Agrodulce (page 196) made with dried jujubes.*

10-inch fluted tart pan. Press to distribute the crust evenly into the bottom and up the sides. Prick the bottom with a fork and bake on a baking sheet for about 8 minutes, until the crust just looks dry. Remove from the oven (leave the oven on) and cool completely on a wire rack.

PREPARE THE FILLING

Combine the eggs, brown sugar, and coconut milk in the bowl of a blender or food processor. Blend on high speed until thoroughly combined. Peel and discard the skin of the sweet potatoes. Pack the meat into 2 cups and add to the processor along with the ginger, coriander, allspice, nutmeg, and salt. Blend on high speed until smooth. Transfer the filling to the cooled tart crust and smooth with a spatula to even the surface.

BAKE THE TART

Place the tart on a baking sheet and bake for 15 minutes. Lower the oven temperature to 325°F and bake for another 8 to 10 minutes, until the middle is set but still slightly wobbly (it will firm more as it cools). If the crust begins to brown too much before the middle is set, carefully tent the tart with aluminum foil. Remove from the oven and place on a wire rack to cool completely.

PREPARE THE SALTED MAPLE WHIPPED CREAM

Combine all the ingredients in a stand mixer or in a bowl using an electric hand mixer and beat on high speed until stiff peaks form.

TO SERVE

Slice the tart and serve with dollops of salted maple whipped cream and a garnish of agrodulce.

SWEET POTATO

Remnants of sweet potatoes have been dated as far back as 8000 B.C. in Peru, where the sweet potato is thought to have originated before domestication in Central America. Unlike most New World foods that made their way east by European trade routes, the sweet potato provides evidence that Polynesians may have had interactions with South Americans long before the Spanish arrived. With their sophisticated catamarans and enduring spirit, there are clues that the Polynesians may have made the long ocean voyage and brought this delicious tuber back home with them. Or perhaps a plant's seed landed on a bed of seaweed and floated its way over. Either way, a recent genetic study of sweet potatoes gathered in Polynesia in the late 1700s before their increased hybridization proves their link with the DNA of those in Ecuador and Peru. Since then, they have made their way around the world as hybrids of different cultivars selected for flavor and yield and, of course, earned a solid place at the Thanksgiving table to celebrate a food of our early American ancestors.

APPLE CHARLOTTE

Serves 4

This dessert of humble beginnings has been dressed up with a few nontraditional ingredients. Still, it is likely you will already have the ingredients in your pantry to make this impressively flavorful dish. Apple charlotte, or *sharlotka yablochnaya*, was originally made in the Russian tradition using rye or another hearty bread and red wine, but if you use leftover Sweet Jane (page 82) and rum, this recipe will have you sinking to your knees for more. Serve it warm with a scoop of vanilla ice cream, Toasted Fennel and Kumquat Ice Cream (page 184), or a drizzle of cold Spicebush Custard Cream (page 135) for the ultimate garnish.

113 g / ½ cup (1 stick) unsalted butter, plus softened butter for the pan

60 g / ½ cup (2 ounces) Sourdough Bread Crumbs (page 66)

340 g / about 12 ounces stale Sweet Jane (page 82) or Spiced Cherry Rye Levain (page 260)

495 g / generous 1 pound (about 3) Granny Smith or other baking apples

Juice of 1 lemon

½ teaspoon ground cinnamon

¼ teaspoon freshly grated nutmeg

45 g / ⅓ cup walnuts

76 g / ⅓ cup dark rum

50 g / ¼ cup sugar

1½ teaspoons finely grated orange peel

½ teaspoon pure vanilla extract

1 to 2 tablespoons sesame seeds

Preheat the oven to 400°F.

Liberally butter a 9 × 5 × 3-inch baking pan, sprinkle on the bread crumbs, and shake to coat, shaking out any excess. Trim the crusts from the Sweet Jane (reserve them for making Sourdough Bread Crumbs [page 66] or Bread Kvass [page 315]) and cut the bread into 1-inch pieces. Place on a baking sheet and toast in the oven for 10 to 12 minutes, tossing occasionally to evenly brown them. Remove from the oven and cool on the sheet, then tear into smaller pieces with your fingers.

Peel, core, and slice the apples between ⅛ to ¼ inch thick before tossing in the lemon juice (reserve the skins and cores for Apple Cider Vinegar, page 6). Melt 1 tablespoon of the butter in a large skillet over medium heat. Add the apples, cinnamon, and nutmeg and cook until tender to a fork, about 5 minutes. Transfer to a bowl to cool and melt the remaining 7 tablespoons butter in the same pan. Toss the torn bread and walnuts to coat in the butter and cook until fragrant and saturated, 3 to 4 minutes. Turn off the heat, add the rum, sugar, orange peel, and vanilla, and stir to coat.

Spread a layer of the torn bread over the bottom of the baking pan followed by a layer of the apples, finishing with a final layer of torn bread. Sprinkle the sesame seeds on top and place into the oven. Bake for 1 hour, or until the apples are soft and bubbly and the bread topping is toasty brown and crisp. Place on a wire rack to cool and set for 20 minutes, then slice and serve warm.

CANDIED PERSIMMONS

Makes about 1 pint

Persimmons carry the torch of autumn, their glossy light yellow to deep reddish orange skin matching the turn of maple leaves and blazing sunsets as they arrive to market. Although originally from China, more than two thousand cultivars exist with increasingly enticing hybrids whose chocolate-speckled flesh and endearingly sweet flavor have increased their desirability. They were introduced to California in the 1800s where some of the most delicious fruits are now produced in years with adequate rainfall but are also grown in countries such as Korea and China where they are imported to the States in large quantity. Firm Fuyu persimmons are used here, distinctively different from their soft and squishy ripe cousins the Hachiya. Although I prefer to leave the edible skins on, you may choose to peel them before cooking if you find them undesirable.

1¼ cups honey
½ cup Apple Cider Vinegar (page 6)
1 tablespoon orange blossom water

Pinch of salt
4 Fuyu persimmons, sliced about ¾ inch thick

Combine the honey, vinegar, orange blossom water, and salt in a medium saucepan and heat over medium-low heat to loosen the honey and combine the ingredients. Add the persimmons, reduce the heat to low, and cook until the persimmons are translucent and the mixture has thickened considerably, about 20 minutes, stirring occasionally to avoid scorching. When they are close to done, the skins will curl slightly. When the flesh becomes rosy orange, tender, and somewhat translucent, take them off the heat. Cool and store, covered, in the refrigerator for up to 1 month.

SORGHUM, VANILLA, *and* ROSEMARY APPLE PIE

Makes one 9-inch deep-dish pie

Few American food traditions can outdo our beloved apple pie. A home-baked apple pie with its warm, sweetly spiced aroma is a pure expression of love. This version cooks a blend of sorghum syrup and butter into a caramelized glaze. White pastry flour or a blend of white and red whole wheat pastry flours stands up to the rosemary, which adds an almost savory quality to the crust that is balanced by the unmistakable flavor of real vanilla in the filling. You may use common types of baking apples, such as Granny Smith, Honeycrisp, or Braeburn, or more obscure heirloom varieties, such as Russets, Black Twigs, or Pippins. Baking the pie in a large brown paper bag helps ensure that the apples are cooked through without the piecrust becoming overly browned. Serve with Toasted Fennel and Kumquat Ice Cream (page 184) or vanilla ice cream.

FOR THE ROSEMARY DOUBLE CRUST

1 recipe Fermented Whole-Grain Piecrust dough (page 58)

1½ tablespoons minced fresh rosemary

FOR THE EGG WASH AND TOPPING

1 large egg yolk

Generous splash of whole milk, half-and-half, or heavy cream

20g / 1½ tablespoons coarse sugar (demerara, muscavado, or turbinado work well)

FOR THE FILLING

30 g / 3 tablespoons fresh lemon juice

1362 g / 3 pounds (7 to 8) medium baking apples

1 plump vanilla bean

65 g / ⅓ cup granulated sugar

2 teaspoons orange zest

½ teaspoon ground cinnamon

Generous pinch of salt

85 g / ¼ cup sorghum syrup

30 g / 2 tablespoons unsalted butter, cut into small slices

PREPARE THE ROSEMARY CRUST

Make the fermented piecrust dough, adding the rosemary to the dry ingredients before mixing in the liquid. Divide into two pieces, one slightly larger than the other. Press into rounds, wrap in plastic wrap, and refrigerate for at least 1 day or up to 3 days. Roll the dough according to the directions on page 58 and chill for at least 30 minutes or up to 1 day before assembling the pie.

When ready to bake the pie, roll one piece of dough to a 10- to 11-inch circle that's ⅛ to ¼ inch thick, and the second piece just slightly larger. Drape the larger piece into the pie pan, gently pressing to fill the bottom and the sides. Trim the

(recipe continues)

OPPOSITE *Deep-dish apple pie requires a long baking time, so don't let its golden crust fool you into pulling it from the oven too early!*

edges with kitchen scissors or a knife, leaving a
½-inch overhang. Cover both the top crust and
the pie pan with plastic wrap and place in the
refrigerator while you prepare the egg wash.

PREPARE THE EGG WASH

Whisk the yolk with the milk in a small bowl and
set aside.

PREPARE THE FILLING

Place the lemon juice in a large bowl. Quarter and
core the apples, reserving the discarded pieces
for Apple Cider Vinegar (page 6) or Apple Pectin
Stock (page 16). Slice the apples on a mandoline
⅛ to ¼ inch thick (too thin and they will cook down
to mush). Place the apples in the bowl, tossing to
coat with the lemon juice. Sprinkle the sugar over
the apples and toss to combine, using your fingers
to separate and coat each piece with the sugar.
Leave to sit covered with a plate or plastic wrap for
at least 45 minutes or up to 3 hours. Drain off the
liquid and halve the vanilla pod. Scrape the seeds
over the apples and add the orange zest, cinnamon,
and pinch of salt, tossing to combine.

Transfer the apples to the pie pan in overlapping
and snugly arranged flat stacks (to minimize
shrinkage), mounding the apples toward the center.
Drizzle with the sorghum syrup and finish by
evenly distributing the butter over the top, then set
the top crust over the filling. Fold the overhanging

crust under the bottom crust and use your fingers
or a fork to decoratively crimp the edges. Brush
the egg wash on the surface of the crust using a
pastry brush and sprinkle with the coarse sugar.
Cut several 2-inch vents in the top and place in the
freezer for at least 15 minutes or up to 1 day to firm
the crust before baking. If freezing for longer than
30 minutes, be aware that the cooking time will be
extended by 20 to 25 minutes.

BAKE THE PIE

Position a rack in the middle of the oven and
preheat the oven to 400°F. Line a baking sheet
with parchment paper.

Place the pie sideways in a large brown paper bag,
fold the opening of the bag, and staple it closed.
Place on the prepared baking sheet in the oven
on the middle rack, making sure the bag does not
touch the sides or top of the oven, and bake for
20 minutes. Decrease the oven temperature to
375°F and bake for an additional 70 minutes. To
fully brown the crust, remove the paper bag and
continue to bake for an additional 15 to 20 minutes.
There should be no blond spots remaining on the
crust. The pie is done when the crust is a deep,
dark brown and a knife inserted into one of the
vents easily pierces the soft apples. Remove from
the oven and place on a wire rack to cool for at
least 2 hours to allow the juices to set. Slice and
serve warm with ice cream.

ORANGE *and* VANILLA ROSE HIP SAUCE

Makes about 2 pints

This fragrant and highly nutritious sweet jam is brimming with vitamin C from autumn-harvested rose hips. For best flavor and yield, choose plump fruits of *Rosa canina* (the dog rose commonly found in Europe) or *Rosa rugosa* (the beach rose that has naturalized the United States) with a deep red color in September and October. I love pairing rose hips with vanilla and orange, but I have recently enjoyed making this sauce with pinches of ground allspice, cinnamon, clove, and cardamom added to the mix. (Recipe shown on page 109.)

8 to 9 cups rose hips
About 4 cups sugar

3 tablespoons fresh lemon juice
Zest of 1 orange

½ cup fresh orange juice
1 plump vanilla bean

Trim away any dark spots from the rose hips and remove the stems and dried calyx. Place the rose hips in a large pot and add water to cover by at least 2 inches. Bring to a simmer over medium-high heat, then reduce the heat to low to maintain a simmer, cover, and simmer for 30 minutes, or until the flesh pierces easily with a fork. Transfer the rose hips and cooking liquid to a food mill positioned over a large bowl. Process the hips to remove the seeds and hairs, starting with the coarsest disk and graduating to the finest disk. When you have a smooth, silky pulp, I strongly suggest taking the time to run it through a fine-mesh sieve to remove any remaining hairs.

For every 4½ cups (1150 g) of rose hip pulp, add 4 cups (800 g) granulated sugar, the lemon juice, orange zest, and orange juice. Split the vanilla bean lengthwise and scrape the seeds into the mixture, then add the scraped bean to the pot as well. Bring to a boil over high heat, reduce to medium-low, and stir continuously for about 10 minutes, until the mixture becomes thick and the bubbles turn glassy. Turn off the heat, remove the vanilla bean pod, and skim away any foam that has accumulated. Transfer the jam to sterilized jars and seal. You may process in a water bath for long-term room temperature storage or leave 1 inch of headspace in the jars and freeze for up to 1 year.

BROWN BUTTER CORN CAKE

Makes one 10-inch cake

This cake is quiet, hearty, and satisfying without being too sweet. Like a large, sliceable financier, it can be cut into small wedges and enjoyed for breakfast or with afternoon tea. When autumn arrives, I like to make it with halved foxy muscadines or jammy Concords, but Champagne grapes, pears, or summer stone fruits and berries work well too.

160 g / ½ cup + 3 tablespoons Brown Butter (page 34)

70 g / ½ cup toasted almonds

140g / 1 cup powdered sugar, plus more for serving

50 g / ½ cup fine to medium cornmeal

55 g / ½ cup whole wheat, pastry, or spelt flour

1 teaspoon ground allspice

1 teaspoon ground cardamom

½ teaspoon fine sea salt

185 g / ¾ cup egg whites

2 heaping teaspoons lemon zest

150 g / small bunch of grapes, or ½ cup fresh blueberries, raspberries, blackberries, or the fruit of your choice

---

Preheat the oven to 425°F.

Melt the brown butter in a 10-inch ovenproof skillet.

Combine the almonds, powdered sugar, cornmeal, flour, allspice, cardamom, and salt in the bowl of a food processor and process until the almonds are finely ground. Transfer to a large bowl and vigorously beat in the brown butter, scraping in the browned bits from the skillet. Beat in the egg whites and lemon zest.

Pour the batter into the warm skillet and position the fruit on top, allowing it to sink just a bit before placing in the oven. Bake for 10 minutes, then decrease the oven temperature to 375°F. Continue baking for another 12 to 14 minutes, until the sides pull away from the skillet and a toothpick inserted into the center tests clean. Turn off the heat, vent the oven by popping open the door, and leave the cake on the oven rack for an additional 5 minutes. Remove from the oven and place on a wire rack to cool completely. Invert from the pan or serve straight from the pan with a dusting of powdered sugar.

OPPOSITE *The nuttiness of both brown butter and cornmeal pair beautifully with a number of different fruits in this snack cake.*

POMEGRANATE PASTE
(SEVEN MONTHS *of* LONGING)

Makes about 1 cup

Seven months of longing. This number oddly corresponds to two seasonal pleasures that might appear unrelated. As the last leaves fall to the ground, I enjoy a final refreshing swim in the Atlantic Ocean before my least favorite season ensues. At this time, pomegranates appear in the local markets, their taut skins stretched around a powerhouse of flavor brimming with nutritional promise. Seven months until the next swim. Every year as I wrap a towel around my shivering shoulders and wipe the sand from my feet one last time, the pomegranate returns and I amusedly curse its allure! Seven months of hoarding and tearing through the leathery skin of pomegranates, juice staining my fingers and dripping from my savage chin. And when I am brave enough to dip a toe into chilly May waters, seven months of gestation until the garnet-colored elixir of life returns to splatter my kitchen walls.

The large red orbs bursting with dark red, astringent arils are what we most often find in groceries in the West, meeting eager hands and lips in autumn after a lengthy six- to seven-month ripening on the shrub. There are other smaller, sweeter varieties sporting a yellowish to blushing leathery skin and softly pink to clear arils. These can be found at specialty grocers or farmers' markets in places, such as California, where they are grown. When possible, I like to use a combination of sweet and tart varieties for this paste. It's a recipe that takes time, is almost laughably messy, and is oozing with sensuality if you choose to engage a willing lover. If you're the unromantic type, simply buy some juice cleverly packaged in shapely bottles and boil it down to a syrup. Taste for tartness, add a little sugar and lemon juice, and you'll have a delicious flavor enhancer. It just won't be as potent as the homemade stuff.

Seeding a pomegranate is an excellent stress reliever when you've had a frustrating day. This technique is a kitchen hack I learned from a Persian friend: use a knife to pierce entry into the middle of the fruit, then use your hands to split the fruit down the middle lengthwise. Fold each half outward, splaying the pith and revealing the jeweled arils. Hold one half in your palm split-side down and position it over a bowl. (Some people like to fill the bowl with water, but I find this unnecessary.) Use the back of a wide wooden spoon to vigorously spank the pomegranate, encouraging the arils to release from their membrane. Repeat with the other half and pick out any remaining bits of pith.

This recipe is pure pomegranate flavoring that adds a bright tartness to any number of dishes, including Tangy Bread Salad with Peaches, Tomatoes, and Purslane (page 272) and Muhammara with Hazelnuts (page 100). You may experiment with other fruits, such as Concord grapes, in place of some of the pomegranate arils to add another dimension of flavor (cook until their skins burst before mashing). My favorite variation is to substitute half of the pomegranate arils with an equal volume of fresh raspberries and making it into a brightly colored powdered sugar glaze to use for cakes and cookies.

8 cups pomegranate arils (about 2½ pounds; 5 to 6 large fruits)

2 tablespoons sugar

¼ teaspoon fine sea salt

OPTIONAL ADDITIONS

One 2-inch stick cinnamon

3 to 5 whole allspice berries

¼ teaspoon black peppercorns

Place the pomegranate arils in a wide pot and set over medium-low heat. Bring to a simmer and smoosh with a potato masher, kraut tamper, or the bottom of a jar to release the juices. Turn off the heat and process through a food mill in small batches to extract the juice. Compost the pits. You should have about 3⅓ cups juice and pulp. If short, you may adjust by adding pomegranate or another fruit juice, such as orange. Return the juice to the pot and add the sugar, salt, and spices, if using. Bring to a boil over medium-high heat, then reduce the heat to low and cook for about 1 hour, stirring occasionally and skimming the surface of foam, until the paste is thick and darkened considerably. Transfer to a sterilized jar, cool, cover, and store in the refrigerator for up to 6 months.

POMEGRANATE

The pomegranate, or *Punica granatum*, is an ancient fruit originally from Persia and North India that was domesticated somewhere between three and four thousand years ago. Based on excavations from the Bronze Era in Israel, it may be one of the first cultivated fruits in human history. It has enjoyed a sanctified reverence in cultures that have embraced its persuasive benefits. Born from exotically ornamental, pendulous reddish orange flowers, pomegranate fruits grow on handsomely large evergreen shrubs that can be trained as single-trunk trees. They come in many sizes, colors, and even flavors, ranging from mildly sweet and watermelon-like to puckery tart and astringent. They can be pressed to make a refreshing beverage, reduced into a syrup to flavor salads or pastries, or made into a savory Persian walnut sauce called fesenjoon that's smothered over tender duck or chicken. The thick skin and staining blooms can also be utilized as a dye for fabric, rugs, and leather.

Pomegranates have long symbolized prosperity, abundance, and even fertility, reflecting their proliferation of juicy arils and antioxidant-rich health profile. They are mentioned in many religious scriptures and depicted in numerous works of art, elevating the fruit from a food staple to one of divine significance. The Quran mentions it as one of the six fruits of paradise, Zoroastrianism considers it a symbol of eternal life, and Buddhism reveres it as one of the three blessed fruits, etched into the Zen temples of China after they found their way east along the Silk Road. Pomegranates are neatly packaged and easily transportable, which would have made them excellent companions to the tradesmen of the spice routes. Unsurprisingly, pomegranates migrated to ancient Egypt most likely via Syria, where their importance extended into the afterlife, most famously depicted on a vase contained in King Tutankhamun's tomb.

Considering its Latin name, which translates to *seeded apple*, I am convinced Eve would have been more likely to lure Adam out of Eden with a pomegranate than with an ordinary apple. The story of temptation unfolds in Greek mythology with Hades enticing Persephone with the pomegranate and binding her to him in the underworld. I imagine his ruggedly strong hands tearing open the plump fruit as Persephone admired the edible rubies tumbling from his hands. Perhaps he scooped them up and fed them to her as she cooed and considered her possible fate, eventually yielding to his irresistibly delicious argument. This enraged her mother, Demeter, so much that she abandoned her duties in pursuit of reclaiming her daughter, making crops wither into death and dormancy. This woefully dramatic tale explains the passing of the seasons: when Persephone pays her mother an annual visit in the spring, the barren earth once again provides life.

OPPOSITE *Pomegranate fruits vary widely in both their exterior and interior and include a color spectrum beyond the most commonly grown ruby seeds of 'Wonderful' known in the United States. Pomegranate flavor is equally broad depending on the cultivar, ranging from tart and tannic to sweet and mild.*

SCUPPERNONG JELLY

Makes about 3½ pints

I have many fond memories of growing up with scuppernong grapes, the tart autumn treats that are now cultivated and sold regionally. As a child I would swing wildly from the vines to help shake the grapes free as my father would gather them, gifting them to my grandmother to make jelly for her famed biscuits. Although she was the only one in the family who wasn't a prolific drinker, she always had a little bottle of muscadine wine tucked away to secretly "nip," as she would call it.

This recipe uses the juice of the scuppernong, which you can easily find at farmers' markets in Southern states such as Arkansas, Tennessee, Georgia, and North Carolina, or you can extract it by boiling down the fruit and straining the skins and seeds. Forage or purchase grapes that are at the just-ripe stage, with even a few that are underripe to ensure that you will have enough pectin for the jelly to set. If you are concerned your grapes may be overripe, you can use 1 cup of reserved citrus seeds to assist in the pectin content—bring the juice and seeds to a boil, then leave to steep overnight.

You will need a generous 3½ quarts of grapes to make enough juice for this recipe. Place the grapes in a large pot and mash them gently to release their juices. Bring to a boil, then reduce the heat to maintain a simmer and simmer, stirring occasionally, for about 10 minutes until the skins have collapsed and inner flesh has disintegrated to a soft mush. Pass the grapes and juice through a food mill on the coarsest setting into a large bowl. Place the bowl in the refrigerator overnight and allow any solids to settle. The next day, strain through a jelly bag or nut milk bag, leaving behind any residue at the bottom of the bowl (do not squeeze the bag).

Although the sugar content of this recipe is quite high, do not attempt to reduce the sugar, as if you do it will not set. This jelly is excellent served with Beef Liver Pâté (page 103).

7 cups scuppernong juice
   (see headnote)

6 cups sugar
6 tablespoons fresh lemon juice

Place a small plate in the freezer.

Heat the juice in a large pot over medium-high heat. Just before it comes to a rolling boil, stir in the sugar and lemon juice to dissolve. Reduce the heat to maintain a medium boil, skimming the surface of foam and allowing water to evaporate. After about 25 minutes, check for a set according to the directions on page 18, or alternatively you may use an instant-read thermometer to confirm the juice has reached 221°F. Continue cooking as needed until the jelly sets. Pour into sterilized jars and process in a hot water bath for 10 minutes. Store in a cool location for up to 1 year.

SCUPPERNONG GRAPES

Scuppernong grapes are a type of *Vitis rotundifolia*, or muscadine, grape with a unique musky flavor that grows well in the hot and humid southeastern United States. Their thick, woody vines reach high into the canopy of hardwood forests where they drop their large round fruits when the first frost rolls around. Scuppernongs are named after the Scuppernong River in Sir Walter Raleigh's colony in North Carolina, where they have been gathered since at least 1554.

Scuppernongs are a thick-skinned, greenish bronze, tart variety of muscadine (other varieties of muscadine are typically dark purplish black in appearance and sweeter). Muscadines have the most antioxidants of any grape, including ellagic acid and resveratrol, which can help prevent cancer, heart disease, and high cholesterol.

QUINCE PRESERVES

Makes about 6 pints

There is something both alluring and exotic about quince. It feels firm and dense in the hand with a felted exterior not unlike a peach. Its fragrance permeates every corner of the room, stimulating the appetite with a floral complexity reminiscent of an orchid-filled jungle forest. And yet its inedibility in this raw state has sealed its fate as one of the most underutilized fruits in Western cuisine. What a pity!

Quince season is autumn, when the markets have long since said good-bye to tomatoes and are instead brimming with apples, pears, and root cellar vegetables such as potatoes, turnips, carrots, and beets. I snatch up quince as soon as I see them and let them lie in admirable repose until they become just fragrant enough to make this preserve. Like most fruits intended for preservation with sugar, if you let quince ripen fully, it will lose its pectin content and will not set nearly as well as when it is still slightly green. I add the sugar slowly, tasting along the way, as some quince are more astringent than others and may need more or less sugar than what is suggested here. If you happen to get your hands on more than you can muster to preserve, try letting some fully ripen to a golden color, then core, chop, and add it to a lamb stew or chicken tagine.

For this recipe, you can cook the quince for more or less time and with more or less sugar depending on your desired result. If you have the option of time and an abundance of fruit, dehydrate some or all of it to make a membrillo-type paste, delicious served with salty cheese and crusty bread. Use the spreadable version on toast, in yogurt, or as a glaze for roast chicken or pork.

6 to 7 large quinces (about 7 pounds)

6 to 7 cups water

6¾ cups sugar

1 cup fresh lemon juice

5 to 6 tablespoons rosewater, to taste

1½ to 2 tablespoons ground cardamom, to taste

Cut the quince into large chunks and place it into a large preserving pot. Add water to just cover. Cook over medium heat, stirring occasionally, until the quince is fork tender, about 30 minutes. Turn off the heat and set aside until cool enough to touch (or refrigerate overnight). Run the mixture through a food mill to remove the cores and seeds and return to the pot. Bring to a simmer over medium heat, then turn off the heat. Stir in the sugar a little at a time, tasting along the way, until it is fully dissolved. Add the lemon juice, rosewater, and cardamom. Return to the stovetop, turn the heat to medium-low, and cook for 1 to 1½ hours, stirring frequently to prevent the bottom from scorching, until the preserves hold their shape thickly on a spoon. Transfer to sterilized jars and process in a hot water bath for 5 minutes to seal.

Poaching quince in a gentle simmer of syrup infused with hibiscus fills the kitchen with a warm, floral perfume.

HIBISCUS POACHED QUINCE

Serves 6

The humble quince is transformed into an elegantly simple dessert when poached with tangy hibiscus and served with Spicebush Custard Cream (page 135) or vanilla ice cream. The quince may require more or less cooking time depending on how ripe it is, but be sure to keep the liquid from boiling, as boiling will break the fruit into mush.

7 cups water

2 cups sugar

1 stick cinnamon or 5 whole
   allspice berries

4 fresh, or 6 to 8 dried, and
   whole hibiscus sepals

1¼ pounds (about 3 medium)
   quince

Combine the water, sugar, cinnamon, and hibiscus in a large pot. Bring to a simmer over medium-high heat, stirring until the sugar dissolves. Halve the quince and slip them into the hot syrup. Reduce the heat to low and simmer uncovered for 1 to 2 hours, until the quince is fork tender. Turn off the heat to cool slightly and let the syrup thicken. Serve warm, at room temperature, or cold for a refreshing after-dinner indulgence.

SPICEBUSH CUSTARD CREAM

Makes about 5 cups

Spicebush berries have a remarkable flavor and are one of my favorite wild spices to infuse into autumn and winter recipes. This cream is rich and comforting when served slightly warm with Hibiscus Poached Quince (page 132) but can be equally refreshing as a cold drizzle to a warm slice of Sorghum, Vanilla, and Rosemary Apple Pie (page 118).

3 cups whole milk

1 cup heavy cream

¼ cup + 2 tablespoons fresh or dried spicebush berries

Three 1 × 3-inch strips orange zest

8 large egg yolks, at room temperature

1 cup sugar

Generous pinch of salt

Pour the milk and cream into a large heavy-bottomed saucepan and add the spicebush berries and orange zest. Heat until bubbles just start to form around the perimeter of the pot. Mash the berries with the back of a spoon to encourage them to release their flavor. Turn off the heat and allow to steep for at least 1 hour or up to overnight (dried berries will need longer than fresh berries). Taste periodically for strength of flavor. Strain through a fine-mesh sieve into a bowl, then return to the pot, place over medium heat, add the sugar, and stir until it dissolves.

Fill a large bowl with ice and position a smaller bowl on top.

Beat the egg yolks in a large bowl. While whisking vigorously, pour in 1½ cups of the sweetened cream in a thin, steady stream to temper the egg yolks. Then slowly pour the tempered yolks back into the sweetened cream in the pot. Turn the heat to medium-low and cook the custard, stirring with a wide spatula and watching that it doesn't curdle, until it coats the back of a spoon, 10 to 12 minutes. Pour through a fine-mesh sieve into the chilled bowl. Serve immediately, or place a piece of plastic wrap directly on top of the custard to prevent a skin from forming and keep in the refrigerator for up to 1 week.

OPPOSITE *Spicebush (*Lindera benzoin*) is an attractive understory tree with yellow autumn foliage often found at the edges of forests.*

SPICEBUSH

Spicebush, or *Lindera benzoin*, is an understory shrub belonging to the laurel family, native to the woodlands of the eastern United States. Every part of the plant is showy and fragrant including the bark of its smooth, sprawling branches, which earned its specific epithet *benzoin*, derived from the Arabic word for "aromatic gum." It is appreciated in the winter landscape for its handsomely shaped and distinctively round buds leading to bright green flowers bursting forth in clusters in March. My favorite attributes are its golden leaves and bright red berries that appear in September in the Carolinas and mature as late as October in the Northeast, a feast for birds or humans alike. Do not, however, confuse *Lindera*'s oblong ½-inch shiny red drupes with poisonous round honeysuckle berries. Look for spicebush at the edges of woodlands, where their fall color is best exposed to the sun, and try to identify them before industrious birds make away with the full larder. Luckily, they tend to populate gregariously in separate drifts of male and female plants with multiple shrubs clustered within a short distance to pollinate each other.

When abundant, you may harvest and dry the berries to use later in custards, grind them into a powder to add to cakes or cookies, or replace the fennel in Toasted Fennel and Kumquat Ice Cream (page 184), or pepper in Sweet Meadow Vermouth (page 145). Their flavor—combining notes of ginger and cardamom with coriander and black pepper—is unlike any other spice I have experienced in both the nose and mouth. They are a wild edible worth seeking out, but do remember to harvest sustainably, always leaving behind enough for wildlife to enjoy and to encourage further germination.

HAZELNUT MILK

Makes 2 cups

Nut milks have been enjoying popularity in whole food kitchens over the last decade, and for good reason—they are rich, satisfying, and digestible when properly soaked. Hazelnut milk is the star in Hazelnut Béchamel (page 94) but can also be enjoyed as a vegan creamer for tea and coffee or served hot sweetened with honey and finished with a sprinkle of cinnamon. To make a sweetened hazelnut milk, add 2 or 3 pitted dried dates and a dash of vanilla extract when you are blending the nuts. The leftover nut meat can be dried and used as a flour replacer for Probiotic Granola Bars (page 318) or other baked goods.

1 cup raw hazelnuts
2¼ cups water

Place the hazelnuts in a small bowl and add water to cover by at least 2 inches. Leave to soak overnight. Drain, then place the nuts in a blender, add the water, and blend on high speed until smooth. Pour the milk through a nut milk bag or a double layer of cheesecloth to extract the milk, squeezing well to get it all out. Store in a covered jar in the refrigerator for about 3 days until ready to use.

ROSE HIP TEA

Serves 2

When darkness descends into the winter months, it is time to fortify the body and strengthen the immune system with vitamin C. Rose hips are an excellent concentrated source and are easily dried to make tea, especially if you have free and abundant access from your garden or in the wild. Alternatively, prepare this tea in large batches during the summer months and serve over ice with lemon wedges. To make a calming tonic and digestive aid, steep 1 teaspoon fenugreek seeds and a few dried rose petals or hibiscus sepals in each cup.

2 tablespoons dried rose hips
Honey and/or lemon juice

Place 1 tablespoon of the rose hips in each of two tea bags or infusers and pour 1 cup of boiling water into each mug. Steep for 3 to 4 minutes, then add honey and/or a squeeze of lemon to taste.

OPPOSITE *The fruit of the rose, called a hep or hip, has great diversity in form and color. Featured here are* Rosa eglanteria, R. nutkana, R. *'Carefree Beauty,'* R. moyesii, R. *'Thomas Affleck,'* R. palustris, R. rugosa, R. spinosissima *var.* altaica, *and* R. multiflora.

ROSE HIP FIZZ

Makes about 1 gallon

Rose hips are excellent candidates for creating a yeast water that forms the base of a carbonated, slightly sweet and tart beverage. You may also use it to inoculate flour to create a starter culture for bread (page 68). I encourage you to experiment with other edible botanicals, such as fresh rose petals, honeysuckle blossoms, or honey locust blossoms, in place of or in addition to the rose hips. Although I have the most success with fresh rose hips, you may substitute an equal volume of dried rose hips, allowing extra time for the hips to soften and carbonation to develop.

Sumac is a beloved spice most notably used in Middle Eastern cooking that you can swap in for the rose hips in this beverage. There are many edible species of sumac and a handful that grow well in the United States, including *Rhus typhina*, *Rhus glabra*, and *Rhus copallina*. Their tart berries are called drupes and form in tight, conical-shaped clusters in late summer/early autumn when they are ready to harvest.

After fermentation, you can spike this fizzy beverage with bourbon or whiskey or mix with Prosecco as an aperitif. Alternatively, you can continue to ferment it until it turns into vinegar (see page 6). Because of its high sugar content, it will take longer than other vinegars.

About 3½ quarts warm water (130°F)

2 cups mild honey or sugar

Generous 3 cups fresh rose hips (about 9 ounces), rinsed, or the equivalent weight of fresh or dried sumac clusters (10 to 12)

Three 4-inch cinnamon sticks

Stir the water and honey together in a 1-gallon crock, large jar, or bowl until the honey is dissolved. Submerge the rose hips and cinnamon sticks and weight with fermentation weights, a zip-top bag filled with water, or a small bowl. Cover loosely with a lid or clean dish towel, secure with a rubber band, and ferment at room temperature, checking often for floating particles and skimming as necessary to keep mold from forming. After 4 to 5 days, you should notice plenty of carbon dioxide bubbles releasing from the mixture. Begin tasting for your desired sweetness—the longer you allow it to ferment, the more the microbes will metabolize the sugars, giving it a slightly more sour flavor similar to kombucha. I like to harvest after 10 to 14 days, when the carbonation has subsided somewhat.

Decant the liquid through a fine-mesh sieve into a jar. Cover and place in the refrigerator for up to 6 months. Note that fermentation will continue even after decanting! It is important to occasionally "burp" this ferment by popping the top to release carbon dioxide gas buildup.

ROSE HIPS

I have long been a student of the rose and find all parts of the plant to have strength of character in some way. The scent and romance of the flower has earned enduring favor throughout many cultures. The hip, or fruit, is often overlooked but comes as a patient reward for caring for the plant long after the flowers have faded and the foliage turns crimson with the chill of autumn. As they swell in size, they appear as decorative garden orbs that turn brilliant shades of saffron, orange, red, and sometimes purple-black as the days shorten and the leaves are blown from their branches to begin the succession of decay.

The diversity of these beautiful fruits is astonishing, and I have grown certain roses for the value of their fruit as much as their perfumed blossom. Not all hips are tasty or fit for consumption, however, as they range from sweet to astringent. *Rosa rugosa*, often found on beaches, and *Rosa canina* in the English countryside are two of the best candidates for drying. *Rosa nutkana*, the Nootka rose that populates much of the Pacific Northwest, is a prolific fruiter and wonderfully suited for drying to make tea or adding to Sweet Meadow Vermouth (page 145) but not as useful for making Orange and Vanilla Rose Hip Sauce (page 121) because of its higher seed-to-flesh ratio.

To preserve the hips for winter tea, gather as many fruits as you care to spend time outdoors. Remove the stems and sepals from the blossom end and spread onto a parchment-lined baking sheet. Alternatively, you may split them in half and scrape the seeds and troublesome hairs from the inside. Place in the oven on the lowest setting or in a dehydrator set to 110°F for 2 to 3 hours or longer depending on their size, until the hips are fully dried to a crisp, hard state. It is important to remove as much moisture as possible to prevent mold from forming in dry storage.

If you are planning to use the dry hips for anything other than tea, place them in the bowl of a food processor and process on high speed until they are chopped and a bit dusty. Be careful not to inhale the fine hairs and transfer to a fine-mesh sieve, shaking to sift. Discard the hairs and store the hips in a covered container in a cool, dry location for up to 1 year.

ROSELLE AND ROSE SPRITZ

Serves 4–5 with the aperitif option

This wine spritzer is not only beautiful to behold, but it offers the health benefits of roselle, a type of hibiscus long regarded for its cardiovascular benefits and mighty source of antioxidants and vitamin C. Dried hibiscus sepals are used here, but if you have access to fresh sepals, you may use an equal amount of them. The result is an impressive aperitif option to candy the hibiscus to use as a garnish.

1 packed cup (½ ounce) edible
   flower petals, washed and
   dried

1 cup (½ ounce) dried hibiscus
   sepals

1 orange, sliced, plus wedges
   for serving

One 750-ml bottle white wine

¼ cup orange-flavored liqueur,
   such as Grand Marnier,
   Cointreau, or Triple Sec

2 to 3 tablespoons mild honey,
   to taste

1 teaspoon whole allspice
   berries

1 stick cinnamon

2½ cups water

1¼ cups sugar or honey

FOR THE CANDIED HIBISCUS

Strained hibiscus from making
   hibiscus syrup (see below)

TO STEEP THE PETALS AND SEPALS

Place the flower petals, hibiscus sepals, and orange slices in a large container with a lid and pour in the wine and liqueur. Stir in the honey. Cover and place in the refrigerator to steep for 2 to 3 days, stirring and tasting along the way until you've reached your desired flavor. Strain the wine and reserve both the wine and hibiscus.

TO MAKE THE SYRUP

Place the strained hibiscus, allspice, and cinnamon in a medium saucepan and cover with the water. Stir in the sugar and bring to a boil over medium-high heat. Reduce the heat to maintain a simmer and simmer uncovered until the liquid has thickened to a syrup, about 1 hour. Strain the hibiscus and set aside. Allow the syrup to cool, then

stir into the wine to taste. Transfer the wine to a lidded jar and chill, then serve over ice garnished with strained or candied hibiscus (see below) and an orange wedge. This is a deliciously concentrated way of drinking it, but you can also serve it three parts wine to one part seltzer over ice.

TO MAKE THE CANDIED HIBISCUS

Place the strained hibiscus on a parchment paper–lined baking sheet and place in the oven. Set the oven to the lowest temperature possible. Most ovens can dehydrate at 175°F. Alternatively, you may use a dehydrator set to 110°F. Dry for 2 to 3 hours, checking along the way, until the sepals are somewhat dry to the touch but still pliably soft and not too chewy. Store in a sealed container in the refrigerator for up to 1 month.

ROSELLE

Roselle, or *Hibiscus sabdariffa*, is a delicious member of the mallow family that goes by many names, including Jamaican sorrel or Florida cranberry depending on where it is used. It is a tall, stately plant with crimson stems and charming pale flowers resembling those of okra, whose dark red calyx (whorled sepals) may be harvested and used fresh or dried to make a tart, refreshing tea the color of garnets. The edible leaves may also be cut into a chiffonade and added as a garnish to salads or other dishes, lending a fresh astringency not unlike the flavor of sorrel. It is usually grown in warm, temperate regions, much like its close cousin okra, requiring a long and warm season in order to mature. It is easily sourced in Hispanic or Caribbean markets and enjoys favor in Middle Eastern groceries as well.

SWEET MEADOW VERMOUTH

Makes about 3 cups

When we align ourselves with the vital forces of each season, we are better able to harness the energy of the natural world and facilitate our own transitions in life. After our soul has hibernated through a long winter of setting intentions and observing the stillness of freshly fallen snow, spring arrives, and with it a renewed vigor to explore and enjoy the tender rebirth of plants, animals, and insects. The equinox calls us into perfect balance with light and darkness as the days grow longer and the earth turns greener. When the solstice arrives, it ushers a vibrancy and fiery energy matched by the intensity of the sun, making us feel powerful and confident in our accomplishments. As autumn draws near, change is inevitable, indicated by brilliant leaf colors and the odor of decay—a gentle reminder not only to fortify our pantries for the winter ahead but also to let go of anything holding us back from comfort and turning inward.

This recipe for vermouth attempts to honor autumn with a reflection of its most fleeting botanical highlights. The result is a beverage or mixer as joyous to imbibe as it is to make, combing hillsides, stretching into trees, or strolling beach dunes and perfumed fields observing signs of edible life. The recipe may be adjusted to include ingredients of other seasons as well, harnessing the distinct influence of lilac blossoms or honeysuckle, wild carrot or burdock root. In spring and summer, feel your body awaken to the sun and honor the poetry of blossoms announcing their reproductive power. Sip their heady fragrance in this beverage with dear friends or a lover. In autumn and winter, turn to ingredients with immune-boosting and cleansing benefits, such as vitamin C–rich rose hips, tangy sumac, sharp juniper berries, or bitter dandelion root. The trick is to identify what each ingredient lends to the recipe, balancing bitter medicinal benefits with sharp citrus and those of lighter, more pleasing floral notes. No matter the combination, I always add a small stick of cinnamon and some kind of peppercorn to ground the mixture and give it a woody, earthy personality that plays well with most other ingredients.

In its basic form, vermouth is a fortified wine (usually white but sometimes rosé) infused with bitter and aromatic botanical ingredients. It can be made in several different ways depending on the desired outcome and amount of time you wish to devote to the process. You can use vodka to make initial herbal extractions that you then blend with a wine that has been steeped with additional ingredients for several days. Alternatively, you may simply infuse all of the herbals in wine or even boil them down before fortifying with a liquor such as brandy and adding

(recipe continues)

OPPOSITE *This fortified wine can be made with whatever seasonal ingredients you find inspiring. Choose a combination of floral and bitter edible flowers and herbs for a balanced result.*

sweetness from caramelized sugar. I opted for the simpler approach after a long West Coast wander gathering ingredients and receiving gifts from fellow foragers. When I returned to New York, it was late autumn and I wanted a quick way to experiment with the bounty I had collected in combination with indigenous aromatics of the quickly fading season. Leaning on a few dried spring flowers including chamomile helped lift and brighten the mix, but you can substitute honeysuckle, jasmine, fragrant rose petals, or small amounts of lavender. A crisp, un-oaked white wine, such as a trebbiano, chenin blanc, or pinot grigio, is best here, as you want a clean and unfussy backdrop to the flavors of the season.

3 small feijoa (*Acca sellowiana* or pineapple guava) or 1 small pear (about 2½ ounces), halved

15 g / ¼ cup dried, or 20 g fresh rose hips

5 small bayberry leaves, or bay leaves as a substitute

One 6-inch sprig fresh or dried mugwort

One 4-inch sprig lemon verbena

¼ cup (¼ ounce) dried or ⅓ cup fresh chamomile flowers

Two 3-inch strips orange zest

One 3-inch strip lemon zest

1 teaspoon coriander seeds or 1 large head green coriander

½ teaspoon pink peppercorns

1 stick cinnamon

2 or 3 dried hops flowers or 1 fresh dandelion root

One 750-ml bottle dry, un-oaked white wine

¼ cup sugar

1 tablespoon honey (optional)

1 cup smooth brandy

Place the fruit, botanicals, and spices in a medium saucepan and pour in 2 cups of the wine. Cover and bring to a boil over medium-high heat. Reduce the heat to maintain a simmer, cover, and simmer for 8 to 10 minutes, until the fruit and rose hips are tender. Turn off the heat and allow to steep for at least another 10 minutes or up to 2 to 3 hours, checking for bitterness along the way. Strain into a bowl.

In a separate saucepan, heat the sugar over medium heat until it caramelizes, being careful not to let it burn. Reheat the botanical concentrate until it is barely simmering. Slowly (very slowly!) trickle it into the caramelized sugar, being extra-careful, as the sugar will bubble and spit and can easily lash out and burn you if you pour too fast. Vigorously whisk the mixture. If the sugar clumps, stir over medium-low heat until completely dissolved. Give the concentrate a taste—it should be somewhat bitter but not unpleasant. If you taste it in your stomach (or your toes curl), stir in the honey. Add the remaining wine and the brandy and cool at room temperature. Transfer to a jar, cover, and store in the refrigerator for up to 1 month. Serve chilled over ice, neat, or in A Stranger's Door Cocktail (page 147).

A STRANGER'S DOOR COCKTAIL

Makes 1 shaken drink

When you come from a place of ample wild space with a plentitude of edible rewards, it is not easy to feel comfortable foraging in an urban setting. When I first moved to New York City, this meant tiptoeing around city parks and nervously combing roadsides in fear of being caught plucking a berry or mushroom. Eventually I owned up to the responsibility of harvesting wild edibles and began knocking on doors. The rewards were beyond acquiring the item of desire and often included the benefit of a story or recipe the stranger was happy to share. If I happen to forage in a place I know I'll want to visit again, returning with a delicious jar or loaf with said ingredient usually seals permission for future forays. An added benefit of knocking with politeness and respect is reinforcing a sense of trust in humankind, one that has alarmingly eroded in our current climate of political polarization and social extremism.

The initial reactions from most people answering unsolicited knocks are, not surprisingly, those of confusion. No, I'm not selling a product or evangelizing a religion (unless worshipping nature is a religion). When I explain I just want to make use of their glut of fallen apples or quince, more often than not the reaction is one of relief. "Oh, please do!" they usually exclaim, knowing their conscience has been lifted from the tragedy of waste or the avoidance of messy rot in their own front yard. In one case it meant packing an additional suitcase of feijoas offered from the front yard of an Oakland home. A prized score not seen in seasonal climates with harsh winters, these delectable fruits of the myrtle family were the litter from this handsome landscape plant. They stored for weeks in my refrigerator at home, leading to many delicious experiments including this frothy, lightly sweet cocktail. If you don't have access to feijoas, a juicy ripe pear is a fine substitute.

This recipe uses ingredients that can be found growing wild in fields and forests and front yards and backyards alike. Be bold and take a chance asking permission to gather before properly identifying your intended harvest—you never know what neighborly camaraderie you'll cultivate in exchange.

(recipe continues)

2 ounces smooth brandy

1½ ounces **Wild Carrot Syrup** (page 302)

1 large egg white

½ ounce Sweet Meadow Vermouth (page 145)

1½ teaspoons fresh lemon juice

Dash of grapefruit bitters

4 or 5 ice cubes

Slice of feijoa or pear (optional)

Combine the ingredients in a cocktail shaker (or a mason jar with a lid) and fill halfway with ice. Shake vigorously for 30 to 45 seconds, until the ingredients are incorporated and the egg white is frothy. Strain into a chilled coupe glass and garnish with a slice of feijoa or pear, if using. Serve immediately.

5

WINTER

From left to right: *Meyer lemons (*Citrus *x* meyeri*)*, Citrus taiwanica*)*, kumquat (*Citrus japonica*)*, grapefruit (*Citrus *x* paradisi *'Duncan'*)*, grapefruit (*Citrus *x* paradisi *'Ruby Red'*)*.

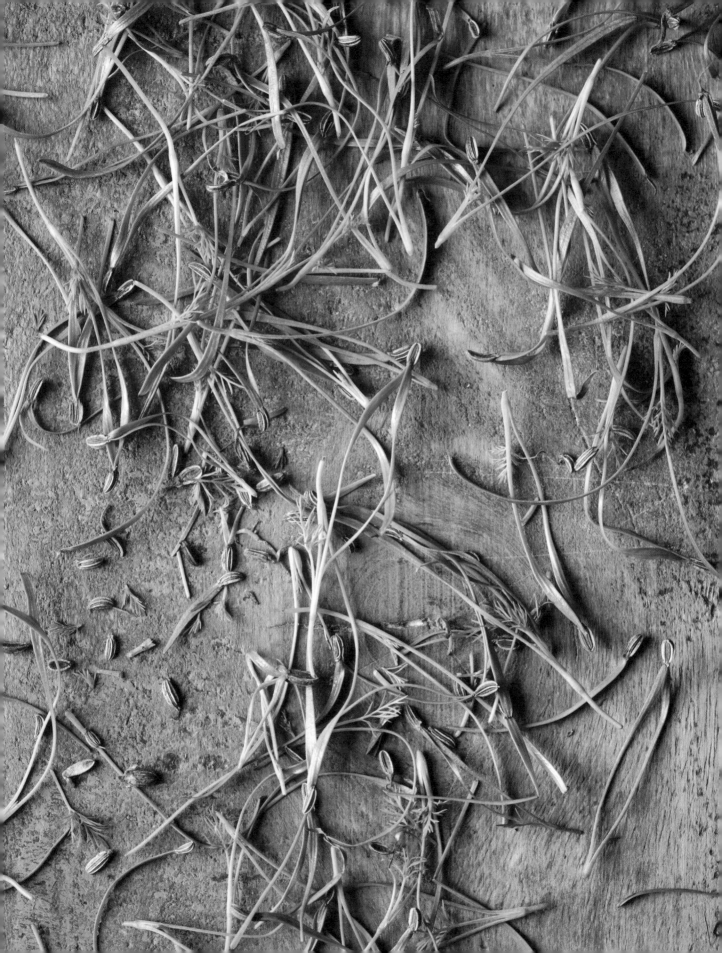

Hearth and Home

BREADS

Brown Butter Sourdough
Banana Bread / 154

Sourdough Challah / 157

A Brick of Rye (The Apple of
My Eye) / 160

Benne Sourdough / 162

Sprouted Buckwheat
and Cranberry Porridge
Bread / 164

Einkorn Cardamom
Rolls / 167

SAVORY DISHES

Kishk and Mushroom
Porridge / 169

Ginger Peanut Garlic
Paste / 173

Beluga Lentil Curry / 174

Oxtail Borscht with
Sour Cherries and
Purple Barley / 176

Bacon-Wrapped Pork Loin
with Charred Cabbage and
Prune Sauce / 179

SWEETS AND DRINKS

Chocolate Einkorn
Fudge Cake with Hazelnut
Streusel / 181

Toasted Fennel and
Kumquat Ice Cream / 184

Honey and Vanilla Poached
Kumquats / 185

Shaker Lemon and
Sage Pie / 187

Orange Cardamom
Cake / 190

Sticky Date, Teff, and
Pecan Cake / 193

Agrodulce / 196

Dried Fig, Walnut, and
Sesame Jam / 197

Fire Cider Tonic / 200

Jujube, Ginger, and
Turmeric Tea / 203

Fire Cider Bloody Mary
/ 204

Kumquat Liqueur / 207

OPPOSITE *Microgreens such as these sprouted bronze fennel seeds are a clever way to add concentrated flavor,
nutrition, and beauty as a garnish.*

BROWN BUTTER SOURDOUGH BANANA BREAD

Makes one 9½ × 5-inch loaf

Brown butter heightens the flavor of einkorn in this classic moist bread, improving on the flour's already toasty, nutty character alongside deep notes of banana caramelization. Use the ripest bananas you can find and an inactive starter that would otherwise be discarded (I like to use a starter fed with rye, spelt, or whole wheat flour). If you wish, you can ferment the batter at room temperature for up to three hours before baking to improve upon its texture and digestibility. This loaf is not overly sweet, making it a perfect breakfast indulgence with a strong cup of black coffee.

Unsalted butter for the pan

195 g / 1¾ cups whole einkorn flour

¾ teaspoon baking soda

½ teaspoon kosher salt

400 g / 4 peeled medium bananas

90 g / 6 tablespoons Brown Butter (page 34), softened

175 g / ¾ cup light brown sugar

2 large eggs

1 teaspoon pure vanilla extract

100 g / ½ cup 100% hydration sourdough starter

20 g / 2 tablespoons buttermilk or whole milk

90 g / ¾ cup toasted nuts (pecans, walnuts, almonds, or a combination works well)

PREPARE THE BATTER

Preheat the oven to 350°F.

Prepare a parchment sling to drape over the long sides of a 9½ × 5-inch loaf pan. Generously butter the parchment and bare sides of the pan and set aside.

Whisk the flour, baking soda, and salt in a medium bowl. Using a fork, measure and mash 290 g of the banana (from 3 bananas) in a small bowl and set aside. Cream the brown butter and brown sugar in a stand mixer on medium-high speed until thick and fluffy, about 4 minutes. Add the eggs one at a time, mixing until smooth. Add the vanilla and mashed bananas and mix until well blended. Add the sourdough starter and mix until just incorporated.

Add the dry ingredients to the wet ingredients in several batches, mixing until no dry lumps remain. Add the milk to thin the batter slightly, then stir in the toasted nuts. Transfer the batter to the prepared pan and smooth the top. Cut the remaining banana lengthwise down the middle and nestle it into the top of the batter.

BAKE THE BREAD

Place the loaf pan on a baking sheet and bake for 65 to 70 minutes, rotating the pan halfway through, until a toothpick inserted into the center of the loaf comes out clean. Cool on a wire rack for 15 to 20 minutes, then use the sling to assist you in carefully removing the loaf onto the rack to cool completely before slicing.

Whole wheat flour and natural leavening make this egg-rich bread inspired by classic challah distinctively wholesome, and it pairs well with Dried Fig, Walnut, and Sesame Jam (page 197).

SOURDOUGH CHALLAH

Makes 2 large loaves

It took years of testing for me to feel confident in sharing this naturally leavened challah with whole wheat flavor and no added commercial yeast. I wanted a fairly light but not necessarily fluffy crumb, only slightly sweet, and definitely not sour. Considering I was using sourdough as leavening, the last stipulation was perhaps the most difficult and led me to a very different feeding schedule for my starter than I normally follow. You will need to start feeding your starter the day before you plan to bake the challah in 4-hour increments with one longer overnight rise. There is lots of inactive time in between the short feedings; I find it helps to set an alarm to keep myself on track while I focus on other tasks around the house or kitchen. You may also use a refreshed sourdough starter maintained according to the notes on page 61, but the effort here is definitely worth the less acidic results.

It is important to secure a rather warm location to proof both the starter and the dough in order to encourage greater yeast activity and less bacterial dominance. In the winter, I keep a plug-in radiator in a small room and crank it as high as it will go with the door closed! This creates a nice 80°F to 85°F temperature, perfect for encouraging less bacterial activity and the characteristic acidity that makes sourdough, well, sour! Instead, the yeasty beasties dominate the culture and, along with a wee bit of added sugar, provide you with a sweet leaven perfect for making enriched brioche-type breads like challah. If you are keeping to tradition, feel free to substitute the softened butter with oil such as sunflower, avocado, or a more flavorful one such as coconut. Instructions are included for a six-stranded braid, but feel free to simplify by making just three strands.

FOR THE STARTER AND LEAVEN

20 g / 1 tablespoon 100% hydration sourdough starter

325 g / 1⅓ cup + 1 tablespoon water

325 g / 2½ cups high-extraction bread flour

35 g / 2 generous tablespoons sugar or honey

FOR THE DOUGH

325 g / 1¾ cups 100% hydration young and sweet sourdough leaven (see above)

290 g / 1¼ cups tepid water (70°F to 75°F)

120 g / ½ cup mild honey

60 g / 4 tablespoons unsalted butter, softened, or oil

2 large eggs

4 large egg yolks

15 g / scant ½ tablespoon fine sea salt

490 g / 3½ cups high-extraction bread flour

340 g / 3 heaping cups whole wheat pastry or spelt flour

Neutral oil for the bowl, such as avocado or sunflower

FOR THE EGG WASH

1 large egg yolk

20 g / 1 tablespoon mild honey

Dash of whole milk or half-and-half

FOR THE GARNISH (OPTIONAL)

2 to 3 tablespoons sesame, poppy, caraway, or nigella seeds

(recipe continues)

PREPARE THE STARTER

In a small bowl, mix together the 20 g starter, 20 g of the water, 20 g of the bread flour, and a pinch of sugar (about 5 g). Cover with plastic wrap and place in a warm (80°F to 85°F) location. After 4 hours, remove all but 20 g of starter from the bowl and repeat twice, covering and returning the bowl to the warm location. On the fourth feeding, remove all but 10 g of the starter and feed it 110 g water and 110 g bread flour and a generous pinch of sugar. Cover and return to the warm location for 8 to 10 hours.

PREPARE THE LEAVEN

The following morning, remove all but 30 g of starter and feed it the remaining 155 g water, the remaining 155 g bread flour, and 15 g sugar. Cover and proof in the warm location for 4 hours before mixing it into the dough.

PREPARE THE DOUGH

Whisk together the leaven, water, honey, soft butter or oil, eggs, egg yolks, and salt in a large bowl. Slowly incorporate the flours, mixing with your hands until a sticky, shaggy mass forms and all of the flour is hydrated. Cover and allow to rest for 5 to 10 minutes.

Remove the dough from the bowl and slap-and-fold on a clean surface for 5 to 7 minutes, taking periodic breaks and allowing the dough to relax if the surface begins to tear. The dough will be very sticky but will tighten up as you work it—do not add extra flour! Clean the bowl and lightly oil it, then return the dough to the bowl. Cover with plastic wrap and allow to proof in a warm (80 to 85°F) location for 4 to 5 hours, until the dough has just doubled in size.

SHAPE A SIX-STRANDED BRAID

On a lightly floured surface, divide the dough into 12 pieces weighing 135 to 140 g each. Cover loosely with plastic wrap while you work. Using as little flour as possible, roll six pieces into tapered strands 12 to 14 inches long. Place the strands parallel to each other and pinch the top ends together, then braid in the following sequence:

- Move the outside right strand left over two strands.

- Move the second strand from the left to the far right.

- Move the outside left strand over two strands.

- Move the second strand from the right over to the far left.

- Repeat until you reach the end of the loaf, then tuck both ends firmly under the braid.

Move the braided loaf to a parchment paper–lined baking sheet and repeat with the next six strands to create a second loaf, placing on an additional baking sheet.

PREPARE THE EGG WASH, PROOF A SECOND TIME, AND BAKE

In a small bowl, whisk together the egg yolk, honey, and milk and use a pastry brush to lightly coat the loaves, leaving some behind for a final wash. Cover both loaves loosely with plastic wrap and proof in your warm location for 2 to 2½ hours, until they feel inflated, loosely soft, and retain a finger impression when lightly poked. When in doubt, let them proof an extra 30 minutes!

When the loaves are almost fully proofed, preheat the oven to 375°F and apply a second coating of egg wash, wiping away any pooling around the base of the loaves. Sprinkle on the seeds, if using, and bake on the middle rack (without steam) for 35 to 38 minutes, until the crust is a deep golden brown. Remove from the oven and cool completely before slicing.

A BRICK *of* RYE (THE APPLE *of* MY EYE)

Makes three 9 × 5-inch loaves

Lovers of rye will characteristically emit an enthusiastic moan with any mention of its earthy, sometimes peculiar behavior in bread. A number of heirloom varieties have been reintroduced in various climates, bringing back a wide spectrum of both flavor and performance depending on where it is grown. 'Abruzzi' and 'Danko' varieties are both highly favored, as is 'Seashore' or 'Dixie' rye. When freshly milled and properly fermented, this coveted grain will yield notes of hazelnuts, honey, freshly cut hay, or sometimes even mushrooms and is an experience unlike any other grain you will ever taste. If you have never made a 100% rye bread before, be prepared for a very sticky dough that needs little mixing work beyond fully hydrating the flour. If you are using a mixer, be careful not to mix for too long or the result will be a gummy, less than desirable crumb.

The following recipe is incredibly simple to prepare using a sourdough starter and requires little hands-on time compared to many other recipes. Because of the specific and active enzymes of rye, it is recommended to use a sourdough starter maintained with rye flour to create the leaven for this dough. You may also jazz up this otherwise basic formula with the optional addition of toasted seeds and nuts for increased flavor and nutrition. After mixing, you simply plunk the dough into a few buttered loaf pans, smooth the tops, and allow it to bulk inside the pans until they are ready to cold proof in the refrigerator overnight. These moist, dense loaves require a very long bake at a low temperature. The crust will darken considerably before they are done, making it difficult to determine when to pull them from the oven without the use of an instant-read thermometer. Make sure you allow the loaves to fully cool before slicing, waiting a full day after baking for the crumb to set. This is a very basic loaf with no bells and whistles, but you may add seeds, rye berries, or nuts if you like.

FOR THE LEAVEN

40 g / scant ¼ cup 100% hydration active sourdough starter (refreshed)

100g / ⅓ cup + 2 tablespoons tepid water (70°F to 75°F)

100 g / scant 1 cup whole rye flour

FOR THE SCALD

315 g / about 3 cups whole rye flour

405 g / 1¾ cups boiling water

FOR THE DOUGH

240 g / scant ¼ cup leaven (see left)

865 g / 3¾ cups tepid water (70°F to 75°F)

1070 g / 10 generous cups rye flour

32 g / 1 tablespoon fine sea salt

OPTIONAL FOLD-INS

240 g / 2¼ cups toasted nuts (pecans, walnuts, or hazelnuts)

90 g / 9 tablespoons toasted black or white sesame seeds

150 g / 1 cup toasted pepita seeds

135 g / 1 cup toasted sunflower seeds

PREPARE THE LEAVEN

About 8 to 10 hours before mixing your dough, prepare the leaven with the ingredients called for here according to the directions for the Table Loaf on page 62.

PREPARE THE SCALD

After you mix the leaven, place the rye flour in a medium bowl. Pour the boiling water over the flour and mix until no dry lumps remain. This mixture will be stiff and resist mixing, but do not be tempted to add more water. Cover with a plate or plastic wrap and cool at room temperature until you are ready to mix your dough.

PREPARE THE DOUGH

Mix the leaven, scald, and tepid water in a large bowl to create a slurry. Add the flour and mix with your hands until no dry lumps remain, and gently mix in the nuts and seeds if using. Generously grease three loaf pans with butter. Using your hands, divide the dough evenly between the three pans. Wet your hands and smooth the tops of the dough, slicking it down and moving it into the corners and adding a little more water if necessary. Cover with plastic wrap and allow to ferment at room temperature for about 4 hours, or until the surface appears just slightly puffy in the pan. Cover with kitchen towels then place in plastic bags and move to the refrigerator to cold ferment for 8 to 12 hours. This dough does not hold well for extended fermentation.

BAKE THE LOAVES

Remove the loaves from the refrigerator and allow to come to room temperature for about 2 hours or until the dough appears puffy and the surface has shallow cracks. Meanwhile, preheat the oven to 470°F.

Score the top of the loaf with a razor blade ¼ to ½ inch deep down the center. Bake with steam for 15 minutes (see Basic Techniques and Bread Vocabulary for reference, page 321). Decrease the oven temperature to 450°F and bake for another 65 to 70 minutes, or until the internal temperature reads 205°F on an instant-read thermometer. The loaves will be a deep, dark brown and the sides should pull free from the pan. Remove from the pans and cool completely on a wire rack. Do not slice until the following day.

BENNE SOURDOUGH

Makes 2 loaves

This seeded loaf is stunning to present at the table, especially when you roll it in additional sesame seeds after shaping. It has a deliciously nutty aroma that complements so many recipes in this book, from bright and sweet Spiced Ground Cherry, Lemon, and Apple Preserves (page 300) to Grilled Eggplant with Buttermilk Tahini Sauce and Tomato Coulis (page 294).

FOR THE LEAVEN

25 g / 1 heaping tablespoon 100% hydration active starter, refreshed (fed)

55 g / about ¼ cup tepid water (70°F to 75°F)

55 g / ½ cup whole-grain flour (rye or whole wheat works well)

FOR THE SOAKER

65 g / ½ cup toasted benne, white sesame seeds, or black sesame seeds

80 g / ⅓ cup + 1 tablespoon tepid water (70°F to 75°F)

FOR THE DOUGH

135 g / ⅔ cup leaven (see left)

570 g / 2½ cups tepid water (70°F to 75°F)

620 g / 4¼ cups + 2 tablespoons high-extraction bread flour

120 g / 1 cup + 1 tablespoon whole wheat bread flour

40 g / 2½ tablespoons whole rye flour

16 g / 1 tablespoon fine sea salt

FOR THE TOPPING (OPTIONAL)

Benne, white sesame seeds, or black sesame seeds (or a combination)

PREPARE THE LEAVEN

About 8 to 10 hours before mixing your dough, prepare the leaven with the ingredients called for here according to the directions for the Table Loaf on page 62.

PREPARE THE SOAKER

Place the sesame seeds in a small bowl and stir in the water. Cover with an inverted bowl or plastic wrap and leave to soak at room temperature until ready to mix your dough.

PREPARE THE DOUGH AND BAKE

Prepare the dough with the ingredients above according to the Table Loaf directions on page 62. After you mix in the salt, evenly spread one third of the seed soaker over the surface of the dough. Gently lift the dough from the bottom of the bowl and stretch to the middle, folding it over the added ingredients. Rotate the bowl and fold two or three more times, until you have worked your way completely around the dough. Continue with the remaining seed soaker until it is incorporated into the dough. Avoid large pockets of seed clumps, but it's OK if there are uneven streaks at this point, as the seeds will distribute further as you build dough strength. Continue stretching and folding every 30 to 45 minutes for the remainder of bulk fermentation at room temperature, about 4 hours. This will both strengthen the dough and evenly distribute the fold-ins. When the dough has increased in size by at least one third, continue shaping, retarding, and baking as instructed on page 64.

BENNE

Benne is an heirloom variety of *Sesamum indicum* native to sub-Saharan Africa that populated the antebellum Southern colonies, specifically South Carolina, where it is now primarily grown. Brought over by slaves and introduced as a subsistence food, the botanical diversity and edibility of both greens and seeds earned benne's place in rows between other more valuable crops such as rice, field peas, and corn. Benne improved the soil where it was planted and offered relief from insect pressure on its neighboring crops. Unfortunately, it fell out of favor in preference for seeds that were selectively gleaned for oil production, and their vibrant, nutty flavor was almost completely lost. But thanks primarily to the efforts of Anson Mills, this delightful seed has reinvigorated cuisines in the South and is wonderful when used in Benne Sourdough.

SPROUTED BUCKWHEAT *and* CRANBERRY PORRIDGE BREAD

Makes 2 loaves

This earthy but sweet loaf uses both buckwheat flour and sprouted buckwheat groats. Its high percentage of rye makes it dense but incredibly flavorful. You will need to start with raw buckwheat groats—they will have a slightly green tint to them—in order for them to sprout.

To sprout the groats, place them in a small bowl and add water to cover by at least 2 inches. Leave to soak overnight, then drain through a colander or sieve. The groats will be somewhat slimy (that's OK). Rinse the groats, drain, and spread them onto a baking sheet in a single layer. Dampen a kitchen towel and cover the groats, then place in a warm ventilated location and stir once a day. They are ready when a small protrusion appears from the pointy end of the seed. You may keep the sprouts covered with a dampened paper towel in the refrigerator for up to 2 weeks, occasionally popping the lid to aerate. The texture of the groats will give the loaf a firm bite, but if you would like the groats to dissolve into the crumb, you may cook them first according to directions for raw buckwheat on page 54.

FOR THE LEAVEN
- 25 g / 1 tablespoon 100% hydration sourdough starter, refreshed (fed)
- 45 g / 4½ tablespoons tepid water (70°F to 75°F)
- 45 g / 5 tablespoons raw or toasted buckwheat flour, or an equal weight of high-extraction bread flour

FOR THE DOUGH
- 115 g / 1½ cups + 1 generous tablespoon leaven (see left)
- 550 g / 2¼ cups + 2 tablespoons tepid water (70°F to 75°F)
- 480 g / scant 3¾ cups high-extraction bread flour
- 160 g / 1½ cups whole rye flour
- 20 g / generous 2 tablespoons whole buckwheat flour
- 13 g / 1 tablespoon fine sea salt

FOR THE FOLD-INS
- 35 g / ¼ cup sprouted buckwheat (see headnote)
- 150 g / 1 cup dried cranberries

Prepare the leaven and dough according to directions for Table Loaf on page 62. When the salt has been completely incorporated, sprinkle the sprouted buckwheat and cranberries over the dough. Gently incorporate by repeatedly folding the dough over the fold-ins. The dough should feel soft and slack and a bit sticky from the rye. Cover with plastic wrap and set in a warm spot, ideally 75°F. Continue stretching and folding every 45 minutes to 1 hour for the remainder of the bulk fermentation, about 3½ to 4 hours. When the dough feels puffy and has visibly increased in volume, proceed with shaping, retarding, and baking according to directions for the Table Loaf on page 64. Because of the high percentage of whole grain in this loaf, it is best baked after 8 to 12 hours resting time in the refrigerator.

EINKORN CARDAMOM ROLLS

Makes 12 rolls

These soft, slightly sour breakfast rolls are easily assembled and make a rustic but impressive presentation. If you prefer a less fermented flavor, prepare a sweeter leaven as described for the Sourdough Challah (page 157), using honey or sugar and placing your starter in a warm location while you perform frequent feedings. You may prepare this in a large cast-iron pan or place each individual roll in the depressions of a muffin pan for easily transportable snacks. They are amazing served warm from the oven after being iced!

FOR THE DOUGH
200 g / 1 cup 100% hydration active sourdough starter, refreshed (fed)

170 g / ⅔ cup + 1 tablespoon whole milk, at room temperature

1 large egg, at room temperature, beaten

60 g / 4 tablespoons unsalted butter, softened

60 g / 2½ tablespoons sugar

185 g / 1⅓ cups + 1 tablespoon high-extraction bread flour, plus more for rolling

200 g / 1¾ cups + 1 tablespoon whole einkorn flour

1 teaspoon ground cinnamon

1 teaspoon ground cardamom

9 g / scant 1 teaspoon salt

FOR THE FILLING
115 g / 1 stick or 8 tablespoons unsalted butter, softened, plus more for the pan

130 g / ½ cup + heaping 1 tablespoon brown sugar or coconut sugar

1 teaspoon ground cinnamon

1 teaspoon ground cardamom

FOR THE GLAZE (OPTIONAL)
90 g / 6 tablespoons Brown Butter (page 34)

170 g / ⅔ cup + 1 tablespoon cream cheese

125 g / 1 cup powdered sugar

15 to 45 g / 1 to 3 tablespoons fresh lemon juice (optional)

15 to 45 g / 1 to 3 tablespoons strong coffee (optional)

MAKE THE DOUGH
When your starter is bubbly and active, add the milk, egg, butter, and sugar to the bowl and stir to combine. Add the flours, cinnamon, cardamom, and salt and mix with your hand until well hydrated and no lumps remain. Cover with an inverted bowl or plastic wrap and allow to bulk ferment at room temperature for about 4 hours, turning and folding every hour.

MAKE THE FILLING AND PREPARE THE ROLLS
Grease a muffin pan well with butter. In a small bowl, stir together the softened butter, brown sugar, cinnamon, and cardamom, until consistently combined.

Transfer the dough to a lightly floured surface and pat it into a flattened rectangular shape. Using a rolling pin, roll the dough to a 6½ × 12-inch rectangle. Spread the butter mixture evenly over the dough. Using a dough scraper to assist, roll the

(recipe continues)

dough lengthwise to create a long coil. Pinch the seam to seal and lightly roll to slightly elongate it. Place on a baking sheet and freeze for 30 minutes to harden, then remove from the freezer and unwrap. Cut into rounds about 1 inch thick. Twist two rounds around each other and press them into the muffin pan. Repeat with the remaining dough to fill the pan. Cover with a kitchen towel, then plastic wrap, and place in the refrigerator overnight.

TO BAKE

Remove the rolls from the refrigerator about 1 hour before you are to bake them for a final proof and preheat the oven to 375°F. The rolls should feel puffy and soft when gently poked with your finger.

Bake for 15 to 17 minutes, rotating the pan halfway through, until the tops are oozing and golden brown. Cool in the pan on a wire rack for about 5 minutes, then remove the rolls to a wire rack.

IF YOU ARE MAKING THE GLAZE

Heat the butter in a small saucepan until melted. Turn off the heat and whisk in the cream cheese until no lumps remain. Sift in the powdered sugar a little at a time, alternating with the lemon juice and/or coffee if you wish the mixture to be more pourable. Run the glaze through a strainer to remove any lumps, add a dollop of glaze to the top of each roll, and glaze the sides generously.

KISHK *and* MUSHROOM PORRIDGE

Serves 2

When I visited the Middle East for the first time, I was overwhelmed with invitations to experience traditional foods. One such opportunity was to visit the mountainous Marjayoun area of Lebanon, a region near the border of Israel that I needed to apply for a special visa to enter. The family of a dear friend sponsored my visit, and no effort was spared to inaugurate my Lebanese experience with food and drink. Most of our time was spent cooking and eating while listening to stories over small glasses of arak, a potent Levantine anise-flavored spirit.

One chilly morning while visiting a generous Druze baker and her shepherd husband, I was prepared a traditional bowl of kishk porridge from food from their farm: awarma (ground lamb meat preserved in fat) and Kishk Powder (see page 42) made from bulghur wheat fermented with goat's milk labneh. We huddled around an oil-burning furnace slowly spooning steaming mouthfuls of this hearty porridge alongside small cups of boiled Turkish coffee. The mother of the house threw me nervous glances as everyone else moaned and smiled over their bowls. She was no doubt wondering how my Western palate would react to this distinctively sour gruel with an aftertaste of barnyard funk.

Admittedly, it was a puzzling experience initially—the texture of the porridge struck me as similar to the boxed cream of wheat I reluctantly slurped as a child. But what left me craving more the next day (and for years to come) was not only kishk's characteristic fermented flavor but the digestibility and unmistakable energized feeling and satiation it gave me until well into the afternoon. One hearty bowl carried us through a full morning of activities—cuddling baby goats, walking through cliffside villages ogling piles of fresh produce, and perusing shelves that groaned under the weight of jars of mouneh (preserves) from the previous season's bounty. Upon returning to the farm's kitchen, we sipped mate from gourds around another oil-burning furnace, mixed dough, and cooked flatbreads outside on a traditional saj griddle while neighbors gathered to partake of our efforts.

I lugged home suitcases of ingredients from that trip, including large containers of both kishk and awarma, and hoarded them until I mournfully scraped the very bottom of the jars. I knew the same flavor could not be replicated without the local wheat or farm-fresh labneh and meat from Lebanon, but it was worth trying. This warming winter porridge is flavored by the umami of mushrooms—I prefer Lacto-Fermented Mushrooms (page 11) to match the fermented character of the kishk, but you may use whatever mushroom you like. If you don't have Whey-Fermented Cipollini Onions (page 45) on hand, plain sliced onions will work. Kishk powder is quite salty, so use a light hand with the seasoning.

(recipe continues)

1 tablespoon Clarified Butter
(page 34), Rendered Animal
Fat (page 33), or extra-virgin
olive oil

⅓ cup Whey-Fermented
Cipollini Onions (page 45),
halved

1 cup Lacto-Fermented
Mushrooms (page 11)

Generous pinch of salt,
or to taste

2 plump cloves garlic, thinly
sliced

2 to 3 cups water, or stock
or broth of choice (pages 36
to 37)

1 cup Kishk Powder (page 42)

**FOR THE GARNISH (FOR EACH
BOWL; OPTIONAL)**

2 tablespoons Milk Kefir
(page 39)

2 to 3 tablespoons fresh herbs
or microgreens (parsley,
chervil, cilantro, bronze
fennel, or dill work well)

A sprinkling of cracked black
peppercorns, or to taste

Heat the clarified butter in a medium saucepan over medium-high heat until lightly sizzling. Lower the heat, add the cipollini onions, and cook for 2 to 3 minutes without stirring. Stir and continue to cook until softened, 3 to 4 more minutes. Add the mushrooms and salt and cook for 4 to 5 more minutes, stirring occasionally, until the mushrooms are browned, adding a dash or two of water or stock if they start to stick. Add the garlic and stir until fragrant and slightly softened, about 1 minute. Transfer to a small plate and return the saucepan to medium-high heat.

Add 2 cups water or stock and heat until just simmering, then slowly whisk in the kishk powder. Continue to cook, whisking constantly, until the mixture thickens, adding up to 1 cup more water or stock if you desire a more soup-like texture (the porridge will thicken upon cooling). Turn off the heat and taste for salt. Divide between bowls and drizzle with the milk kefir, if using. Top with the mushroom mixture and fresh herbs or microgreens and cracked pepper, if using, and serve immediately.

OPPOSITE *Warming and hearty, Kishk and
Mushroom Porridge is a canvas for any
manner of savory toppings.*

GINGER PEANUT GARLIC PASTE

Makes about 1¾ cups

This is an all-purpose seasoning that I like to add to stir-fries, soups, and legume dishes, such as Beluga Lentil Curry (page 174). The recipe easily halves or doubles.

1½ cups sliced fresh young
    ginger (8½ ounces)
5 plump cloves garlic

2 to 3 Thai chilies, to taste,
    sliced
3 tablespoons soy sauce
1½ tablespoons honey

3 to 4 tablespoons peanut butter
1 tablespoon vinegar of your
    choice (optional)

Place the ginger, garlic, and chilies in the bowl of a mortar and pestle and pound to a thick paste. Stir in the remaining ingredients and transfer to a jar, cover, and store in the refrigerator for up to 3 months.

OPPOSITE *Using fresh young ginger to make this paste imparts a mellow, sweet character.*

BELUGA LENTIL CURRY

Serves 4

These small, pearly black lentils earned their name for their resemblance to caviar, although unfortunately they lose their striking color after they are cooked. Hearty and satisfying, their flavor benefits from the thickening power of Ginger Peanut Garlic Paste (page 173) and the earthy addition of Malabar spinach. This handsome and robust plant is not a true spinach but a heat-loving, eager Asian vine that appreciates a sturdy trellis on which to grow. Harvest its succulent leaves when young and keep the flower buds pinched back to encourage vigorous growth. At the end of the growing season, you can let it go to seed, harvest the young pods for quick pickling (see page 14), and garnish the dish with them. If you do not grow or cannot source Malabar spinach, substitute a common cooking leaf, such as Swiss chard or regular spinach, or the more exotic callaloo or sweet potato leaves.

2 tablespoons Clarified Butter (page 34) or coconut oil

1 medium red onion, chopped

2 tablespoons Ginger Peanut Garlic Paste (page 173)

5 cups Ruby Chard Broth (page 27), Vegetable Broth (page 28), or Chicken Broth (page 36)

1½ cups dry beluga lentils

2 large handfuls Malabar spinach leaves

FOR THE GARNISH (FOR EACH BOWL; OPTIONAL)

2 to 3 tablespoons heavy cream or coconut milk

1 large handful of fresh cilantro leaves

Handful of Baked Root Chips (page 92)

Quick pickled Malabar spinach seed heads (see page 14)

Heat the butter in a large heavy-bottomed saucepan over medium heat. Add the onion and cook until translucent, 6 to 7 minutes. Stir in the ginger peanut garlic paste, broth, and lentils, increase the heat to medium-high, and bring to a boil. Lower the heat to maintain a simmer, partially cover, and cook for about 25 minutes, until the lentils are tender. Stir in the Malabar spinach leaves until wilted. Ladle into bowls and garnish as you like.

OXTAIL BORSCHT *with* SOUR CHERRIES *and* PURPLE BARLEY

Serves 4

I've held many odd jobs as a freelancer in food. Some to learn new skills, others to pay the bills. If I'm lucky, the two magically combine and I have the creative freedom to let my talents marry the two. I have worked alongside cooks from many different countries, including Belize, Trinidad, Poland, Iran, and the Republic of Georgia, to prepare both intimate dinners and elaborate feasts. Although the version of borscht from the Caucasus I learned was made with osso buco, I use easier-to-source oxtail or will leave the meat out entirely in the summer months and add more vegetables. Grating unlocks the juices of each vegetable and deeply flavors the broth. The grater attachment of a food processor will make this jeweled garnet soup a breeze to pull together.

Purple barley imparts an earthy malty flavor that works so well with root vegetables; it's what makes this borscht really shine. If unavailable, you may substitute a non-purple variety of whole barley if you wish, adjusting the cooking time according to the package directions. You can soak the barley in warm water to cover by a couple inches for 6 to 8 hours to shorten the cooking time. Begin by making a batch of Beef Broth (page 37) in advance, reserving the tender oxtail for this recipe. For the cabbage, a mild savoy, napa, or beautiful purple cabbage will work. Or substitute chopped beet greens or Swiss chard (stir them in at the very end of cooking until wilted).

In the winter, serve this soup warm with a splash of Fire Cider Tonic (page 200) or lemon juice, or in the summer with vegetable broth and without the meat as a refreshing cold vegetarian soup. The garnishes are the key to keeping the soup vibrant with color, flavor, and complexity.

2 tablespoons beef fat skimmed from Beef Broth (page 37) or Rendered Animal Fat (page 33)

1 medium onion, coarsely grated

2 large carrots, coarsely grated

1 stalk celery, minced

3 plump cloves garlic, sliced

2 quarts Beef Broth (page 37)

1½ quarts water

¾ cup purple barley

Oxtail reserved from Beef Broth (page 37)

3 cups thinly sliced cabbage

2 medium beets, coarsely grated

¾ cup dried sour cherries

2 tablespoons Apple Cider Vinegar (page 6) or Pineapple Vinegar (page 8)

1 tablespoon sugar

Juice of 1 lemon

FOR THE GARNISH

Several dollops of sour cream

1 tablespoon prepared horseradish

2 to 3 tablespoons fresh dill leaves

2 to 3 tablespoons fresh flat-leaf parsley and/or cilantro leaves

Sprinkle of nigella seeds

Lemon wedges

Heat the skimmed beef fat in a large soup pot over medium heat until clear, about 2 minutes. Add the onion, half of the grated carrot, and the celery and cook until the onion is translucent, about 7 minutes. Add the garlic and cook until fragrant, about 1 minute. Add the beef broth, water, and barley. Bring to a simmer, then reduce the heat to maintain a simmer and cook for 1 hour partially covered, or until the barley is tender. Stir in the reserved oxtail and cook to heat through. Stir in the remaining carrot, the cabbage, beets, and cherries, bring to a simmer, and cook until the cabbage is tender, 12 to 15 minutes. Add the vinegar, sugar, and lemon juice. Ladle into bowls and top with the sour cream and horseradish. Garnish with the dill, parsley, and nigella seeds and serve with lemon wedges alongside.

BACON-WRAPPED PORK LOIN *with* CHARRED CABBAGE *and* PRUNE SAUCE

Serves 4 to 6

Pork loin is a lean, tender cut that needs careful attention to keep it from drying out. Using Bread Kvass (page 315) as a marinade not only further tenderizes the meat but also gives it a subtly sweet flavor. It's also an excellent way to utilize mature kvass that may be too strong for casual sipping. If you don't have kvass on hand, consider using mead or cider instead. Wrapping the pork loin in bacon seals in moisture; just make sure to let it rest for a sufficient amount of time before slicing so it does not seize and stiffen. Serve with Stone-Ground Grits/Polenta (page 55) and drizzle the cabbage with Agrodulce (page 196) for a sweet and sour finish to complement the flavors of the prunes and kvass. It would be unthinkable not to serve this with a Dijon or hot mustard alongside, so make sure you have some on hand.

12 ounces pork loin

1¼ teaspoons kosher salt

½ teaspoon freshly ground black pepper

2 plump cloves garlic

1 tablespoon coarsely chopped fresh rosemary

1 tablespoon coarsely chopped fresh sage

1 cup Bread Kvass (page 315)

1½ teaspoons extra-virgin olive oil

12 ounces thick-cut smoked bacon

1 medium onion, sliced

1 cup plump prunes, chopped

1½ pounds (1 small head) savoy cabbage, quartered

⅓ cup Apple Cider Vinegar (page 6)

1½ teaspoons whole yellow mustard seeds

Dijon or hot mustard, for serving

Lay the pork loin on a plate and sprinkle it on all sides with ¾ teaspoon of the salt and the pepper. Grate the garlic using a Microplane and rub it onto the pork loin, then press on the herbs. Allow to stand at room temperature for 20 minutes. Transfer the pork loin to a small bowl and pour in the kvass. Cover with plastic wrap and refrigerate for 8 hours, flipping once to coat.

Preheat the oven to 350°F.

Remove the loin from the marinade, pat dry, and allow to come to room temperature for 20 minutes. Strain the marinade through a fine-mesh sieve into a bowl and reserve it.

Heat the oil in a large heavy-bottomed skillet or a Dutch oven over medium-high heat for 2 to 3 minutes. Briefly sear the loin on all sides, about 2 minutes or until browned. Remove from the pan, set aside on a plate, and allow to cool until you can handle it. Lay the bacon strips out onto a plate,

(recipe continues)

slightly overlapping, making sure the width of the bacon covers the length of the pork loin. Wrap the pork loin in the bacon, finishing with the seam side down, and secure with toothpicks.

Return the skillet to medium heat and sear the bacon with the toothpicks facing upward, then remove the toothpicks and brown on the remaining sides. Drizzle ¼ cup of the marinade over the pork loin as you go, keeping your hands out of the way, as the kvass may ignite in a dramatic flambé! Transfer the pan to the oven and bake for 10 to 12 minutes, until the internal temperature reaches 150°F to 160°F. Remove from the oven, transfer to a serving plate, and tent with aluminum foil. Increase the oven temperature to 425°F and allow to rest for 15 minutes while you make the prune sauce.

To make the prune sauce, cook the onions in the pan with the reserved meat juices over medium heat until they have softened and slightly caramelized, 10 to 12 minutes, adding the marinade in small amounts while the onions cook and allowing it to reduce. Stir in the prunes and any remaining marinade and continue cooking until the marinade has thickened and the liquid has reduced, 6 to 8 minutes. Transfer the prunes and onions to a serving bowl and cover.

Sprinkle the remaining ½ teaspoon salt over the cabbage wedges. Heat the pan with the remaining bacon fat over high heat until screaming hot. Add the cabbage and sear until almost black, about 8 minutes, drizzling the fat over the top of the wedges to coat. Carefully pour in the vinegar, sprinkle in the mustard seeds, and transfer to the oven. Bake for 15 to 20 minutes until the cabbage is tender to a fork, turning once with tongs about three quarters of the way through.

Slice the pork loin and drizzle the prune sauce over the meat, or serve on the side with the cabbage. Serve immediately.

CHOCOLATE EINKORN FUDGE CAKE
with HAZELNUT STREUSEL

Makes one 10 × 3½-inch cake

This is one of the most satisfying chocolate cakes I have ever made. Einkorn has the reputation of being difficult to direct substitute into traditional recipes because it doesn't absorb liquids nearly as well as most whole-grain flours. The trick with this cake is to pre-gelate the starches in the einkorn using hot coffee to scald the flour. During this process, water molecules intervene and separate the starch molecules. Once the starches cool down, they become firm again with pockets of water trapped in between in a process called retrogradation. What all of this means is that you end up with a decadently moist, tender, and fudgy cake that no one will believe is whole grain. I prefer to use a flat-bottomed tube pan to avoid sticking, but you may gamble with a generously buttered Bundt pan instead. Although the hazelnut adds texture and fragrance, you may omit it completely. It is absolutely delicious served with Toasted Fennel and Kumquat Ice Cream (page 184).

FOR THE CAKE

226 g / 1 cup unsalted butter, cut into pieces, plus more for the pan

85 g / 3 ounces bittersweet chocolate, chopped

275 g / 2½ cups whole einkorn flour

70 g / ⅔ cup cocoa powder, sifted

400 g / 2 cups granulated sugar

1½ teaspoons baking powder

1½ teaspoons baking soda

¾ teaspoon salt

345 g / 1½ cups very hot (140°F to 150°F) strongly brewed coffee

3 large eggs, lightly beaten

2 teaspoons pure vanilla extract

FOR THE STREUSEL

130 g / 1 cup hazelnuts, toasted, skins removed, and coarsely chopped

140 g / ⅔ cup light brown sugar

30 g / ¼ cup cocoa powder

1 tablespoon ground cinnamon

Place your oven rack at its lowest position and preheat the oven to 350°F.

Place the butter and chocolate in a heatproof bowl and set over a small pan of simmering water (make sure the bottom of the pan doesn't touch the water). Stir with a silicone spatula until melted. Set aside to cool.

Very (very!) generously butter a large flat-bottomed tube or Bundt pan—don't skimp or miss any nooks or crannies or the streusel topping will end up sticking. Place the pan in the refrigerator while you work.

In a large bowl, whisk together the flour, cocoa powder, sugar, baking powder, baking soda, and salt. Slowly pour in the hot coffee, stirring with a

(recipe continues)

large spoon. Mix until combined, then beat in the melted butter and chocolate with a large spoon until combined. Allow the batter to cool slightly, then add the eggs and vanilla and beat to combine.

If you are making the streusel topping, in a separate bowl, whisk together the streusel ingredients. Sprinkle half over the bottom of the chilled pan. Pour half of the cake batter over the streusel, then sprinkle on the remaining streusel. Pour in the remaining batter and lightly tamp the pan on the counter to remove any large air bubbles. Bake for 60 to 65 minutes, until a toothpick inserted into the center of the cake tests clean. Place the cake on a wire rack to cool for 15 minutes, then carefully unmold it onto a plate. Cool completely on the plate and serve. The cake will keep covered in a container for up to 3 days at room temperature.

OPPOSITE *Rich and fudgy, this whole-grain chocolate cake is complemented by a scoop or two of Toasted Fennel and Kumquat Ice Cream (page 184).*

TOASTED FENNEL *and* KUMQUAT ICE CREAM

Makes 1 quart

Kumquats are tiny little packages of big flavor. Unlike an orange or grapefruit that invites you to slowly peel away its protective outer layer to reveal its generous juicy flesh, kumquats are completely edible epiphanies of instant gratification delivered straight from the tree to the mouth. Their uniquely sweet peel and abrasively sour pulp together create a memorable awakening of the taste buds. For this reason, kumquats are incredibly useful beyond enthusiastic grazing, sliced raw into salads, baked into winter desserts, or joined with fennel in this ice cream. Fennel's nutty sweetness complements these little golden gems perfectly. Because their season of availability is short, I have become devoted to their preservation in this recipe and the following one. Although this ice cream is best served with the bold flavors of chocolate, as with Chocolate Einkorn Fudge Cake with Hazelnut Streusel (page 181), it can be paired with other recipes, such as Apple Charlotte (page 115), Brown Butter Corn Cake (page 123), or Sorghum, Vanilla, and Rosemary Apple Pie (page 118). (Recipe shown on page 183.)

1 tablespoon fennel seeds

2 cups heavy cream

1 cup whole milk

1 cup fresh kumquats (about 6 ounces), seeded and minced

½ cup + 1 tablespoon sugar

1 tablespoon orange blossom honey

Generous pinch of salt

5 large egg yolks, at room temperature

In a medium heavy-bottomed saucepan, toast the fennel seeds over medium-low heat until light and fragrant, 2 to 3 minutes. Pour in the heavy cream followed by the milk. Turn off the heat, cover, and allow to steep at room temperature for at least 2 hours, tasting along the way for desired strength of flavor. Transfer to a container and refrigerate overnight.

Place the kumquats in a small bowl and stir in 1 tablespoon of the sugar and the honey. Set aside for 30 minutes, stirring occasionally, until the kumquats begin to macerate and release their

juices. If not using right away, cover and store in the refrigerator until ready to use.

Prepare an ice bath by placing a few cups of ice in a large bowl and positioning a smaller bowl on top.

Strain the cream mixture through a fine-mesh sieve, return it to the pot, and stir in the remaining ½ cup sugar and the salt. Cook, stirring, over medium heat until the sugar dissolves.

Put the egg yolks in a medium bowl. To temper the egg yolks, pour 1½ cups of the sweetened cream in a thin, steady stream while whisking vigorously. Then slowly pour the tempered yolks back into the remaining sweetened cream. Cook the custard over medium-low heat, stirring with a wide spatula, until it coats the back of the spatula, 10 to 12 minutes, watching that it does not curdle. Pour through a fine-mesh sieve into the chilled bowl. Cover and refrigerate until completely cold, at least 3 hours.

Churn according to your ice cream maker's instructions, adding the kumquats during the last 5 minutes. Transfer the ice cream to a freezer container, cover, and place in the freezer. Allow to harden in the freezer for at least 8 hours or overnight before serving.

HONEY *and* VANILLA POACHED KUMQUATS

Makes 1½ pints

This quick and easy preserve is ambrosial on a piece of sourdough toast with a generous pat of butter. It makes a wonderful companion to roasted meats, chicken tagine, and pork and fish dishes. Tip: Rinse and dry the used vanilla bean pod and add it to a jar of sugar to infuse it with its scent.

1 cup mild honey
1 cup water

1 vanilla bean, split
510 g / 3 cups fresh kumquats
    (about 18 ounces)

Place the honey and water in a large saucepan. Scrape the vanilla seeds into the pot and add the bean. Using a sharp paring knife, score the kumquat skin in quadrants, placing them into the pot as you work. Bring to a simmer over medium-high heat, then immediately reduce the heat to the lowest heat possible. Partially cover to allow steam to escape and cook for 20 to 25 minutes, stirring occasionally, until the kumquats are somewhat translucent. Remove the vanilla bean. Transfer hot to warm sterilized jars, cover, and store in the refrigerator for up to 6 months.

SHAKER LEMON *and* SAGE PIE

Makes one 9-inch double crust pie

The United Society of Believers in Christ's Second Appearing, more commonly known as the Shakers, is a Christian sect founded in England in 1770 by a woman named Ann Lee. Ann Lee, who was thought to embody the second coming of Christ, established four basic tenets: communal living, celibacy, regular confession of sins, and isolationism from the outside world. The Shaker story is an intriguing study of a social and religious experiment in utopian community in early American history. They were radical for their time in many ways: they practiced social, sexual, economic, and spiritual equality 75 years before emancipation and 150 years before suffrage. They strongly believed in gender equality, even though their responsibilities were separated by sex.

They were initially known as "Shaking Quakers" because of their ecstatic dancing and speaking in tongues during worship services but were just as known for their craftsmanship. According to Shaker tradition, God dwelt in the details and quality of their work, and their influence can be widely seen in fashion, furniture, textiles, music, and sometimes food. The following recipe is adapted from one they are most known for in Kentucky, where I once lived in close proximity to the remnants of a well-preserved Shaker community. Shaker cooks considered lemons an important part of a healthy diet, even though they were expensive and elusive. This pie speaks to the pure flavor of lemon and making use of every bit of the fruit. I have made a few adjustments to include whole grains and sage to cheer the darkest days of winter. I prefer spelt in the use of this piecrust, but any whole wheat pastry flour will do.

1 recipe Fermented Whole-
  Grain Piecrust dough
  (page 58)

FOR THE FILLING
235 g / 4 small Meyer lemons
400 g / 2 cups granulated sugar
¼ teaspoon fine sea salt

1 tablespoon chopped fresh
  sage leaves or finely crushed
  dried sage leaves
5 large eggs, at room
  temperature
22 g / 1½ tablespoons unsalted
  butter, melted and cooled
1 tablespoon fine cornmeal or
  corn flour

FOR THE EGG WASH
1 large egg yolk
Dash of heavy cream
1½ to 2 tablespoons coarse sugar

Whipped cream, for serving

Trim and discard the ends of the lemons, cut them in half, and remove the seeds. Using a mandoline or a sharp knife, slice the lemons as thinly as possible and place them into a large bowl. Add the sugar, salt, and sage and stir well to combine. Cover

(recipe continues)

with plastic wrap and allow to macerate at room temperature for 24 hours.

Roll out half of the piecrust to about an ⅛-inch-thick 10- to 10½-inch round and drape it into a 9-inch pie plate. Lightly press the crust into the plate and trim the edges with scissors or a knife, leaving a ½-inch overhang.

In a large bowl, beat the eggs, butter, and cornmeal with an electric hand mixer until slightly frothy. Stir into the lemon mixture until well combined and transfer to the pie plate. Roll the remaining dough into a 12-inch round, drape it over the filling, and trim it to leave a 1-inch overhang. Alternatively, you may cut decorative shapes from the crust first, allowing it to firm up in the freezer for 5 minutes to assist in better ease of handling before draping. Tuck the overhang under the bottom crust and crimp to create a decorative edge. Place in the freezer for about 20 minutes to firm the crust.

Preheat the oven to 425°F.

To make the egg wash, combine the egg yolk and cream in a small bowl. Cut a few slits in the top of the crust for venting and brush with the egg wash. Sprinkle with the coarse sugar and bake for 15 minutes, then decrease the oven temperature to 350°F and continue baking for another 30 minutes, or until the crust is golden brown, checking after 15 or 20 minutes and tenting with a pie shield or aluminum foil if the crust is browning too fast. Remove from the oven and cool on a wire rack for at least 2 hours to set. Serve slightly warm or at room temperature, with whipped cream.

OPPOSITE Citrus hystrix *(makrut limes) are worth growing or seeking in Asian markets for their alluring perfume. Use their zest to adorn pastries, to finish savory stews, or as a potent ingredient in Sweet Meadow Vermouth (page 145).*

CITRUS

The genus *Citrus* encompasses many species, crosses, and varieties that represent the menagerie of jewel-fleshed fruits we know today. The fruit is botanically referred to as a hesperidium—a modified berry with a thick leathery rind called a pericarp. Within is a spongy ovary wall (the pith) and carpels (segments) filled with juicy, vitamin-rich vesicles. The variety of colors, flavors, and textures in citrus is remarkable as a result of the natural inclination of the genus to cross-pollinate. As exotic heirloom selections and their hybrids find a wider audience and distribution, our appetites can explore the possibilities their exotically wrinkled, oil-fragrant skins or animated postures can bring into our culinary repertoires.

Citrus trees and shrubs have been cultivated for more than four thousand years and are thought to have originated in parts of India, China, Australia, New Caledonia, and New Guinea. Citrus plants readily interbreed, producing hybrids as sour as the Seville orange or as sweet and ambrosial as the Cara Cara, a red-fleshed orange discovered growing on a ranch by that name in Venezuela. Each has a distinctive flavor and culinary characteristics dependent on its genetics, where it's grown, and when it's harvested.

Citrus grow naturally in tropical and subtropical climates and are commercially viable only in areas where there is some seasonal change but no sustained frost. Cooler fall weather induces color change but not ripeness, so growers must taste the fruit to test its balance between sweet and sour before picking. Citrus fruits stop ripening after they are picked because unlike fruits such as pears and peaches, they don't possess starches that turn to sugars. Oranges, grapefruits, lemons, kumquats, and other citrus fruits are wonderful preserved with salt, stewed in marmalades, added to tagines, chopped into salsas, and baked into cakes.

ORANGE CARDAMOM CAKE

Makes one 9-inch cake

This is an adaptation of an old Sephardic cake recipe prepared without dairy and with ground almonds instead of flour. It is a traditional recipe of North African and Spanish origins, where the cultivation of citrus was once associated with Sephardic Jews. If you wish to make this cake flourless, simply substitute almond flour for the pastry flour. Either way, it will be a remarkably firm but moist cake with a tender crumb that is perfect humbly adorned with powdered sugar. If you are serving within the same day, the blood orange glaze makes a festive finish and adds yet another moist element to the cake.

FOR THE CAKE
465 g / 2 whole oranges
Unsalted butter, for the pan
165 g / 1½ cups whole wheat
    pastry flour, plus more for
    the pan
6 large eggs

340 g / 1 cup honey
1 teaspoon pure vanilla extract
55 g / ⅓ cup sifted Sourdough
    Bread Crumbs (page 66)
1½ teaspoons baking powder
2 teaspoons ground cardamom
¼ teaspoon fine salt

FOR THE GLAZE (OPTIONAL)
125 g / 1 cup powdered sugar
Juice of 1 blood orange
1 teaspoon blood orange zest

PREPARE THE BATTER

Place the oranges in a small saucepan and add water to cover. Cover and bring to a boil over medium-high heat. Reduce the heat to low and simmer for 2 hours, occasionally rolling the oranges and making sure the water has not boiled dry. Remove the oranges from the pan, cool completely, then quarter them to remove the seeds (reserve them for their pectin to use in jam or jelly making—see page 16).

Set an oven rack to the middle position and preheat the oven to 350°F. Line a 9-inch cake pan with parchment paper. Generously butter the

bottom and sides and dust with flour, tamping out any excess.

Place the orange quarters, eggs, honey, and vanilla in a food processor or blender and process on high speed to a smoothie-like consistency. Transfer to a large bowl.

Whisk together the flour, bread crumbs, baking powder, cardamom, and salt into a separate large bowl, and pour in the wet mixture. Stir until just combined, then transfer to the prepared cake pan.

(recipe continues)

OPPOSITE *This moist cake needs little other than a dusting of powdered sugar but is beautiful adorned with a blood orange glaze.*

190 SEASONAL RECIPES

BAKE THE CAKE

Place the cake in the oven on the middle rack
and bake for 10 minutes. Decrease the oven
temperature to 325°F and bake for another
15 minutes, or until the edges have browned and
pulled away from the pan and a toothpick inserted
into the center tests clean. Place on a wire rack to
cool completely. If serving without the glaze, place
a plate on top of the pan and flip; dust lightly with
powdered sugar and serve.

GLAZE THE CAKE (OPTIONAL)

Turn the cake out onto a serving plate with the
bottom facing up. Sift the powdered sugar into
a small bowl and whisk in enough blood orange
juice until it is pourable but not runny. Stir in
the orange zest, pour over the cake, and use an
offset spatula to assist in spreading it over the top
and encouraging it to drip over the sides. Serve
immediately.

STICKY DATE, TEFF, *and* PECAN CAKE

Makes one 9-inch cake

Recipes for sticky date cake and date bread can be found on handwritten cards in heirloom recipe boxes throughout the South. Although there are many variations, the premise of soaking dates in a hot liquid to both sweeten and moisten the crumb is a given. This variation is based on a recipe from the Vanderbunt family of Oxford, Georgia, who generously allowed me to peruse their treasured collection. I have adapted it to make it a whole-grain cake, using spelt and rich, almost chocolaty teff flour to deepen its character. Walnuts are the traditional nut of choice, but I prefer the sweetness of pecans paired with these flours. Hot tea is used to scald both the dates and the teff, but you may use hot coffee or water instead—whatever is left over at the end of a day's kitchen work is usually what sneaks its way in!

FOR THE CAKE
Unsalted butter for the pan

95 g / ½ cup whole teff flour, plus more for the pan

250 g / 1½ cups chopped dried dates

½ teaspoon fine sea salt

230 g / 1 cup boiling hot black tea

1½ teaspoons baking soda

90 g / ¾ cup coarsely chopped pecans

50 g / ¼ cup coconut oil, or unsalted butter, melted

155 g / 1 cup coconut sugar or brown sugar

2 large eggs

1 teaspoon pure vanilla extract

110 g / 1 cup whole spelt flour

FOR THE GLAZE
135 g / 9 tablespoons unsalted butter

115 g / ¾ cup coconut sugar or brown sugar

95 g / ¼ cup + 1½ tablespoons heavy cream

¼ teaspoon kosher salt

25 g / 2½ tablespoons brandy or dark rum

½ teaspoon pure vanilla extract

FOR THE GARNISH (OPTIONAL)
40 g / ½ cup coconut flakes, toasted

Salted Maple Whipped Cream (page 112)

PREPARE THE BATTER

Preheat the oven to 350°F. Line a 9-inch cake pan with parchment paper, and butter it generously. Lightly flour the pan to coat the bottom and sides, tapping out any excess.

Place the teff flour, dates, and salt in a medium bowl. Pour the hot tea over the bowl, sift in the baking soda, and stir well to combine. Stir in the pecans and set aside for the ingredients to soak while you prepare the rest of the cake.

In the bowl of a stand mixer, beat the melted coconut oil and coconut sugar until well combined. Add the eggs one at a time, incorporating the first before adding the second, then add the vanilla and mix until smooth. Beat in the date mixture, then

(recipe continues)

add the spelt flour and mix until just combined.
Pour the runny batter into the prepared cake pan.

BAKE THE CAKE

Place the cake in the oven and bake for 20 minutes.
Carefully tent the cake with aluminum foil to
prevent overbrowning and continue baking for
another 15 to 20 minutes, until a toothpick inserted
into the center of the cake tests clean.

PREPARE THE GLAZE AND FINISH THE CAKE

While the cake is baking, prepare the glaze:
Combine the butter, coconut sugar, cream, and salt
in a medium saucepan and bring to a rolling boil
over high heat. After about 45 seconds, take off the
heat and stir in the brandy and vanilla. When the
cake is done, use a toothpick to generously poke
holes all over the surface while still in the pan. Pour
about half of the warm glaze over the cake and
allow to soak for 15 minutes. Place a plate over the
cake and flip the cake out so it's bottom-side up.
Poke additional holes into the surface and drizzle
the rest of the glaze over the top of the cake in a
few additions, allowing it to soak into the surface
before drizzling more. Allow to cool completely.
Garnish with the toasted coconut and salted maple
whipped cream, if using.

AGRODULCE

Makes about ¾ cup

This versatile sweet and sour classic Italian sauce is made from a few simple ingredients—namely vinegar, a sweetener, and some dried fruit. It can be tailored to suit the meal with which it is served, adjusting the choice of vinegar or fruit to complement seasonal vegetables, grilled or roasted meats, or even desserts such as Sweet Potato Tart with a Coconut Pecan Crust (page 112). Make good use of Homemade Vinegars such as apple, pineapple, or jujube (see pages 6 to 8) to create a bright sauce, or use sherry vinegar or balsamic vinegar for more robust flavor. Sometimes I like to add a glug of port wine to the end of cooking to impart a rich complexity to the fruit. Raisins are the classic Italian choice, but try prunes when pairing with Bacon-Wrapped Pork Loin with Charred Cabbage and Prune Sauce (page 179) or cherries when serving over sautéed Whey-Fermented Cipollini Onions (page 45). For a spicy kick, include a hot chili such as jalapeño or Fresno to dress up roasted Brussels sprouts or winter squash. (Recipe also shown on page 113.)

1 cup vinegar of choice
⅓ cup honey

½ cup chopped (medium dice) dried fruit of choice
Generous pinch of salt

Combine all the ingredients in a small saucepan and cook over medium heat until the mixture reduces into a thick sauce, 6 to 8 minutes, or slightly longer depending on your choice of fruit. Serve immediately, or cool, cover, and store in the refrigerator for up to 1 week.

DRIED FIG, WALNUT, *and* SESAME JAM

Makes about 7 cups (3½ pints)

There is a historic row of Arabic shops located on Atlantic Avenue in Brooklyn, and I consider a trip there to source ingredients an opportunity to both learn and share joy in nostalgic dishes. I always walk away inspired by buckets of Moroccan olives, Lebanese pine nuts, and Arabic coffee. After one trip bringing home a large, unpremeditated purchase of plump dried figs I just couldn't resist, I researched a recipe for this jam, ultimately turning to one of my favorite old cookbooks from Claudia Roden, *A Book of Middle Eastern Food.* I adapted her method to incorporate sesame seeds and honey, two of my favorite ingredients, and left out the mastic, a tree resin that provides flavor and thickening power. But if you can source mastic, pulverize a few small nuggets (no more than ½ teaspoon worth) with a pinch of sugar in a mortar and pestle. Stir it in thoroughly after removing the jam from the heat and before transferring to the sterilized jars.

This jam is incredibly sweet and nutty, and my favorite way to eat it is with salty companions, such as a thick slice of pecorino or cured ham. Look for Lebanese- or Spanish-grown pine nuts for purity and supreme flavor. If this is not possible, toasted sunflower or pumpkin seeds make an equally delicious substitute. Many jams need lots of time to prepare, but this one comes together in a snap and makes a beautiful holiday gift, especially if you use a combination of black and white sesame seeds. (Recipe shown on page 156.)

3 cups water

1¾ cups sugar

1 cup orange blossom honey

Zest and juice of 1 lemon

2 pounds dried figs, stemmed and coarsely chopped

1½ teaspoons ground aniseed

2 cups walnuts, toasted

½ cup pine nuts, toasted

¼ cup sesame seeds, toasted

Combine the water, sugar, honey, and lemon juice in a large saucepan and bring to a boil over medium-high heat. Stir in the figs, lemon zest, and aniseed. Reduce the heat to medium and simmer until the figs soften and the liquid reduces to a syrup, about 8 minutes. Add the walnuts, pine nuts, and sesame seeds and continue to simmer, stirring constantly, until the mixture has thickened and resists the motion of the spoon, about 5 more minutes. Transfer to sterilized jars, and cover. Store in the refrigerator for up to 6 months.

EXPLORING GLOBAL INGREDIENTS

To feel a sense of place wherever I am, I cook and bake from the markets I visit. It is by engaging in the rituals of eating that I am able to discover a personal prose to a region that cannot be comprehended from a photograph or a news story. For this reason, I have been wandering in and out of spice shops and open-air markets for years. No matter where I travel, my first inclination is to find these heady little corners of culinary possibility and their windows into cultural understanding.

In a spice shop in Marrakech, I heard for the first time the quote from the Hadith of Muhammad "Hold on to the use of the black seed, for indeed it has a remedy for every disease except death." For an estimated three thousand years, the seed of the nigella flower has been held in utmost reverence in both Indian and Arabic cuisine. How lucky I was to discover its potency under the hands of a Berber ambassador! When I entered, the shopkeepers smiled with their smoky eyes and fueled our long transaction with copious pours of sweetened mint tea and a neck massage by the youngest, most handsome helper. The gesture struck me as odd but proved to be innocent enough; the proprietor simply wanted me to feel well taken care of as a customer. It was an amusing display of affection for a young single woman navigating the customs of the North African world for the first time. He sensed my hesitation and positioned my chair in the front window both to reinforce my comfort and for passing tourists to observe. I blushed at the ease with which I melted under his hands, and we all giggled a little as I left with embarrassingly heaping bags of spices and teas. It was my first purchase of nigella seed and the beginning of a long romance with the plant as an herbal remedy, culinary spice, and beguiling garden annual. The hospitality of that exchange has endured through years of memories, and although I doubt I could find the shop's location again in the maze of the medina, I often yearn for a return visit to tell the shopkeeper of the delicious doors he opened by casting nigella's spell.

Visiting the spice shops in Bourj Hammoud, the Armenian neighborhood of Beirut, was a less affectionate experience but still one of enthusiastic exchange. Here is where many cultures and ingredients from neighboring countries, including Syria, come together under one roof. Istanbul's Ottoman-era Spice Bazaar was impressively sophisticated, and I was amazed at the level of international business each vendor was ready to engage. In addition to single spices, there were clever blends for every culinary and medicinal use imaginable that could be shipped by the vacuum-sealed bag or boxed crate straight to my door.

Ecuador has banned the import of GMO crops in order to preserve its unique agricultural heritage, and it shows in the unparalleled menagerie of color, mineralized flavors, and remarkable freshness of their markets. Several sojourns to this small but biodiverse country revealed agricultural practices and culinary preparations of many indigenous as well as European introductions of ancient grains. Corn, maize, barley, wheat, quinoa, and amaranth were all present in abundance alongside hundreds of varieties of indigenous fruits, roots, and vegetables. Knobby little potatoes in flashy spotted pink or purple skins would tumble out of sacks stacked next to mounds of green or brown coconuts and fragrant red bananas. Closer to the Amazon, two- to three-feet-long legumes containing rock-hard seeds disguised under a thick, fuzzy coating are piled high in dazzling display. Only after aggressively sucking and nibbling on what feels like cotton candy–flavored mothballs are the inedible seeds released onto your thirsty tongue. It is an experience not unlike the passing of time cracking unhulled sunflower seeds between your teeth. Although not an activity I crave in repetition, it certainly begged me to step outside of my culinary comfort zone.

When I visited the multileveled markets of Otavalo, Cuenca, and later Oaxaca, Mexico, it became painfully obvious that modern North American society has been cheated out of so many years of deliciousness. Grain grown in the United States since the industrialization of agriculture has suffered greatly from a focus on mass production. This is sadly the case with most of our commodity grain crops; corn bred for ethanol or cattle feed a delicacy it does not make!

The mercados of Oaxaca revealed the vibrational magic of the region with indigenous ingredients, mounds of smoky chilies, and brujitas crouched behind bundles of herbs ready to cure any ailment of the body or spirit. As the tart and addictive experience of milky pulque (fermented maguey sap) pulsed through my veins, I wondered if the leathery woman from the Sierra knew I had a weakness for insect foods as she shoved a roasted grasshopper my way with a knowing glance. Prepared masa could be bought in the colors of the rainbow, my favorite of the region the distinctive lavender-gray purple corn.

But it is the markets of New York City, much closer to home, where I am able to return time and again, reinforcing relationships with the owners (and their mouse-hunting cats) who greet me with my favorite ashta pastry, fresh pinch of spice, or savory snack in hand. The assault of fish guts as you push through plastic-draped curtains is the baptism of shopping in Chinatown. Women wrapped in colorful saris plunge their hands eagerly for the most beautiful Thai green baby eggplants in Jackson Heights with such immediacy you would think there was suddenly a rare shortage. When you meet the gaze of the shopper in Flushing with little regard for personal space, an approving smile flashes across their face as they inspect your stash. Although only a few miles from home, this great hunt for ingredients takes me on a journey not unlike the souks, bazaars, and mercados of distant lands, ending in an imaginative meal in my own kitchen.

FIRE CIDER TONIC

Makes about 6 cups

People often solicit health advice from me, especially those who have had digestive and immune issues similar to my own. The suggestions are often the same and quite simple: get more sleep, cut out unnecessary stress in your life, remove processed foods from your diet, and move your body (and mind!) in purposeful ways. Yet knowing this, I still struggle with the modern hustle that seems to conspire against a healthy lifestyle. When I catch myself desperately digging through the glove compartment in search of calories in any form I can swallow, I know it's time to hit the reset button and participate in a more mindful activity.

To stay healthy, I try to find a rhythm that can help me anticipate times of stress and busyness that would otherwise prevent self-care. Being a freelancer makes predictability unlikely, and life of course always springs the unexpected. But one thing I can count on is the seasons. I *know* that come winter, I need to take more proactive measures to boost my immune health regardless of how much I am traveling or how many orders I have to fill. The following recipe is one of the most powerful tonics using Western herbs and plant medicine you can make at home. It is a folk remedy and, as such, is highly adaptable and can utilize any manner of ingredients, but there are a few key ingredients that pack the punch needed to make fire cider a potent tonic.

Before frost, you can harvest rosemary, sage, parsley, thyme, lemongrass, winter or summer savory, or whatever else tickles your tummy and thrives in your climate. Do you live in a place abundant with vitamin C–rich rose hips? Include a few of those as well. This is all about blending to suit your needs and connect with the generosity of the plant world around you. Nature provides us with exactly what we need to live healthy and happy lives. It is we who need to take the time and energy to harvest and cultivate this connection. Fire cider is powerful, so be sure to consult with a natural healer if you have undergone any recent health crisis before dosing, in particular if you have kidney or bladder issues. I like the bright bitterness grapefruit adds, but you can substitute orange and lemon, lime, or any combination of them.

If you can time it just right, make a double batch of this tonic and let it steep in several jars during the month of September or October. Wait for at least a month, or up to six if you have the time and space, and strain each jar as you need it. Once strained and mixed with a little honey if you like, you can bottle with affectionately decorated labels and give them to friends for the holidays. Or just take a swig a few times a day to warm your bones, stimulate digestion, and energize your body as you watch the snow fall outside your window. It is also excellent in salad dressings, sprinkled over rice, or added to a Fire Cider Bloody Mary (page 204) either fortified with gin or not. You can recycle the spent shredded veggies as an ingredient for cocktail sauce or as a zippy condiment with roasted meats or vegetables.

When making fire cider, throw the windows open and drink deep the fresh air—the ingredients, in particular the horseradish, will clear your sinuses in a hurry! It is helpful to have a cross-breeze going and all of your ingredients, jars, and nonreactive lids clean and prepped and a pair of kitchen gloves to protect your skin from the stain of the turmeric and the fire of the chilies.

One 8-inch piece horseradish, grated

3 large fresh turmeric roots (about 4½ ounces), peeled and grated

One 9- to 10-inch fresh ginger root (about 4½ ounces), peeled and grated

3 small fresh ginseng roots (about 1½ ounces; optional), coarsely chopped

1 large onion, coarsely chopped

2 medium heads (16 cloves) garlic, finely grated

2 large grapefruits, halved and cut into 3-inch wedges

1 to 2 habanero chilies (or chili of choice), coarsely chopped

1½ teaspoons black peppercorns, crushed in a mortar and pestle

About 6 cups Apple Cider Vinegar (page 6) with the mother

¼ cup raw honey, or to taste

In a large bowl, combine all of the ingredients except the vinegar and honey using gloved hands. Toss well, then transfer to jars. Pour in vinegar to cover and cover with nonreactive lids. Leave to sit for at least 4 weeks or up to 6 months, depending on your desired strength. Strain and add the honey, if desired. The tonic will keep in the refrigerator for up to 1 year.

PLANT MEDICINE

Fire cider is considered an adaptation of an oxymel, an ancient method of steeping plant parts in vinegar and honey to extract their beneficial qualities and to make these sometimes otherwise bitter ingredients more palatable. You may choose one plant for its particular quality (such as valerian to assist with relaxation or ginger for digestion) or several according to your needs. Although recipes vary widely, you may blend according to your taste by filling a jar about one quarter of the way full with fresh or dried herbs, roots, or flowers. I prefer to add honey and vinegar in equal parts by visual approximation to fill the jar, but you may prefer more or less of each. Allow fresh, delicate herbs to steep for at least 2 weeks before straining, and let coarser ingredients, such as roots, steep for at least 4 weeks. The following are profiles of plants traditionally used in a fire cider tonic to stimulate immunity.

Horseradish, *Armoracia rusticana*

This member of the cruciferous Brassicaceae family (home to broccoli, cabbage, and mustard greens) has large, beautifully ornamental obovate leaves and is a wonderful perennial addition to any herb garden. Its long taproots can be harvested in the autumn for their pungent and distinctive flavor. Horseradish root is a powerful antibacterial agent that increases gastric secretions and appetite and is excellent to help tone the urinary tract system. It also acts as an expectorant and can help relieve respiratory congestion.

Ginger, *Zingiber officinale*

This much-loved member of the Zingiberaceae family has long been revered for its ability to warm the stomach, ease nausea, fight chills, and break congestion. It is a perennial herb that evolved in Southeast Asia that is most often grown in tropical climates as an annual but has gained increased cultivation in the southern states, where summers are hot and long. The underground tuberous stem (rhizome) is harvested young and can be used as a succulent ingredient in Ginger Peanut Garlic Paste (page 173). After eight to ten months, the older more fibrous rhizomes are dried to create ground ginger that is used in cakes and cookies, blended into curry powders, and used in savory soups.

Turmeric, *Curcuma longa*

This master plant shares the same family as ginger and has a morphological resemblance. Its deeply staining rhizomes are used to color curry powder, mustard, and textiles. The pigment is derived from curcumin, a compound proven to be beneficial in rheumatic conditions, a dizzying list of digestive disorders, treatment of gallbladder disease, cardiovascular health, and even cancer. In India, its antimicrobial properties have been used topically for millennia to treat skin ailments and internally for liver and stomach issues. Western medicine shows a record of its beneficial use as far back as 1748, but there is no record of it being used to treat disease until 1937.

Garlic, *Allium sativum*

Cultivated since 2000 B.C. in Egypt and Mesopotamia, garlic is known as a powerful flavoring agent the world over. Its sulfuric compounds have been proven beneficial in the treatment of cardiovascular disease, and they have been shown to suppress initiation and development of cancer cells, lower cholesterol, and boost immune function. These compounds are found throughout the Amaryllidaceae family, which includes onions, shallots, chives, and leeks. This family's strong antimicrobial character, most potently found in garlic, can be used to treat bladder, kidney, yeast, respiratory, and throat infections.

Chilies and Sweet Peppers,
***Capsicum annuum* or**
Capsicum frutescens
Both of these species are grown as annuals in most countries, as they are sensitive to frost. *C. frutescens* is often kept as a perennial in more temperate climates with fruits that are extremely pungent including cayenne, Tabasco, and what are generically referred to as red pepper flakes. *C. annuum* has a broad range of colors, flavors, and heat indexes ranging from the mild sweet bell pepper to strongly flavored varieties referred to as chilies. Capsaicin is the compound in chilies that is responsible for their role in treating chronic pain, weight issues, and cancer. Although capsaicin was most likely developed by the plant as a protective mechanism, it is helpful in increasing blood circulation and stimulating mucus and can be used as an anti-inflammatory agent.

JUJUBE, GINGER, *and* TURMERIC TEA

Makes 6 cups

Turmeric and ginger combine to make a powerful immune-boosting, joint-soothing drink. Black pepper aids absorption and jujubes add a touch of natural sweetness. You can add a 3-inch strip of orange zest to the pot or when serving for a little zing, or you can add a stick of cinnamon for its warming notes.

6 large dried jujube dates
One 3-inch knob fresh turmeric, peeled and thinly sliced, or 2 teaspoons ground turmeric

One 5-inch knob fresh ginger, peeled and thinly sliced
½ teaspoon freshly ground black pepper

6 cups water
Squeeze of fresh lemon
Honey (optional)

Pierce the jujubes with a sharp knife and place them in a large nonreactive pot. Add the remaining ingredients and bring to a boil over high heat. Lower the heat to maintain a simmer and simmer for 12 minutes. Remove from the heat and allow to steep for at least 30 minutes or up to 3 hours.

Strain and dilute; a 1:1 ratio is recommended. Alternatively, store in a covered container in the refrigerator for up to 5 days; dilute and reheat when you're ready to serve. Finish with a squeeze of lemon. Although you may compost the jujube, I like to pit and include a few slices in the tea.

FIRE CIDER BLOODY MARY

Serves 2

The immune tonic Fire Cider Tonic (page 200) fortifies this classic brunch cocktail with a nod to Asian ingredients. You need not use alcohol, but if you do, look for a good soju or shochu, a clear Korean beverage distilled from rice, wheat, or barley. If you can't find it, a quality vodka or the unsweetened version of Kumquat Liqueur (page 207) would be fine. A rim of togarashi (a Japanese spice blend of ground chilies, orange peel, sesame, ginger, and seaweed) along with a garnish of toasted nori and kimchi provides a unique and savory finish with just the right amount of saltiness to counter the bite of the fire cider. To toast the nori, place a skillet over medium-high heat for 2 to 3 minutes. Place the nori on the skillet until it turns from a dark to bright green color. Remove to cool before serving.

1 lime or lemon wedge

¼ cup togarashi

Ice cubes

1¼ cups tomato juice

½ cup soju or shochu, gin, or vodka (optional)

½ cup Fire Cider Tonic (page 200), or more to taste

1 teaspoon tamari

1 teaspoon toasted sesame oil

FOR THE GARNISH (OPTIONAL)

Toasted nori (purchase it or toast it yourself)

¼ cup kimchi

A few cucumber slices

2 lime or lemon wedges

Use the lime wedge to wipe the rims of two large glasses. Dip the rims into the togarashi to coat, then fill the glasses with ice. In a pitcher, stir together the tomato juice, soju, fire cider, tamari, and toasted sesame oil. Divide the mixture between the glasses. Garnish as you wish and serve immediately.

KUMQUAT LIQUEUR

Makes about 3½ cups

This liqueur reminiscent of limoncello can be made in a number of different ways. Some traditional recipes call for soaking the fruit in liquor first, straining, and then mixing with simple syrup. I prefer the following method because after a few days of vigorous shaking, I can forget about it in a corner of my kitchen for at least a month. It makes for a rather concentrated beverage with sweet floral, almond, and citrus notes. Choose your liquor wisely—I prefer a small-batch gin made with spicy botanical notes of coriander, and thankfully there are more than a few labels that fit this description. But don't despair if a more generic brand is available; simply pop a teaspoon of coriander seeds into the bottle as well.

You can eliminate the sugar and steep the scored kumquats and gin together in a bottle for a month or longer and use the gin as you would plain gin, topping off with more as you use it to extend the life of the fruit. My preferred autumn/winter gin and tonic formula is to muddle a steeped kumquat in a tall glass, add ice and a few whole cloves or star anise, and then pour 2 to 3 ounces of the gin and top it off with a good-quality tonic.

Regardless of the method, after the kumquats have flavored the liqueur, you can strain them and cook them over medium-low heat with some added sweetener until broken down to make a boozy jam for toast or pancakes.

2 cups gin, vodka, rum, or
    bourbon

1½ cups sugar or honey
1½ cups fresh kumquats

Pour the liquor of your choice into a 1½-quart bottle and stir or shake in the sugar—it will not dissolve immediately, but over time it will. Using a sharp paring knife, score the skin of the kumquats into quadrants and drop them into the bottle. Cover and shake again. Repeat this for the next few days or when you think of it. After several weeks, the sugar will dissolve and the kumquats will become mildly effervescent in the liquor. Steep for at least 1 month or longer if you prefer a stronger flavor. I often leave kumquats in the liquor and pour from the bottle, but you also may strain them and store the liquor in a clean bottle in a cool location.

OPPOSITE *Kumquat liqueur is a refreshinng after-dinner treat served cold. If made without sugar, it is an excellent substitute in a gin and tonic, garnished with star anise or cloves and a sprig of thyme.*

6

SPRING

Clockwise from left to right: *puntarelle chicory* (Cichorium intybus), *radicchio* (Cichorium intybus *'Rosa del Veneto'*) *pansy* (Viola *sp.*), *sweet William* (Dianthus *'Rainbow Loveliness'*), *purple daikon radish* (Raphanus sativus *var.* longipinnatus), *watermelon radish* (Raphanus sativus *var.* acanthiformis), *green meat radish* (Raphanus sativus *'Green Meat'*), *morel mushrooms* (Morchella esculenta), *radicchio* (Cichorium intybus *'Treviso Tardivo'*), *beet* (Beta vulgaris *'Chioggia'*), *radicchio* (Cichorium intybus *'Rosa di Gorizia'*), *and radicchio* (Cichorium intybus *'Variegata di Castelfranco'*).

A Return to Vitality

BREADS

Amaranth, Millet,
and Sorghum Bread
(The Paradigm Shift) / 213

Whey Kaak/Pita / 215

Emmer and Green Garlic
Gougères / 218

Herman's Heirloom
Cornbread / 220

Nomad Flatbread / 224

SAVORY DISHES

Fried Farro, Radicchio,
and Puntarelle Salad with
Currants / 226

Asparagus and
Amaranth Soup / 229

Beet Falafel / 231

Freekeh Salad with
Pea, Gooseberry,
and Radish / 235

Chickpea Pancakes with
Dandelion Greens and
Caramelized Onions / 236

Quickie Congee / 241

Pa Kimchi / 242

Butter-Roasted Sumac
Chicken / 245

Chicken and Fennel
Sourdough Dumplings / 249

Jujube, Ginseng,
and Rice Chicken Soup
(Samgyetang) / 251

Brown Butter Apricot
Kasha / 252

SWEETS AND DRINKS

Cranberry Marmalade / 254

Salted Kumquat and
Honey Tea / 255

AMARANTH, MILLET, *and* SORGHUM BREAD (THE PARADIGM SHIFT)

Makes 2 loaves

This moist loaf uses millet flour, cooked whole sorghum, and whole soaked amaranth seeds to create a sticky, loose dough that is best baked in a loaf pan to hold its shape. The bread has an incredible keeping quality and a very approachable flavor. It has a soft and slightly sweet crumb and a toothsome, addictively crunchy crust from an extra coating of amaranth seeds, which also make it incredibly handsome to behold. Source your grains locally to support a regional grain economy if you can, or purchase them online or from a health food store. This recipe is also excellent for using up leftover cooked whole grains, such as rice, farro, or freekeh, in place of the sorghum. For an added dimension of flavor, consider toasting the amaranth and sorghum before soaking.

FOR THE SOAKER
110 g / ½ cup amaranth
50 g / ¼ cup sorghum
170 g / ¾ cup water

FOR THE LEAVEN
40 g / scant ¼ cup 100% hydration sourdough starter, refreshed (fed)

40 g / scant 2½ tablespoons tepid water (70°F to 75°F)
40 g / 4 to 6 tablespoons whole wheat flour

FOR THE DOUGH
120 g / 1 cup + 1 heaping tablespoon leaven (see left)
490 g / 2 cups + 3 tablespoons water

60 g / 3 tablespoons sorghum syrup
490 g / 3½ cups high-extraction bread flour
170 g / 1¼ cups whole millet flour
75 g / ⅓ cup whole wheat bread flour
14 g / 1 tablespoon fine sea salt
Softened unsalted butter for the pans

PREPARE THE SOAKERS

At the same time as you prepare your leaven, place the amaranth in a small bowl and add water to cover by at least 2 inches. Place the sorghum in a separate bowl and add water to cover by at least 2 inches. Leave to soak at room temperature until you are ready to mix your dough, about 8 hours.

PREPARE THE LEAVEN

Place the starter and tepid water in a large bowl and stir to form a slurry. Add the flour and mix with a spoon until no dry lumps remain. Cover with a plate or plastic wrap and allow to ferment at room temperature for about 8 hours.

PREPARE THE AMARANTH AND SORGHUM

About an hour before you are ready to mix the dough, drain and rinse the amaranth through a

OPPOSITE *This recipe prepares a sorghum porridge but is adaptable to leftover cooked grains, such as rice or buckwheat, instead.*

(recipe continues)

nut milk bag or jelly bag, squeezing out any excess moisture. Drain and rinse the sorghum and place it in a small saucepan. Add the ¾ cup water and bring to a simmer over medium-high heat, then lower the heat to maintain a simmer, cover, and cook for about 45 minutes, until the grains are soft. Transfer the sorghum to a colander, rinse with cool water, and set aside.

MIX THE DOUGH

Add the water and sorghum syrup to the bowl with the leaven and stir to create a slurry. Add the flours and, using your hands, mix and squeeze the dough in a circular motion until no dry lumps remain. Cover with an inverted bowl, plate, or plastic wrap and autolyze (rest) the dough for about 20 minutes for the flour to fully hydrate. Sprinkle the salt evenly over the surface of the dough and mix to combine. Spread about ⅓ cup soaked amaranth and all of the cooled sorghum over the dough and gently incorporate it by repeatedly folding the dough over it. Reserve the remaining amaranth for the top of the loaf. The dough will feel overhydrated and mushy, but don't be too concerned, as it will change texture and become more adhesive during bulk fermentation. Cover with plastic wrap and set in a warm spot, ideally 75°F.

Bulk ferment for 3 to 4 more hours, until the dough has increased in size by at least one third and feels puffy and alive. To help develop the dough, stretch-and-fold it every 30 to 45 minutes to strengthen the gluten network while further incorporating the soakers.

SHAPE THE DOUGH

Generously grease two 9 × 5 × 3-inch loaf pans with butter. Remove the dough from the bowl onto a lightly floured surface. Divide it into two pieces and fold them into even rectangles. Place them seam-side down, cover with a towel or plastic wrap, and allow them to bench rest for about 10 minutes.

With the seams of the rectangles facing up, fold the top third of the rectangle to the center, using the heel of your hand to seal the seam. Fold the bottom third of the rectangle to the center, overlapping the first fold only slightly and again sealing the seam with the heel of your hand. Then fold the dough in half, tucking with one hand and sealing with the heel of your opposite hand to gain some tension. Lightly dampen the top of the loaves using a misting bottle or your fingers, then roll them into the reserved amaranth seeds to coat. Place the loaves into the buttered pans seam-side down.

Cover each loaf with a kitchen towel, then wrap it in a plastic bag. Retard in the refrigerator for 8 to 12 hours before baking. This dough does not hold well in refrigeration for an extended amount of time.

BAKE THE LOAVES

Remove the loaves from the refrigerator and allow to come to room temperature for about 1 hour. Meanwhile, preheat the oven to 470°F.

Score the top of the loaves with a razor blade ¼ to ½ inch deep down the center. Bake with steam for 15 minutes. Decrease the oven temperature to 450°F and bake for another 30 to 35 minutes, until an instant-read thermometer inserted into the bread registers 200°F. Remove from the oven and allow to rest in the pans for a few minutes, then remove and cool completely on a wire rack.

WHEY KAAK/PITA

Makes 7 to 9 flatbreads

In January 2017, I boarded a plane to Lebanon as an ambassador of sourdough. With a few flecks of dehydrated sourdough starter in tow, I embarked on a culinary adventure focused on naturally leavened bread while educating myself about this culture's ancient cuisine.

Flatbread is the predominant style of bread in the Middle East, with purse-shaped kaak (pronounced as *ka-ak*) one of the most intriguing varieties. It is typically sold dangling playfully from food carts, but you can also find them on highway stops split with your choice of filling, much like bagel houses in New York. Warmed halloumi, a spreadable cheese with olives and za'atar, and any number of other options are made to order. After my return stateside, I longed to recreate the slightly chewy pillows of sesame goodness, but in a whole-grain sourdough version. I use whole wheat pastry flour here and add whey for a more tender crumb. You may substitute spelt flour if you like.

Attempting to recreate a memory from a distant land is tricky territory. No matter how authentic you try to make it, the ingredients, mood, and environment of where you originally experienced it can never be fully replicated. When I am short on patience or time to coat the dough in sesame seeds, sometimes I will bake it into pita breads. They are a delight to watch rise and puff in the oven, but don't be tempted to roll them too thinly, as they will not puff sufficiently in the oven. The first few may take a little practice, but they will be delicious regardless!

Stale kaak is excellent torn into small pieces, tossed with olive oil, garlic paste, and za'atar, and toasted in a 400°F oven for about 15 to 20 minutes to make chips.

FOR THE DOUGH
310 g / 1¼ cups + 1 tablespoon yogurt whey

125 g / 1¼ cups 100% hydration active sourdough starter

20 g / 1 tablespoon honey

300 g / 2¾ cups whole wheat pastry flour

185 g / scant 1½ cups high-extraction bread flour

20 g / heaping 2 teaspoons fine sea salt

FOR THE SESAME TOPPING
40 g / 2 tablespoons grape molasses

30 g / 2 tablespoons water

95 g / ¾ cup sesame seeds

MIX AND KNEAD THE DOUGH

In a large bowl, stir together the whey, starter, and honey to create a slurry. Add the flours and salt and mix using your hands until no dry lumps remain. Cover with an inverted bowl, plate, or plastic wrap, and allow to rest for 5 to 10 minutes. The dough will be soft and somewhat sticky, but do not be tempted to add more flour.

Remove the dough from the bowl and knead on a clean work surface until it is smooth and malleable,

(recipe continues)

5 to 7 minutes. If the dough begins to tear, allow it to rest for a few minutes before returning to kneading. Divide the dough into 7 pieces that are 130 to 135 g each and shape them into rounds. Cover with plastic wrap and allow to proof at room temperature for 2 to 3 hours, until puffy and almost doubled in size. At this point, you have two options: you can cover well and retard in the refrigerator overnight, or you can roll it out and bake right away.

BELOW *Whey becomes a useful ingredient rather than a pesky by-product of straining yogurt when used to make flatbreads such as these pita.*

BAKE THE BREAD

Preheat the oven to 475°F with a baking stone on the middle rack for 45 to 60 minutes.

Cut two pieces of parchment paper fit to the size of the stone and lay each onto the back of a baking sheet or pizza peel. Mix all of the sesame coating ingredients in a small bowl and set aside. Using a rolling pin, flatten each piece into a disk about 8 inches in diameter and transfer to the parchment. Use a pastry brush, flattish spoon, or spatula to cover the surface with a generous coating of the sesame topping. Using a small biscuit cutter, stamp out a hole 1½ inches from the edge and place it beside the bread on the parchment. When you have filled a parchment sheet, carefully slide it onto the preheated baking stone. Bake for about 4 minutes, until they puff up, keeping an eye on them as you continue rolling out the rest of the dough. Flip using tongs and bake on the other side for an additional 2 to 3 minutes, until the edges stiffen and the sesame seeds are lightly toasted. Do not be tempted to brown them too much or they will harden as they cool. Remove from the oven and place in a basket lined with a cloth and wrap them to keep them warm. Continue with the remaining flatbreads and serve immediately.

OPPOSITE *Washed with a slightly sweet syrup and sprinkling of sesame seeds, these Lebanese-inspired flatbreads are best eaten the day they are made.*

EMMER *and* GREEN GARLIC GOUGÈRES

Makes about 24

The first time I made these custardy clouds was at a fundraiser dinner I helped prepare for the Red Hills Small Farm Alliance near Tallahassee, Florida. A dozen different farms donated fresh produce, cheese, meat, nuts, and dairy. I had brought with me a bag of high-extraction emmer flour and wanted to make a tender dinner roll to accompany the meal, but I needed to use up a large wheel of cheese as well. So I opted to make these custardy treats and added a fleeting seasonal ingredient: green garlic (although you may use any green tops of the allium family instead, such as chives, spring onions, or ramps). The result is an addictively moist and savory interior surrounded by a shattering crust that is best served warm out of the oven. If you cannot source emmer, try substituting with high-extraction bread flour instead.

230 g / scant 1 cup whole milk
230 g / scant 1 cup water
90 g / 6 tablespoons unsalted butter
1 teaspoon salt

210 g / 1½ cups high-extraction emmer flour
4 large eggs
40 g / ½ cup chopped green garlic

210 g / 1½ cups grated hard cheese, such as Gruyère or Emmental
Cracked black pepper

PREPARE THE BATTER

Preheat the oven to 400°F and line two baking sheets with parchment paper.

Combine the milk, water, butter, and salt in a large saucepan and bring to a boil over medium-high heat. Reduce the heat to medium and vigorously beat in the flour all at once using a sturdy spoon, working quickly to produce a paste, until it is thick enough to release easily from the sides of the pan into a loose ball when stirred. If it doesn't release, reduce the heat to low and continue to cook, stirring, until the dough just pulls away from the sides of the pan. Turn off the heat and set aside to cool until it is just warm to the touch. Add the eggs one at a time, beating well after each addition, until fully incorporated. This takes some concerted effort when done by hand, or you may choose to perform this step using a hand mixer at medium speed instead. Stir in the green garlic.

BAKE THE GOUGÈRES

Spoon or pipe 2-tablespoon dollops of the batter onto the prepared baking sheets and top with the cheese.

Bake in the preheated oven for 26 to 28 minutes or until they just begin to color before reducing the temperature to 350°F. Continue baking for another 25 to 27 minutes or until they are puffed and golden brown on all sides—this is an important step to ensure they do not collapse upon cooling. Turn off the heat and crack the oven door. Allow to cool in the oven for about 15 to 20 minutes longer. Serve warm or at room temperature.

HERMAN'S HEIRLOOM CORNBREAD

Makes one #8 skillet (or a 9-inch cornbread)

Much of what I know about sustainable agricultural practices comes from having grown up surrounded by thirsty, nutrient-hungry cornfields and by working as a horticulturist. But as with most crafts, the most important information is passed on by those whose passion for their work is joyfully shared over the dinner table, in the fields, or at the market.

I had been using Herman's Texas gourdseed corn that Herman grows and mills himself to make Sweet Jane (page 82) and Stone-Ground Grits/Polenta (page 55) for almost a year before we actually met. Over the course of the few days we enjoyed together, he and his farmer-baker-community-organizing-homeopathic-healing-extraordinaire-wife, Louise, filled my ears with stories of their life experiences. I was enthralled by their dedication not only to a sustainable farming community but also to the flavor and character of their heirloom crops. We discussed the history of corn, and I discovered several resources of agricultural wisdom I had not been familiar with (see Resources, page 324). We chatted about the importance of rotational crops and the process of milling in between well-delivered farm jokes and bites of lamb's quarter pesto. I learned that his cornmeal I so coveted was a by-product of milling grits that unfortunately didn't enjoy as much fervor due to local Southern foodways. Lucky for me, they sent me home with a car full of cornmeal as well as bags of heirloom Duncan grapefruit and some excellent sugar cane syrup they had made themselves.

But the true revelation came when I visited their farming operation, tucked between the live oaks, tall pines, and blooming highbush blueberries of a Florida spring buzzing with bees and the first blossoms of the China roses. I wandered around dazed and drunk on Hamlin orange blossom perfume, skipping from hoop house to crimson clover field dizzy with inspiration. When we went into the house, I spied a wheel of half-eaten cornbread on the counter, yellow not from the corn but the yolks of their happy chickens. My eyes brightened and my tummy rumbled, and as I tasted it, in one instant of time travel, I was transported back to my Granny Owens's kitchen, where I could have just as well been sneaking a nibble from her well-worn cast-iron skillet.

Herman enthusiastically shared with me a number of old books as well as this recipe using his Texas gourdseed cornmeal without the wheat added to most cornbread. If you can't source theirs, use a freshly milled white cornmeal instead.

In true heirloom fashion, this recipe calls for a #8 cast-iron skillet. Antiquated skillet numbers refer not exactly to the diameter of the skillet but rather the old wood stoves that were used at the time many of these pieces of cookware were forged. The skillet used would depend on the brand of stove and its corresponding size of stovetop eyes. Even after electric and gas stoves eventually replaced wood-fueled stoves, the familiarity of their numbers continued to identify cast-iron cookware. If you own a more modern 9-inch skillet, that will work just fine.

70 g / ¼ cup + 1 tablespoon neutral vegetable oil, such as avocado oil or melted and cooled lard

230 g / 2 cups medium-grind cornmeal

1 teaspoon salt

1 teaspoon baking soda

25 g / 1 tablespoon sugar

2 large eggs

360 g / 1½ cups whole buttermilk

Pour 1 tablespoon of the oil in a #8 (8⅞-inch, or modern 9-inch) cast-iron skillet and use your fingers to rub the bottom and sides well. Place the skillet in the oven and preheat to 400°F while you prepare the batter.

Whisk together the cornmeal, salt, baking soda, and sugar in a large bowl. In a separate bowl, beat the remaining ¼ cup oil, the eggs, and buttermilk until well combined. Mix the dry ingredients into the wet ingredients, stirring until no dry lumps remain.

Pour the batter into the hot pan: you should be rewarded with a sizzling sound when the batter hits the skillet. Bake for 10 minutes, then lower the oven temperature to 350°F and continue to bake for an additional 20 minutes. In Herman's recipe he references his wife's alternative method, much as he honors her differing opinions in other matters of life, with a slow Southern drawl: "Well . . . I think my wife just does 375°F for 30 minutes." I like Herman's method, as it lends a crunchy, thicker crust and moist interior. Either way is excellent, though, especially if you're using good cornmeal and a hot skillet!

CORN

Corn has been a staple crop of my culinary consciousness for as long as I can remember, growing up in Tennessee and spending many years driving past the cornfields of Kentucky and Indiana. My grandmother had a hand-cranked cast-iron grinder on her front porch, and my great-grandfather had a mill that supplied cornmeal and grits to most of Anderson County during his lifetime. We rarely sat down to a Sunday supper without chow-chow, a corn relish served alongside pinto beans and cornbread. I took the ubiquitous presence of corn in my young life for granted until I grew older and more suspicious of its cultivation and misuse in our modern diets.

Corn does not exist naturally but is a mutation of its ancient ancestor teosinte, a tall grass-like plant with seeds encased in an inedible hull. Corn began its evolution into densely packed naked ears between six and eight thousand years ago in central-southern Mexico. This spontaneous loss of teosinte's protective seed coating meant that corn could not survive without the tending and protection of man. Its domestication into a staple crop led its geographic distribution southward through Central America and into South America and eventually into North America and Europe.

My curiosity for corn was reawakened one weekend when a wise farmer in her late seventies came to a workshop I was giving in Rockaway. She brought with her a box of goodies, including grits and cornmeal stone-ground from an obscure heirloom variety that she and her husband grow and mill called Texas gourdseed (see Resources, page 324). It was white flecked with red speckles, and I was immediately curious to cook and bake with it. Gourdseed is a soft heirloom dent corn, domesticated in a line different from other pre-Colombian corns. Cooked, it has a silky texture reminiscent of the cornbread from my grandmother's skillet. It is rich, sweet, and robust in flavor, and unlike many heirloom varieties that evolve in response to specific growing conditions, it is greatly adaptable to poor or rich soils in both hot and humid and dry climates. Since then, she has generously sent packages through the mail, keeping my freezer well stocked with this distinctive heirloom ingredient.

Corn products made from heirloom varieties, including popcorn, sweet corn, and flours and grits made from dent, and polenta from flint corns, offer an impressive array of textures and flavors. To make corn nutritious and digestible, there are a number of ways to properly prepare it, including soaking it in an alkaline solution before cooking. It can also be ground, fermented, and made into breads, such as Sweet Jane (page 82) or Cornmeal Flatbread (page 266).

OPPOSITE *Corn (Zea mays) may be grown for different uses depending on the variety that best suits its climate. This Texas Gourdseed is an heirloom soft dent corn best for making Herman's Heirloom Cornbread (page 220) or Stone-Ground Grits (page 55).*

NOMAD FLATBREAD

Makes 5 to 6 breads

Recipes are reflections of time, place, ingredients, and the culture that appreciates them. They can be passed down over generations with little interpretation or significant tweaks. Regardless of their heritage, each heirloom recipe carries with it a story or memorable mark in time—a holiday, special event, or custom. This recipe was not handed down from a grandmother or other such cherished source; it was created while living a nomadic lifestyle with a sourdough starter in tow and has accompanied me on many journeys to share my craft as a baker.

I was visiting a friend on an island in the Salish Sea who had invited me to stay in her family's small cabin for a few days. To thank her for her generosity, I wanted to cook a meal using ingredients from the island's abundance of agricultural delights. I had spent the day hitchhiking, stopping to visit an old barn and a goat farm where you pay for your purchases by the honor system. I met a remarkable cast of characters along the way: a wild-eyed gardener from the Age of Aquarius, a shepherd with handsome curly locks and a warm charismatic smile, a potter, a girl taking refuge from a commune she had recently fled, and a few friendly dogs. At the end of the day, I returned home with blackberry-stained fingers ready to get cooking with a sack full of apples, goat's liver, kefir, rose hips, hawthorn fruits, and late-season vegetables. Without a scale, a proofing basket, or the time to make a fully realized loaf of bread, I whipped some active starter with a bit of flour and some farm-fresh milk and kneaded until I felt satisfied. The only thing preventing a delicious dinner was an abrupt power outage fifteen minutes into prep.

I poured myself a glass of wine and tried flipping the breaker, to no avail. More sips and waiting. Twilight ascended, and as I stared into the quiet oncoming night, I spied a stone ring at the end of the yard and thought how lovely it would be to cook and enjoy the meal around a campfire. I set to work, and with a little diligence, the damp Pacific Northwest kindling ignited with enthusiasm.

An hour later, my friend joined me, delighted to discover a roaring flame in the early autumn night. When campfire smoke curls and evergreens grow tall as animated shadows in the night sky, conversation inevitably turns to tales of love and loss, the cosmos, and its infinite mysteries. As we slowly nibbled the meal and sipped more wine, a most mesmerizing sight appeared in the sky: the northern lights! Waves of teal, green, and purple wafted forward, blanketing the sky like a surreal curtain of color. My body seemed to separate from my bewildered mind, and for a brief moment I took a roll call of what I would abandon if these were my final earthly moments. The phenomenon eventually faded, and my friend and I met each other's astonished gaze, laughing wildly with equal parts fear and delight.

Each time I make this recipe, it is with great fondness for that experience and a little different depending on what tools and ingredients I have at hand. In this way it has become a cherished recipe of heirloom status, marking time and place by how and where I make it. (Recipe shown on page 175.)

150 g / about ¾ cup 100% hydration sourdough starter

175 g / ⅔ cup + 1 tablespoon lukewarm milk

75 g / ¼ cup + 1 tablespoon water

30 g / 1½ tablespoons mild honey

15 g / 1 tablespoon orange blossom water (optional)

2 teaspoons salt

330 g / 3 cups whole wheat pastry or spelt flour

110 g / 1 cup whole wheat bread flour

30 to 45 g / 2 to 3 tablespoons lard, clarified butter, or high-heat oil such as coconut oil or avocado oil, as needed

FOR THE TOPPINGS (OPTIONAL)

1 teaspoon sesame seeds

1 teaspoon anise, nigella, caraway, or cumin seeds

PREPARE THE DOUGH

In a large bowl, stir together the starter, milk, water, honey, orange blossom water, if using, and salt to create a slurry. Add the flours and mix with your hands until no dry lumps remain. Allow to rest and hydrate for 10 minutes, then transfer the dough from the bowl to a clean work surface. Knead the dough until it feels soft and pliable, adding a touch or two more water if needed. Clean the bowl, coat it with oil, then return the dough to the bowl. Cover with a plate or plastic wrap and allow to ferment at room temperature for about 3 hours, until the dough is puffy and almost doubled in size. Alternatively, you may cover and place it in the refrigerator overnight.

SHAPE THE DOUGH

Divide the dough into 5 or 6 small balls and preheat the oven to 450°F.

Use your hands to flatten each piece, then roll out with a rolling pin until the breads are ¼ to ½ inch thick, keeping the dough covered while you work. If you are adding toppings, roll them into the surface of the dough.

FRY AND BAKE THE BREADS

Heat 1½ tablespoons lard, clarified butter, or oil in a large, heavy skillet over medium-high heat. When the fat is clear and hot, slip one bread into the skillet. Lower the heat and cook until it is toasty on the bottom, 5 to 6 minutes. Flip and continue to cook until the other side is equally toasty. Transfer the bread to the oven and bake for 8 to 10 minutes, until the edges are crispy but the bread is still soft and pliable, while you continue preparing the additional breads. The timing of the frying makes it fairly easy to slip one bread into the oven as the other leaves it. Place in a large basket and keep covered with a cloth. Serve warm.

FRIED FARRO, RADICCHIO, *and* PUNTARELLE SALAD *with* CURRANTS

Serves 3 to 4

Spring often arrives in the Northeast as the timid guest of winter, unsure whether its presence is welcome for a brief visit or an extended stay. This is when I become desperate for crunchy vegetables—their refreshing texture is a sign of longer days and warmer temperatures to come. This salad combines the beautiful array of radicchio now available to us through both the revitalization of old heirloom varieties and their newer, splashier relatives who bring a bit of theatrical bling to the late winter/early spring table.

Puntarelle is a Catalonian type of heirloom chicory with extremely bitter leaves and a heart of milder, finger-like but hollow inner stalks that pull apart much like that of celery. Although not terribly common outside of Italy, you will find these in very early spring at farmers' markets and specialty food shops. Their flavor and fleeting season make them well worth seeking out, though other chicories or even romanesco can be substituted in this recipe.

1 cup whole farro

1 pound puntarelle

4½ tablespoons extra-virgin olive oil

Salt

¼ teaspoon cracked black pepper

2 medium shallots, minced

1½ tablespoons fresh lime juice

3 tablespoons dried currants

2 scallions, sliced

1 plump clove garlic, thinly sliced

One 8-ounce head radicchio

1 smallish watermelon radish, sliced

3 tablespoons fresh flat-leaf parsley leaves

Place the farro in a medium bowl, add water to cover by at least 2 inches, and soak overnight. Drain and rinse the farro and transfer it to a medium saucepan.

Preheat the oven to 425°F.

Separate the puntarelle into individual stalks and halve them lengthwise. Toss with 2 tablespoons of the oil, ¼ teaspoon salt, and the pepper. Spread onto a baking sheet in a single layer and roast until tender but not brown to retain its color, 15 to

20 minutes. Remove from the oven and allow to cool.

In a small bowl, stir together 1½ tablespoons of the remaining oil, the lime juice, currants, scallions, and a generous pinch of salt. Set aside to allow the currants to plump and the flavors to infuse.

While the puntarelle is roasting, cover the farro with at least 1½ inches of water and bring to a boil over medium-high heat. Reduce the heat

(recipe continues)

to maintain a simmer and cook uncovered until tender, 28 to 30 minutes. Drain well, shaking to remove excess water, and set aside.

Heat the remaining 1 tablespoon oil in a large heavy skillet, add the shallots, and cook until translucent and beginning to caramelize, 5 to 6 minutes. Stir in the drained farro and ¼ teaspoon salt and cook over medium heat until dry and beginning to pop, about 5 minutes. Stir in the garlic and cook until

fragrant and softened, about 1 minute more. Turn off the heat, check for salt, and allow to cool.

In a large bowl, toss together the farro, radicchio, radish, 2 tablespoons of the parsley, and most of the puntarelle and dressing, reserving 3 to 4 puntarelle fingers for garnishing each serving. Divide among plates or shallow bowls. Spoon the remaining puntarelle on top and garnish with the remaining parsley. Serve immediately.

AMARANTH

Amaranth is a unique pseudocereal of ancient origins that earns a heroic description beyond the clever marketing title of "superfood." When properly prepared, it delivers a powerful package of nutrition with more iron, calcium, protein, and fiber than rice or even wheat. It is one of the most protein-rich plant foods—13% to 16% complete protein—rivaling that of meat or cheese. And unlike most grains, it also contains the amino acid lysine, which is essential for growth and tissue repair, encouraging healthy skin.

Three species—*Amaranthus cruentus*, *Amaranthus hypochondriacus*, and *Amaranthus caudatus*—are commonly grown for their edible seeds. This native of the high Andean mountains of Peru has a long history of ceremonial prominence but is regarded as a garden weed in other parts of the world for its potential to seed into any possible speck of earth or crack in the sidewalk. It is sweet and nutty and becomes sticky once cooked, adding thickening powers to dishes like this soup. It can also be popped much like corn for a lovely garnish or snack. Amaranth is much lower in saponins than quinoa, so it does not necessarily need to be soaked and dried before eating, although soaking is suggested if you are eating a lot of it. Cover with water by at least 2 inches, add a generous pinch of salt, and allow to soak overnight. Then drain and rinse in a fine-mesh sieve or nut milk or jelly bag (and dry if intending to pop it later).

ASPARAGUS *and* AMARANTH SOUP

Serves 4

The first time I experienced amaranth being harvested and winnowed was on a visit to Otavalo, Ecuador, where I was working in a garden of a very old hacienda. The head jardinero grew copious amounts of these tall, proud plants in various colors from green to ochre and a dark maroon. Their heavy plumes rose high above all else, competing with even the corn for attention. When they matured and shook freely of their seeds, he would lop off their heads before depositing the thousands of small grains onto a tarp spread over the ground. When the heads finally refused any further yield, he gathered the seeds into a bucket and positioned another bucket on top of the tarp. Being mindful of prevailing winds, he demonstrated how to pour the seeds into the empty bucket, allowing the breeze to catch or winnow the chaff back into the garden. It was a mesmerizing and meditative activity that took a fair amount of concentration. Witnessing his delight at the bounty of potential he had just produced made me that much more appreciative of amaranth's highly regarded place in ancient Aztec, Incan, and Mayan cultures.

The hacienda used this amaranth mostly as a dairy-free thickener. When combined with asparagus and Walnut and Cilantro Sauce (page 25), it makes for satisfying nourishment on a chilly spring day. Alternatively, if you would like to make it into a creamy velouté, you can blend it. Black garlic is an ingredient worth making (page 263) or hunting down, as it lends a particular pop of umami that adds complexity to this otherwise tangy soup. Be sure to have the garnishes on hand, and when you can find it, the fresh perfumed brightness of Meyer lemon zest makes an excellent finish. (Recipe shown on page 74.)

½ cup whole amaranth seeds

2 tablespoons Clarified Butter (page 34), extra-virgin olive oil, or Rendered Animal Fat (page 33)

1 medium onion or 2 shallots, minced

12 ounces asparagus spears, cut into ½-inch pieces

4 plump cloves garlic, sliced

1 tablespoon fresh thyme leaves

Salt, to taste

4 cups Ruby Chard Broth (page 27), Corn Cob Broth (page 28), or Chicken Stock (page 36)

1½ tablespoons white miso paste

½ cup Walnut and Cilantro Sauce (page 25)

1 tablespoon fresh lemon or lime juice (to taste)

FOR THE GARNISH

4 cloves black garlic, sliced

1 tablespoon fresh flat-leaf parsley leaves

1 teaspoon citrus zest, such as common or Meyer lemon or orange

Freshly ground black pepper

(recipe continues)

Place the amaranth in a small bowl and add water just to cover. Stir several times to encourage the seeds to soak up the water, then cover and set aside for 6 to 8 hours, until the amaranth has mostly absorbed the water.

Melt the clarified butter in a large saucepan over medium heat. Add the onion and cook, stirring occasionally, until translucent and just beginning to brown, about 7 minutes. Add the asparagus, garlic, and thyme and cook until the asparagus has just softened but is still vibrantly green, 3 to 4 minutes. Remove from the pot and set aside.

If you have a sieve or nut milk bag that is fine enough, you can rinse the amaranth before cooking. Pour the stock into the pan and stir in the amaranth. Bring to a boil over medium-high heat, then reduce the heat to maintain a gentle simmer. Cover and cook for 20 minutes, or until the amaranth is tender. Remove about ½ cup of the soup to a small bowl and stir in the miso until it is completely dissolved. Transfer the asparagus mixture to the pot and heat it through. Turn off the heat and stir in the walnut and cilantro sauce. Stir in the dissolved miso, add the lemon juice, and check for salt, adjusting for taste. Spoon into bowls and garnish as you like. Serve immediately. You can prepare this soup up to 3 days in advance or freeze for up to 3 months.

BEET FALAFEL

Serves 4

Falafel is a traditional Arabic fritter that has earned its reputation as one of the most satisfying and affordable convenience foods anywhere in the world. Crispy on the outside with a generously spiced, moist interior, these beloved balls made from ancient ingredients carry much contention over the origination of their existence. Its most popular mixture is made from chickpeas, although sometimes fava beans or a mixture of the two are combined with various splashes of creativity. Each Middle Eastern culture seems to have its own imprint, but falafel is most heartily enjoyed stuffed into a soft pita pocket. They have long been a mediocre survival food staple of New York, gobbled as late-night bar food or for a quick and cheap lunch. When made with quality ingredients and attention to flavor, however, you will understand why so many enthusiastically claim falafel's origins as their own.

I prefer making falafel with freshly grated raw beets, a strong mix of spices, abundant bread crumbs, and heart-healthy flax. When you have made the mixture, test to see if the balls come together much like you would test piecrust dough, by squeezing a small handful in your palm to check for crumbling. If the mixture doesn't immediately bind, pulse in a small slice of torn crustless fresh bread and allow to rest for 10 minutes before checking again. If you have the time and patience, form the balls at least an hour before they are dunked in the bath of hot oil. This will allow the bread crumbs and flax to hydrate and help keep the falafel firm when frying.

The earthy character of this falafel begs for a silky Buttermilk Tahini Sauce (page 294) and a soft Whey Kaak/Pita pocket (page 215). Make sure you have harissa, plenty of fresh arugula, herbs, sliced radish, green almonds, and/or fennel on hand as well as any remaining stray chickpeas to round out the fillings. Make a large batch and reheat as necessary for a satisfying and quickly assembled lunch. Try serving some over a bed of leafy greens or to accompany Freekeh Salad with Pea, Gooseberry, and Radish (page 235).

2 to 3 plump cloves garlic

1 cup cooked chickpeas, rinsed if canned and drained

1 small raw beet, grated

¼ cup Sourdough Bread Crumbs (page 66)

1½ tablespoon flaxseeds

1 cup herbs (a mix of parsley, cilantro, and/or dill works well)

2 scallions, coarsely chopped

¾ teaspoon kosher salt

1 tablespoon baharat spice (see sidebar)

1 teaspoon orange zest

Oil for frying

(recipe continues)

MIX THE FALAFEL

Place the garlic into a food processor and pulse to finely chop. Add the remaining ingredients except the oil and pulse until the mixture is somewhere between smooth and slightly chunky but not pasty—you want the chickpeas and beets to retain their identity and texture. Form the mixture into 2-inch balls and place on a baking sheet.

FRY THE FALAFEL

Line a plate with paper towels. Fill a large heavy pot or Dutch oven with oil to a depth of about 2½ inches and heat on high until an instant-read thermometer or deep-fry thermometer reads 350°F. Adding them one at a time, gently slip 4 or 5 falafel balls into the oil and fry until they are deep golden brown in color, about 5 minutes. Using a slotted spoon or sieve, transfer the falafel to the prepared plate and continue cooking the remaining balls. Serve immediately, or cool and store in a covered container in the refrigerator for up to 5 days. Reheat in the oven at 350°F before serving.

BAHARAT

The Arabic root of this spice mix, *bahar*, means "pepper," a suggestion of its potent character, and depending on where it is blended, it may contain as many as fourteen different spices. In the Levant, you will find cinnamon, cumin, coriander, black pepper, and cardamom, with Tunisian blends adding rose petals for texture and heady perfume. My favorite regional additions include fenugreek, ajwain, and long pepper. Baharat is easily found at Middle Eastern markets (see Resources, page 324), but if you cannot find it, try blending your own using a mixture of these spices to taste to use for your falafel and as an all-purpose seasoning for vegetables or meat.

OPPOSITE *Serve falafel with Whey Pita (page 215) and inspired condiments including pickled beets, garden herbs and scallions, seasonal green almonds, fresh or pickled carrots, and Buttermilk Tahini Sauce (page 294).*

FREEKEH SALAD *with* PEA, GOOSEBERRY, *and* RADISH

Serves 6 to 8

Freekeh is an ancient immature green wheat that has been smoked or roasted. It is one of the most delicious grains found in the Middle East, and although it is typically served with roasted lamb, its earthy character makes it delicious combined with fresh spring vegetables, such as peas and radishes or tender small Hakurei turnips. Gooseberries lend a pleasing pop of acidity, but if you cannot find them, use a tart grape of your choice or some succulent strawberries if you plan to eat the salad just after making it.

FOR THE VINAIGRETTE
⅓ cup Apple Cider Vinegar (page 6)

3 tablespoons Preserved Stone Fruit in Herb Syrup (page 305), Pomegranate Paste (page 124), or a floral honey

1 tablespoon fresh lemon juice

1 teaspoon Dijon mustard

1 teaspoon fine sea salt

½ cup extra-virgin olive oil

1 large shallot, thinly sliced

FOR THE SALAD
2 cups sweet or snow peas, cut into 1-inch slices

1½ cups (½ bunch) radishes or small Hakurei turnips, cut into matchsticks

1½ cups gooseberries, halved

3 cups cooked freekeh (see page 54), at room temperature

1 cup fresh flat-leaf parsley leaves, coarsely chopped

½ cup crumbled feta cheese

½ cup toasted almonds, coarsely chopped

FOR THE GARNISH
A sprinkling of feta cheese

A handful of fresh mint, cut into a chiffonade

MAKE THE VINAIGRETTE
Combine the vinegar, syrup, lemon juice, mustard, and salt in a large bowl. Whisk in the oil until emulsified, then stir in the shallots. You can prepare the dressing up to 1 day in advance.

ASSEMBLE THE SALAD
Add the peas, radishes, and gooseberries to the dressing and toss to coat. You can combine this mixture up to 3 hours before serving, keeping covered in the refrigerator until ready to toss with the remaining ingredients.

Combine the freekeh, parsley, cheese, and almonds in a separate large bowl and toss. Add most of the marinated vegetable and fruit mixture and stir to combine. Top with the remaining vegetables and fruits, a sprinkling of cheese, and fresh mint. Serve immediately, or store covered in the refrigerator for up to 1 day.

CHICKPEA PANCAKES *with* DANDELION GREENS *and* CARAMELIZED ONIONS (GRANDMA WISDOM)

Serves 4 to 6

I grew up in rural Appalachia, where I looked forward to pokeweed every spring. My grandmother and I would wander around the perimeter of the house visiting wild patches she nurtured, snipping the succulent new shoots of this nutrient-dense perennial native plant. We would return to her coal-stained kitchen, where she would parboil them to remove toxins (once if young and tender, twice if more mature and leafy), drain, chop, and then fry in bacon grease before scrambling in a few eggs. It is still one of my absolute favorite foraged meals, and each bite carries a sense of nostalgia.

Native Americans, Melungeons, and Native Africans of the Appalachian Mountains and foothills collected wild greens, mushrooms, and acorns and hunted for game and freshwater fish before both of my grandmothers and my parents shared these practices with me. Each wild plant was chosen by our ancestors for both flavor and health benefits, cleansing the blood in spring with bitters and stocking up on fortifying nuts, seeds, and berries in the autumn. This ethnobotanical knowledge was passed along from my native ancestors to my European ancestors who had settled in Tennessee and ultimately to myself, a gift I took for granted until I began studying the foraging customs of other cultures.

When I discovered hindbeh, a Lebanese dish of dandelion greens and caramelized onions eaten with Arabic flatbread, its preparation struck me as similar to the pokeweed of my childhood. Lebanese home cooks cultivate patches of dandelion greens, a perennial herb that is best harvested in early spring or when cooler temperatures return in autumn. The following recipe combines dandelion, heavily laden with caramelized onions, with chickpea crepes, traditionally enjoyed in southern France, northern Italy, North Africa, and Gibraltar. Its crispy edges and custardy interior make for an edible scoop for the sweet onions and bitter greens, and its nutty flavor complements both. The crepe batter needs time to rest after whisking but is quick and easy to cook. If you want to make the chickpea flour more digestible, add 20 g / 1 tablespoon of sourdough starter to the batter. Make the hindbeh several days in advance if you wish and enjoy it with friends after an aperitif of Sweet Meadow Vermouth (page 145), and make sure to allow plenty of time to share stories of your grandmothers and the nostalgic dishes of your childhood.

125 g / 1 cup chickpea flour
1 cup water
1½ teaspoon fine sea salt

½ cup + 3 tablespoons extra-virgin olive oil, plus more for the pan
7½ cups sliced onions (about 6 to 7 small onions)

1 pound dandelion greens (about 2 bunches)
Splash of Homemade Vinegar (page 6)

Whisk together the flour, water, ½ teaspoon salt, and 2 tablespoons of the oil in a medium bowl. Cover with a kitchen towel and rest for at least 2 hours or up to 6 hours for the flour to fully hydrate.

In a large heavy-bottomed skillet, cook the onions and remaining salt in ½ cup of the remaining oil over medium-low heat, stirring occasionally, until the onions are well caramelized, 40 to 45 minutes.

While the onions are cooking, bring a large pot of water to a rolling boil. Turn off the heat and dunk the dandelion greens in the water, stirring to wilt them, about 45 seconds to 1 minute. Pour through a colander positioned over the sink and run cold water over the greens to stop the cooking, then use your hands to wring out excess water. Coarsely chop the dandelion greens and add them to the skillet with the onions. Reduce the heat to low and cook for 10 minutes or longer to remove more of their bitterness. Serve warm or at room temperature. You can make the greens up to 3 days in advance; store covered in the refrigerator.

Place a 10-inch cast-iron griddle or skillet 3 to 4 inches under your broiler and preheat the broiler to high for 15 minutes. Carefully remove the pan and pour in ½ tablespoon of oil, swirling to coat. Return to the broiler for 1 to 2 minutes to heat the oil, then pour in enough of the batter (about ⅓ to ½ cup) to create a thin 8- to 9-inch pancake, tilting the pan to swirl it or using the back of a spoon or measuring cup to quickly spread it. Broil for 3 to 4 minutes, until the crepe is blistered and cooked through with the edges curling slightly. Remove the crepe from the pan with a spatula and repeat with the remaining batter, adding more oil for each crepe—you should have enough batter to make about 4 crepes. Serve immediately, with the dandelion greens and onions, using the crepe as an edible scoop.

FORAGING FOR FEASTING

Over the last few years, there has been a surge in interest in foraging wild edibles including native, non-native, and invasive species. I consider this a reflection of our hunger to connect with the natural world and find a sense of belonging in the digital age. Unfortunately, in tandem with this trend has been an increase in climate change, which has put incredible stress on certain plant populations, including drought, flooding, and unusual freezing temperatures for extended periods of time. Many plant populations are struggling as a result, and the last thing they need to thrive (let alone survive) is a hungry human collecting for culinary amusement. For this reason, I urge you to educate yourself on the health of the plants of your growing region, and when in doubt, stick to the invasive species that dominate your urban or rural wilderness.

Regardless of what you are collecting, keep in mind that wildlife (both animals and insects) depends on these populations for food or reproductive purposes. Search for robust plant communities and do not collect more than 20% of any given stand. When in doubt, it is better to go home empty-handed than to have pillaged the forest or field.

QUICKIE CONGEE

Serves 2

Much like the ubiquitous dumpling, porridge can be found in every culture as a nourishing subsistence food. Africa has its soured corn or millet porridge, the Cantonese have the savory juk, Filipinos have lugaw, the Swiss or Germans have muesli, and the Russians have kasha. I grew up on ho-hum cream of wheat for breakfast, so when I visited Scotland, their oats served with tangy poached rhubarb and fresh, thick cream were a revelation.

The following is a kitchen hack I developed for rice porridge, a dish that traditionally takes hours to complete. By soaking, portioning, and freezing the rice ahead of time, it quickly thickens to a beautiful canvas for any number of toppings. Although cooking times may vary, this recipe is meant to work with whatever type of rice you may have on hand.

1 cup long-grain rice
4 to 4½ cups broth of choice
    (pages 36 to 37)
Salt

FOR THE GARNISH
Handful of fresh herbs, such as
    spicy arugula, shiso, cilantro,
    chives, or chive blossoms
One 2½-inch piece fresh ginger,
    peeled and sliced into
    matchsticks
2 cooked eggs (poached, sunny-
    side, or boiled and sliced)

2 scallions, sliced, white and
    green parts
2 small Pa Kimchi onions
    (page 242), minced
3 tablespoons bonito flakes
Lacto-Fermented Mushrooms
    (page 11) sautéed with garlic

Place the rice in a medium bowl and add water to cover by at least 2 inches. Cover with a kitchen towel and leave to soak overnight. Rinse and drain well, then divide between two small freezer bags. Label and seal, then place in the freezer. Freeze at least overnight or for up to 6 months.

Remove the rice from one bag, place it in a saucepan, and add 4 cups of the broth. Bring to a boil over medium-high heat, then reduce the heat to a simmer. Season with salt and continue cooking for 20 to 30 minutes, until the rice has broken down into a viscous texture, adding more stock to thin it if you like (it will thicken upon cooling). Serve hot topped with your choice of garnishes.

OPPOSITE *Known traditionally as a food to nourish the unwell, this rice porridge is also an excellent breakfast or light lunch.*

PA KIMCHI

Makes about 1 pint

March is mud month in the Northeast, the time when your bones are aching for sunshine and warmth and yet you must continue to suffer the chilling effects of frigid rain. Regardless of this seemingly endless winter, the soil temperature begins to increase and with it the resumed growth of wild onions that salute the rain like enthusiastic green exclamation points jutting from the wet earth. This is an excellent time to wrap a warm parka around your shoulders and pluck these wild onions from the ground before warmer temperatures toughen their stalks and make them bitter.

The following Korean preservation technique uses ingredients found at an Asian grocery store. The Korean red pepper flakes contribute to this lacto-fermented pickle's special flavor. Do make a point to seek it out, even if you need to order it online, but in a pinch you may use cayenne pepper to taste instead. A little of this potent pickle goes a long way, and I will often reach for it to make a quick lunch of rice, an egg, and a few strands of pa kimchi or to garnish Quickie Congee (page 241). The flavor is best after it has aged for a few weeks in the refrigerator and only improves with time.

225 g / 8 ounces wild spring onions

75 g / ¼ cup + 1 tablespoon fish sauce

230 g / 1 cup water

20 g / 2 tablespoons sweet rice flour

20 g / 1 tablespoon honey

1 teaspoon mild vinegar of choice

16 g / 2 plump cloves garlic, grated on a Microplane

15 g / 1-inch piece fresh ginger, peeled and coarsely grated

50 g / ½ cup gochugaru/kochukaru (Korean red pepper, coarse powder grade)

20 g / 2 tablespoons sesame seeds

Soak the spring onions in a bowl of water to cover for 5 to 10 minutes, then rinse well to release their papery outside sheath. Trim the ends of any stringy yellowed tips and slice off the root ends of the onions. Drain and pat dry, then place in a large bowl. Pour over the fish sauce and toss to coat.

Combine the water and rice flour in a small saucepan and heat until it comes to a simmer. Stir and turn off the heat; set aside to cool and thicken to a paste, then stir in the remaining ingredients,

adding the gochugaru to taste. Spoon the mixture over the spring onions and, using gloved hands, toss and gently massage the paste to coat. Gather small bunches of the spring onions and neatly arrange them with the white bulbs together at one end. Gently tie the green ends into a knot and pack each bunch into a clean jar. Cover loosely and allow to ferment at room temperature for 2 to 3 days, tasting along the way. When the onions and paste are tangy to your liking, transfer to the refrigerator, where they will keep for up to 1 year.

BUTTER-ROASTED SUMAC CHICKEN

Serves 4 generously

I developed this recipe while working as a personal chef for a family with fairly conservative tastes. They unfailingly requested a roasted chicken at least once a week, and after six months I was itching to change it up. When I returned from a visit to Istanbul loaded with vibrant spices, I decided to take a chance on a couple of birds, and the response was more than encouraging! I went on to make this dish for an outdoor dinner event at Edgemere Farm in Rockaway, New York. A year later, guests were still asking for the recipe, so I decided to include it here. It is an excellent companion to so many dishes in this book.

Everyone needs a roasted chicken recipe in their repertoire. And filling the roasting pan with seasonal vegetables and serving a side of Brown Butter Apricot Kasha (page 252) makes for a well-rounded meal inspired by Middle Eastern flavors. To make the most of your bird, use the carcass to make chicken broth (page 36).

FOR THE SPICE MIX
2 teaspoons cumin seeds
1 teaspoon nigella seeds
1 teaspoon coriander seeds
1 teaspoon black peppercorns
½ teaspoon pink peppercorns
1½ teaspoons Aleppo or
    Urfa Biber pepper
Leaves from 6 sprigs
    fresh thyme
1 teaspoon orange or
    grapefruit zest
2½ tablespoons ground sumac

FOR THE PAN
One 4- to 4½-pound roasting
    chicken
3½ teaspoons kosher salt
6 large cloves garlic, sliced
5 tablespoons unsalted butter,
    softened
8 new potatoes, halved or
    quartered if large
8 small or 2 large fennel bulbs,
    fronds reserved, halved or
    quartered if large
8 to 12 small baby turnips

3 medium leeks, split
    lengthwise with dark
    green parts trimmed, or
    6 scallions, greens attached
1 small onion, quartered
1 small bunch fresh thyme
2½ tablespoons extra-virgin
    olive oil
Two 6-inch sprigs fresh
    bayberry, or 6 dried
    bay leaves
Six to eight 4-inch sprigs fresh
    summer savory
3 large carrots, cut into 2- to
    3-inch pieces

PREPARE THE SPICE MIX
Combine the cumin seeds, nigella seeds, coriander seeds, and black and pink peppercorns in a small heavy skillet set over medium-high heat. Toast the seeds, shaking the pan, for 2 to 3 minutes, until you can detect their warm fragrance. Place in a mortar and pestle to cool, then grind to a fine powder. Add

(recipe continues)

OPPOSITE *This heavily spiced roast chicken recipe brightens up an otherwise humble meal.*

BUTTER-ROASTED
SUMAC CHICKEN,
continued

the Aleppo pepper, thyme, orange zest, and sumac
and set aside.

PREPARE THE CHICKEN

Rinse the chicken and pat dry. Sprinkle with
2¾ teaspoons of the salt inside the cavity and
over the skin, making sure to cover the whole
surface and in between where the wings and legs
meet the breast. Flip the bird and repeat. Lift the
skin and gently separate it from the meat, being
careful not to tear the skin. Rub the outer and inner
skin surface generously on both sides with the
softened butter. Slip 4 of the sliced garlic cloves
underneath the skin and sprinkle generously with
3½ to 4 tablespoons of the spice mix. Set the bird
aside at room temperature for 20 minutes or store
uncovered in the refrigerator for up to 1 day (which
will encourage a crispier roasted skin and a deeper
spiced aroma).

ROAST THE CHICKEN

Preheat the oven to 375°F.

Place the potatoes, fennel, turnips, and leeks
in a large roasting pan and drizzle with the oil.
Sprinkle with the remaining salt and the rest of
the spice mix and toss to coat. Stuff the bird
with the onion, several sprigs of thyme, and the
remaining 2 cloves garlic and truss the chicken.
Place the bird in the roasting pan and surround it
with the potatoes, fennel, turnips, and leeks. Nestle
the remaining thyme and the bayberry and savory
sprigs in between the bird and the vegetables.
Roast uncovered for 1 hour, stirring the vegetables
halfway through. Add the carrots and roast for
another 30 minutes, or until the leg easily pulls
away when gently tugged or the juices run clear
when pierced with a knife. Allow to rest for about
15 minutes before serving.

CHICKEN *and* FENNEL SOURDOUGH DUMPLINGS

Serves 4

So many recipes that are passed down as heirlooms persist in our kitchens because of the comfort they bring. I find it fascinating that there are versions of this dish in most cultures, from Korea to Bavaria and southern Appalachia. Much like Jujube, Ginseng, and Rice Chicken Soup (page 251) or matzo ball soup, this recipe combines the comfort of a warm chicken soup with the satisfying fulfillment of carbohydrates in the form of fluffy sourdough dumplings. The result is a riff on one of my mother's favorite recipes to prepare during my brief but precious visits with her. This is an excellent way to use sourdough starter that is less than vigorous and would otherwise be discarded, although you may use an active or refreshed starter as well. These dumplings are best enjoyed immediately after they are made to savor their lightness. Once you've prepared this homey, warming dish, consider it a gateway to using sourdough as both a roux and in dumplings that can be plopped into just about any type of hot, savory broth for a quick weeknight meal.

FOR THE DUMPLINGS

195 g / 1¾ cups whole white wheat pastry flour

30 g / ¼ cup fine cornmeal or corn flour

1 tablespoon baking powder

½ teaspoon baking soda

¼ teaspoon fine sea salt

¼ teaspoon freshly ground black pepper

90 g / 6 tablespoons unsalted butter, melted and cooled

180 g / ¾ cup buttermilk or ¾ cup yogurt, at room temperature

75 g / 3 tablespoons 100% hydration sourdough starter, at room temperature

2 tablespoons minced fresh flat-leaf parsley

1 clove plump garlic, finely grated

FOR THE SOUP

2 tablespoons Clarified Butter (page 34), skimmed chicken fat, or extra-virgin olive oil

1 small onion, finely chopped

175 g / 1 bulb fennel, cored and thinly sliced

1 stalk celery, chopped

100 g / 1 medium carrot, chopped

60 g / ¼ cup whole milk

35 g / 1½ tablespoons 100% hydration sourdough starter

1½ quarts Chicken Stock (page 36)

300 g / 2½ cups shredded chicken meat

½ cup fresh flat-leaf parsley leaves

FOR THE GARNISH

¼ teaspoon red pepper flakes

Reserved fennel fronds

1 to 2 tablespoons fresh flat-leaf parsley

MAKE THE DUMPLINGS

Whisk together the flour, cornmeal, baking powder, baking soda, salt, and pepper in a medium bowl. In a separate bowl, whisk the melted butter, buttermilk, starter, parsley, and garlic until well combined. Add the dry ingredients to the wet

(recipe continues)

ingredients and stir until just incorporated—the mixture should have the consistency of a wet biscuit dough. Divide the dough evenly into 8 pieces and roughly shape them into balls. Cover with plastic wrap and allow to ferment at room temperature until the soup is ready or up to 3 hours while you prepare the soup. To make the flour more digestible, use active (refreshed) starter and ferment for 3 hours.

PREPARE THE SOUP

Heat the clarified butter in a stockpot over medium heat. Add the onion, fennel, celery, and carrot and cook until the onion is translucent, about 7 minutes. Pour in the milk and whisk in the sourdough starter. Reduce the heat to low and cook until thickened, about 10 to 12 minutes. Pour in the stock and add the chicken. Increase the heat to high and bring to a rolling boil. Stir in the parsley. Arrange the dumplings into the soup. Lower the heat to maintain a gentle simmer, cover, and cook until the dumplings are fluffy but firm, about 12 minutes. Spoon into bowls, garnish with red pepper flakes, fennel fronds, and parsley, and serve immediately.

JUJUBE, GINSENG, *and* RICE CHICKEN SOUP (SAMGYETANG)

Serves 2 heartily

This deliciously comforting soup was first served to me by a friend whose Korean mother had coached him on its proper preparation. The fortifying bitterness of fresh ginseng is mellowed by the mild sweetness of jujube dates, two traditional Asian ingredients that have both long been regarded for their health benefits. The benefits of ginseng range from increased mental and physical stamina, improved circulation, and a toned nervous system, and for the past four thousand years, jujube has been known as an antioxidant, energy booster, and treatment for insomnia. The way they flavor chicken makes their added health benefits a gratuitous plus when taking the chill off of early spring evenings, though I understand that traditionally this soup is enjoyed at the hottest times of summer when foods warmer than your body temperature may be preferred to cool the system!

½ cup sweet sticky rice

2 small Cornish hens (1 to 1½ pounds)

2 tablespoons plus 2 teaspoons fine salt

12 large dried jujube dates, coarsely chopped

2 fresh ginseng roots, finely diced

1 tablespoon freshly grated ginger

½ teaspoon grated orange zest

12 to 13 cups water

3 to 4 scallions, white and green parts, sliced or chopped

Place the rice in a small bowl and add water to cover by at least 2 inches. Cover with a kitchen towel and leave to soak overnight. Drain through a sieve and rinse.

Rinse and pat the hens dry, then sprinkle each all over with 1 tablespoon of the salt. Set the hens aside for about 20 minutes.

Combine the jujubes, ginseng, ginger, orange zest, and the remaining 2 teaspoons salt with the rinsed rice. Stuff the chicken cavities with the rice mixture and place them in a large stockpot. Add enough water to cover and bring to a boil over high heat. Reduce the heat to maintain a gentle simmer, skimming away any foam from the surface. Cook for about 2 hours partially covered, until the meat is tender and the leg pulls away freely from the breast. Place the hens in serving bowls and ladle broth generously over the top. Garnish with the scallions and serve, offering more broth as you enjoy the hen and discover the sticky-sweet stuffing with a spoon.

BROWN BUTTER APRICOT KASHA

Serves 4

A porridge of toasted buckwheat groats is commonly known as *kasha*, but in the Slavic language the name can also be used to describe a variety of cooked grains. Kasha is largely associated with Russian and Jewish cuisine but has found its way onto health-supportive menus for its nutritional value and digestibility, as buckwheat contains considerably lower levels of antinutrient phytates than other grains.

Kasha provides an earthy, protein-rich carbohydrate backbone to any meal. It is rich in antioxidants, vitamins, and minerals and works in dishes both savory and sweet. Scrambling an egg into the kasha to coat before adding the liquid keeps the individual grains separate rather than a sticky mass. If you like your kasha moist, add a little more liquid near the end of cooking time.

This recipe can easily be adapted to use whatever ingredients you have on hand that would pair well with your meal. Apricot works well with broiled fish or Butter-Roasted Sumac Chicken (page 245). But you may substitute dried cranberries or cherries to go with game or duck. Or try using ¼ cup barberries or wild blueberries or a mixture for tartness. You may also use water in place of stock—if doing so, add ¾ teaspoon salt when you add the water. Brown butter adds an unmistakable depth of flavor, but if you don't have it, you can use plain unsalted butter.

I like to make a big pot of hearty porridge several times a week that can be paired with or repurposed into other dishes. Kasha is oftentimes on the menu: it is excellent refried with lentils and a sunny-side up egg or can be tossed with bow-tie pasta, a little more butter, and sautéed or caramelized onions to make kasha varnishkes, a humble, comforting Ashkenazi Jewish dish.

2½ tablespoons Clarified Butter (page 34) or extra-virgin olive oil
4 medium shallots, sliced
1 cup kasha
1 large egg, beaten

¼ cup Brown Butter (page 34)
1 to 1¾ cups Chicken Stock (page 36) or vegetable stock of choice such as Ruby Chard (page 27) or Corn Cob (page 28)

½ cup dried apricots, coarsely chopped
½ teaspoon ground cinnamon

Heat the clarified butter in a large heavy skillet with a lid over medium-low heat. Add the shallots and cook, stirring occasionally, until they brown and start to caramelize, 20 to 25 minutes. Transfer to a bowl and set aside.

Stir the kasha into the same skillet and increase the heat to medium. Shake the pan to lightly toast until fragrant, about 2 to 3 minutes. Remove from the heat and briskly whisk the beaten egg in to coat the kasha. Decrease the heat to low and stir in the brown butter until melted. When melted, add the stock or water, apricots, and cinnamon, bring to a simmer, and cover. Reduce the heat to low and cook for 15 to 20 minutes, checking after 10 to 12 minutes to see if the kasha needs more liquid. If so, add up to ½ cup more stock, cover again, and continue cooking for another 6 to 7 minutes, until the kasha is soft but not mushy and can be fluffed with a fork. Check for salt and serve immediately. The kasha will keep covered in the refrigerator for up to 5 days.

BUCKWHEAT

Common buckwheat, or *Fagopyrum esculentum*, is the seed of a pseudocereal originally hailing from Asia. Despite its misleading name, buckwheat's groats are seeds of a plant more closely related to rhubarb than wheat with a charming little white flower and graceful posture in the garden. Buckwheat groats are gluten-free and can be found in two forms: the greenish raw groats that are best for sprouting and what we most commonly refer to as kasha, a toasted whole groat that cooks up quickly. Tartary buckwheat, or *Fagopyrum tataricum*, is becoming more available in the US as well (see Resources, page 324) due to its distinctive nutlike flavor and higher levels of rutin, a phenolic compound that has antioxidant benefits. Because of buckwheat's adaptability to poor soil, cold climates, and cooperative cultivation (it can rotate two or three times in one season in the Northeast) as well as ease of harvest and cooking, it has found its way into many different global cuisines. It is ground into flour to make Russian blinis, Briton-style crepes, Japanese soba noodles, and rustic European-style hearth breads. It is cooked whole in Eastern European, Russian, and Central Asian countries, and in China it is brewed into a tea. It is nutritionally dense, is an excellent cover crop that rejuvenates the soil, and has a remarkable flavor that marries particularly well with chocolate and bright fruits as well as a wide range of vegetables and meats.

CRANBERRY MARMALADE

Makes a scant 3 pints

One March, I was given a bounty of freshly harvested citrus I had little experience using. It resembled a yellowish squat orange but, upon scraping its oily skin, produced a fragrance unlike any I had experienced in fresh citrus. The farmer who grew them found their aroma somewhat offensive, but I was curious to put these fruits of *Citrus taiwanica*, an offspring of the sour orange and the mandarin, to good use. I set to work experimenting with some cranberries I had frozen from the autumn and came up with this beautifully jeweled marmalade.

These somewhat rare fruits resemble the fragrance of bergamot with the bitterness of a sour orange and are confusingly referred to as either sour orange or bergamot lemon in trade. If you can't source them, you may use either of the aforementioned or even a common orange. If you do, include the juice and rind of two large lemons in addition to the oranges. This perfumed, thick and jammy marmalade is excellent served with Herman's Heirloom Cornbread (page 220), Æbelskiver (page 111), or Orange Cardamom Cake (page 190). I prefer the clean flavor of citrus to shine through, but you may add spices such as cinnamon, cloves, or allspice if you wish.

6¼ cups fresh or thawed frozen
    cranberries

10 sour oranges (bergamot
    lemons)
3½ cups sugar

Place the cranberries in a large, wide pot. Using a sharp knife or a vegetable peeler, remove the outer skin of the citrus from the bitter inner pith. Slice into ⅛- to ¼-inch strips and stir into the cranberries. Juice the citrus and reserve the seeds—you should have about 2 cups of juice. If you do not, supplement with lemon or lime juice. Pour the juice over the pot and tie the seeds in cheesecloth. Nestle the bundle into the cranberries and citrus peel. Bring to a boil, then reduce the heat to maintain a low simmer and cook, stirring occasionally and mashing with the back of a spoon until the cranberries have popped and the citrus peel is tender, about 20 to 25 minutes. Turn off the heat and remove the seed bundle or cool with the seed bundle submerged overnight for a thickened set.

Stir the sugar into the jam until dissolved and return to a boil. Reduce the heat to maintain a simmer and skim off any foam. Cook for an additional 25 to 30 minutes, until the jam passes the set test (see page 18). Transfer to sterilized jars and process in a hot water bath for 10 minutes (see page 18). Store in a cool location for up to 1 year.

SALTED KUMQUAT *and* HONEY TEA

Serves 2

This warm tea is excellent relief from a sore throat. Sweeten with honey as your palate desires.

4 to 6 Salted Kumquats (page 13), rinsed of brine

2 cups boiling water
Honey

———————

Place two or three kumquats in tea cups and muddle with a cocktail wand or the back of a spoon. Pour the boiling water over them and sweeten with honey to taste. Serve immediately.

7

SUMMER

Summer's abundance of fruits includes nectarines (Prunus persica), peaches (Prunus persica), Japanese plums (Prunus salicina), figs (Ficus carica), gooseberries (Ribes uva-crispa), red and champagne currants (Ribes rubrum), cucamelons (Melothria scabra), and musk melons (Cucumis melo).

Nature's Bounty

BREADS

Spiced Cherry Rye
Levain / 260

Black Garlic, Fig, and
Walnut Levain / 263

Cornmeal Flatbread / 266

SAVORY DISHES

Heirloom Melon Salad with
Tarragon and Fig Leaf
Powder / 271

Tangy Bread Salad with
Peaches, Tomatoes,
and Purslane / 272

Kale, Corn, and
Fermented Mushroom and
Onion Strata / 275

Lemony Vegetarian
Cabbage Rolls / 277

Tok-sel Butter Beans / 281

Okroshka (Kvass Soup) / 282

Basturma / 285

Fermented Green
Tomatoes / 287

Green Tomato and Eggplant
Shakshuka / 290

Tomato Coulis, Sauce,
or Paste / 293

Grilled Eggplant with
Buttermilk Tahini Sauce and
Tomato Coulis / 294

Pickled Mini Eggplant / 297

SWEETS AND DRINKS

Green Tomato and
Lemon Ginger Jam / 299

Spiced Ground Cherry,
Lemon, and Apple
Preserves / 300

Wild Carrot Syrup / 302

Preserved Stone Fruit in
Herb Syrup / 305

Mini Fruit Galettes / 306

Buckwheat Berry
Tartlets with Lemon Herb
Cream / 309

Purple Barley Milk
Cake / 312

Bread Kvass / 315

Probiotic Granola Bars / 318

OPPOSITE *'Amish Paste' tomatoes from an Amish community in Wisconsin are known for their sweet flesh perfect for making sauce (page 293), paste, or for canning.*

SPICED CHERRY RYE LEVAIN

Makes 2 loaves

The warm spices included in this bread might seem a better fit at the autumn or winter table. It is, however, one of the best breads for making Tangy Bread Salad with Peaches, Tomatoes, and Purslane (page 272), an essential of summer. For a sweetener, it uses carob molasses, which has an earthy, somewhat bitter taste. It can be found at Middle Eastern groceries (see Resources, page 324), but if you cannot source it, substitute plain molasses or buckwheat honey or another strong honey instead. Bake a few of these loaves and freeze one for a future bread salad that you won't have to heat up the kitchen to make. This loaf is also excellent served with charcuterie, such as Basturma (page 285) or Labneh Balls (page 41).

FOR THE LEAVEN
40 g / generous 1½ tablespoons 100% hydration sourdough starter

40 g / ¼ cup tepid water (70°F to 75°F)

40 g / 4½ tablespoons whole rye flour

FOR THE SOAKER
225 g / 1¾ cups dried cherries

30 g / 3 tablespoons rye whiskey, bourbon, or brandy

FOR THE DOUGH
1 teaspoon whole allspice berries

1 teaspoon whole fennel seeds, toasted

120 g / 1 cup + 1 heaping tablespoon leaven (see left)

600 g / 2½ cups + 2½ tablespoons water

30 g / 1 tablespoon carob molasses

620 g / 4⅓ cups + 1½ tablespoons high-extraction bread flour

160 g / 1½ cups whole rye flour

1 teaspoon ground cinnamon

16 g / 1 tablespoon fine sea salt

PREPARE THE LEAVEN
Place the starter and water in a large bowl and stir to create a slurry. Add the flour and mix with a spoon until no dry lumps remain. Cover with plastic wrap and allow to ferment at room temperature for about 8 hours, until it is fragrant, shows bubbles breaking the surface, and has swelled considerably in size.

PREPARE THE SOAKER
While the leaven is fermenting, place the dried cherries in a small bowl, pour the liquor over the them, and toss to combine. Cover and set aside at room temperature until the leaven is finished fermenting. If possible, stir occasionally throughout the day for the fruit to fully absorb the liquid.

(recipe continues)

MIX THE DOUGH

Place the allspice berries and fennel seeds in a mortar and pestle or spice grinder and crush to a powder. Add the water and molasses to the mature leaven and stir to combine. Add the flours to the bowl, then add the crushed spices and cinnamon. Using your hands, mix and squeeze the dough in a circular motion until no dry lumps remain. Cover with an inverted bowl or plastic wrap, and autolyze (rest) the dough for about 20 minutes for the flour to fully hydrate. Sprinkle the salt evenly over the surface of the dough and mix well to combine. Spread the fruit evenly over the surface of the dough and fold the dough over the fruit to the middle several times to incorporate. Cover with a plate or plastic wrap and move to bulk fermentation. Continue with instructions for bulk fermentation, shaping, and baking according to the Table Loaf recipe (page 63).

BLACK GARLIC, FIG, *and* WALNUT LEVAIN

Makes 2 loaves

The aggressive sting of winter was stubbornly lingering as I opened the door to my small beach bungalow and begrudgingly stepped out to face the wet Atlantic air. It had been an unusually long and trying season of various personal challenges, and fighting the elements to stay warm was feeling unnecessarily taxing on my spirit. I longed for the easy summer days of freedom unburdened by extra clothing as I descended the icy stairs to my cozy refuge, a bakery operation located in a communal house in Rockaway. An unfamiliar pungency greeted me at the door, a most peculiar scent that was both appetite stimulating and assaulting all at once. The proprietor had decided to surprise me with a batch of black garlic aging away in a rice cooker. Tucked into a corner of the bakery, it filled every corner of the house with a toasty aroma, but it was eventually sequestered into the garage for its lingering personality on the clothes!

Black garlic is a culinary revelation with a texture and flavor that falls somewhere in the savory raisin category. It is so distinctively satisfying that after about a week in the rice cooker, I forgot about the invasive perfume that had initially greeted me at the door. A slow and sustained exposure to low heat caramelizes the sugars of these otherwise pungent bulbs and yields wafts of balsamic in the nose and molasses and tamarind on the tongue. These flavors are beneficial to soups or sauces in need of umami, such as Asparagus and Amaranth Soup (page 229), and play well with other sources of similar flavors, such as dried fruit. In this bread, it invites a soft-rind and creamy, spreadable cheese or a firm and salty curl of Parmesan.

Black garlic can be sourced from spice shops but is simple to make with a rice cooker set to Warm. When your summer harvest is abundant, you may use whole uncured, freshly harvested garlic heads; they will require a lengthy exposure to heat (sometimes up to two weeks) in the cooker before being ready to be stored in a dry, room-temperature location. Cured whole heads of the winter pantry may need only 5 to 7 days. Check periodically after 5 days for both flavor and texture; a just leathery but still somewhat juicy black clove works best when smeared into this bread dough. Expose to heat for longer if you desire to store the bulbs for long periods before use (6 to 8 months). If the cloves become too tough to slice or smear, soak them in a bit of warm water for 10 minutes to rehydrate.

(recipe continues)

1 recipe Table Loaf (page 62),
    made with the adjustments
    below

FOLD-INS
80 g / ¾ cup toasted walnut
    pieces

150 g / 1 cup dried figs, coarsely
    chopped
45 g / ⅓ cup black garlic, peeled
    and coarsely chopped

After the salt has been mixed into the Table Loaf, sprinkle the walnuts and figs onto the dough and gently smear with the black garlic, leaving small chunks as pockets of flavor. Gently lift the dough from the bottom of the bowl and stretch to the middle, folding it over the added ingredients. Rotate the bowl and fold two or three more times, until you have worked your way completely around the dough. Continue this technique every 30 to 45 minutes for the remainder of bulk fermentation at room temperature, about 4 hours. This will both strengthen the dough and evenly distribute the fold-ins. When the dough has increased in size by at least one third, continue shaping, retarding, and baking as instructed on page 64.

OPPOSITE *With lengthy exposure to gentle heat, garlic mellows to an umami-packed sweetness called Black Garlic (page 263).*

CORNMEAL FLATBREAD

Makes 1 large or 2 small flatbreads

Flatbreads are a beautiful canvas for so many toppings. This version resembling focaccia uses stone-ground cornmeal for texture and added flavor. It is an optimal candidate for summer adornment with shishito peppers, lemon slices, and fresh corn—although you may choose to make a sweeter version by substituting with blueberries, figs, or Concord grapes, chopped rosemary or thyme sprigs, and a generous sprinkling of cane sugar in the autumn for a satisfying jammy bread. Bake, then slice and reheat on the grill to create a crisp edge against the moist inner crumb.

FOR THE SOAKER
65 g / ½ cup fine cornmeal
115 g / ½ cup boiling water

FOR THE DOUGH
200 g / 1 cup 100% hydration active sourdough starter, refreshed (fed)
345 g / 1½ cups water
30 g / 2 tablespoons extra-virgin olive oil

280 g / 2 cups high-extraction bread flour
220 g / 2 cups whole wheat pastry flour or spelt flour
12 g / generous 1 teaspoon fine sea salt
1½ tablespoons cornmeal, plus more for sprinkling

FOR THE SHISHITO PEPPER TOPPING
90 g / about 30 shishito peppers
100 g / 1 ear corn kernels
2 small lemons, thinly sliced
2 garlic scapes, chopped
1 tablespoon togarashi spice blend, or to taste

FOR THE GARNISH
Generous pinch flaked sea salt
Sprinkling of red pepper flakes

PREPARE THE LEAVEN (REFRESHED STARTER) AND SOAKER
About 8 hours before you mix the dough, refresh your starter and prepare the soaker. Place the cornmeal in a small bowl and pour over the boiling water. Stir well and cover with a lid or plastic wrap and allow to sit at room temperature for about 8 hours, until the refreshed starter is bubbly and active.

PREPARE THE DOUGH
In a large bowl, use your hands to thoroughly mix the soaker with all the dough ingredients; the dough will be sticky and loose. Cover with an inverted bowl, plate, or plastic wrap and allow to bulk ferment at room temperature for about 3 hours, turning and folding the dough every 45 minutes to 1 hour to gain strength. When bubbles visibly break the surface and the dough has increased in volume by at least one third, cover well and place in the refrigerator to retard overnight.

(recipe continues)

SHAPE THE FLATBREADS

Line a 10 × 15-inch baking sheet or jelly-roll pan with parchment paper. Pour 1 to 2 tablespoons oil on the parchment and sprinkle the cornmeal evenly over the surface. Using a dough scraper to release the dough from the bowl, coax the dough onto a well-floured work surface. Use your fingers to lightly distribute the dough into a rectangle with an even 1½-inch thickness, being careful not to deflate the dough. Use a bench knife to divide the dough into two pieces and transfer to the prepared baking sheet. Lightly dimple the surface of the dough using your fingertips and drizzle the remaining oil over the top. Firmly press the toppings into the surface of the dough, then sprinkle on the togarashi, flaked salt, and red pepper flakes if using. Allow the flatbreads to final proof at room temperature for about 1 hour, until the dough is puffy and showing signs of fermentation bubbles.

BAKE THE FLATBREAD

While the bread is proofing, preheat the oven to 425°F.

Place in the oven and bake for 25 to 30 minutes, rotating halfway through, until the surface is a deep golden brown and the edges are crisp. Remove from the oven and allow to rest for 10 minutes, then use a spatula to loosen and transfer to a cooling rack. Serve warm or at room temperature. It is best eaten the same day it is baked.

OPPOSITE *Cornmeal Flatbread can be baked and reheated on a grill to be passed around and shared with friends and strangers.*

HEIRLOOM MELON SALAD *with* TARRAGON *and* FIG LEAF POWDER

Serves 4 to 6

Melons are synonymous with August, a month when intense heat can drive you to seek refreshment at every turn. Browse your farmers' market for the best selection of the large *Cucumis melo* muskmelon species and its cultivars—look for firm skin and heavy fruit. Melons are a study in pastels and perfume, varying in sweetness and color. While the more common, sweet cantaloupe and its heirloom French cultivars or honeydews are perfectly suitable for this recipe, I prefer some of the drier varieties with white or pale green flesh more closely resembling the flavor and texture of a cucumber, such as the 'Armenian Cucumber' or Iraqi 'Bateekh Samara,' or for a sweeter substitute, try the Turkish 'Alacati,' the Paraguay 'Apple Melon,' or just a simple honeydew in a pinch.

2 whole scallions

¼ cup extra-virgin olive oil

1 lemon

Pinch of salt

2½ pounds heirloom melon, halved and seeded

Leaves from 1 sprig fresh tarragon

½ teaspoon Fig Leaf Powder (page 23)

FOR THE GARNISH (OPTIONAL)

1 tablespoon slivered pistachios, toasted

Handful of edible flower blossoms, such as chives

A few pinches of Urfa Biber or Aleppo pepper

About an hour or up to a day before you assemble the salad, cut the scallions into slivers and place in a bowl of water to encourage them to playfully curl and mellow in flavor.

Drain, pat dry with paper towels, and put the scallions in a medium bowl. Toss with 1 tablespoon of the oil, a generous squeeze of lemon, and a pinch of salt and set aside. Cut the melon into pieces that are easy to handle and cut the outside rind off. Run each piece over a mandoline to create thin ribbons. Arrange the ribbons playfully on a large platter and dress with a few more squeezes of lemon. Drizzle with the remaining 3 tablespoons oil. Top with the marinated scallions and tarragon and, using a small sieve, dust lightly with the fig leaf powder. Garnish with the pistachios, edible flowers, and pepper. Serve immediately or cover and refrigerate for up to 3 hours before serving.

TANGY BREAD SALAD *with* PEACHES, TOMATOES, *and* PURSLANE

Serves 10 to 12

Bread is gleefully repurposed in this summer salad that follows the method of panzanella and the spirit of fattoush. Use the ripest tomatoes and peaches you can find to go with purslane, one of the season's most ubiquitous but delicious garden weeds. The yield is impressively large and perfect for a potluck or family picnic, but you may make a half recipe for a more intimate weeknight dinner. This salad should be eaten no later than an hour after assembly.

1 loaf Spiced Cherry Rye Levain (page 260)

½ cup + ⅓ cup extra-virgin olive oil

3 tablespoons pomegranate molasses

3 tablespoons fresh lemon juice

2 tablespoons ground sumac

¾ teaspoon salt

½ teaspoon coarsely ground black pepper

½ cup sliced scallions

2 large cucumbers, seeded and sliced into thin strips

2¼ cups cherry tomatoes, quartered (about 1 pint)

1 large juicy ripe peach, chopped

1½ cups fresh corn kernels (from about 3 ears)

1 large head romaine lettuce, cored and cut into 2-inch pieces

3 cups purslane leaves and tender stems

1 packed cup fresh mint leaves, coarsely chopped

1 packed cup fresh flat-leaf parsley leaves, coarsely chopped

Finely grated hard-rind sheep's milk cheese

MAKE THE CROUTONS

Preheat the oven to 425ºF.

Slice the bread into 1½-inch-thick pieces and lay flat on a baking sheet. Brush generously with the ½ cup of oil on both sides. Toast until the edges are dark brown and the bread smells bold and aromatic. Remove from the oven and allow to cool, then cut into 2-inch squares. Set aside until you are ready to assemble the salad. You can make these up to 8 hours in advance.

MARINATE THE VEGETABLES

In a large bowl, whisk together the remaining ⅓ cup oil, the pomegranate molasses, lemon juice, sumac, salt, and pepper. Toss the scallions, cucumber, cherry tomatoes, peach, and corn in the vinaigrette. You may cover and refrigerate up to 6 hours in advance.

ASSEMBLE THE SALAD

About 30 minutes before serving the salad, add the croutons to the bowl of marinated vegetables and toss to coat. When you are ready to serve, toss in the lettuce, purslane, mint, and parsley and garnish with the cheese.

KALE, CORN, *and* FERMENTED MUSHROOM *and* ONION STRATA

Makes one 9 × 13-inch pan

Strata is a type of savory bread pudding made with stale bread and vegetables and/ or meat in an egg custard. It makes a hearty side dish, or add a crisp salad, and it's the main event of a meal. The fermented mushrooms and cipollini add depth of flavor, and strained yogurt adds tang. It can be assembled a day ahead and baked just as your guests are arriving, making your entertaining chores a breeze. It is best served straight from the oven after the eggs puff, but it is excellent the next day as well. Cover with foil and reheat in a preheated 350°F oven for 15 to 20 minutes.

7 cups cubed (1- to 2-inch cubes) stale Sourdough Challah (page 157) or brioche

6 large eggs

1⅓ cups whole milk

¾ cup strained yogurt

¾ tablespoon Dijon mustard

1 teaspoon kosher salt

½ teaspoon cracked black pepper

¼ teaspoon freshly grated nutmeg

3 tablespoons duck or bacon fat

1½ cups Whey-Fermented Cipollini Onions (page 45) quartered

1½ cups Lacto-Fermented Mushrooms (page 11)

1 cup raw cremini mushrooms, coarsely chopped

3 plump cloves garlic

1 bunch kale, stemmed and torn or cut into 2- to 3-inch pieces

1 cup fresh corn kernels (from about 3 ears)

Butter, for greasing the pan

1 cup grated Parmesan cheese

2 cups grated fontina cheese

¼ cup bread crumbs

6 large sprigs thyme

Preheat the oven to 350°F.

Spread the challah cubes onto a baking sheet in a single layer and toast for 15 to 20 minutes, until the bread feels dry and firm to the touch. Remove from the oven and allow to cool. You can do this up to 1 day in advance.

In a large bowl, whisk together the eggs, milk, yogurt, mustard, ¾ teaspoon of the salt, the pepper, and nutmeg. Fold in the bread. Cover

OPPOSITE *Lacto-Fermented Mushrooms (page 11) and Whey-Fermented Cipollini Onions (page 45) make the flavors of a savory bread pudding distinctively different.*

and allow to soak at room temperature while you continue with the recipe.

Heat the fat in a large skillet over medium-high heat until it runs clear. Add the cipollini and lower the heat to medium. Sear without stirring for 2 to 3 minutes. Shake the pan and continue to cook until the onions have softened and browned, about 7 minutes. Add the fermented and raw mushrooms and sprinkle with the remaining ¼ teaspoon salt. Cook, stirring occasionally, for 5 to 6 minutes, until the mushrooms are golden brown. Stir in the garlic and kale, and cook, stirring, until just wilted, about

(recipe continues)

2 minutes, then turn off the heat. Stir in the corn and set aside to cool for 10 to 15 minutes.

Preheat the oven to 350°F. Generously butter a 9 × 13-inch baking dish.

Toss the cheeses together in a bowl to combine. Stir the vegetable mixture together with the soaked bread and all but ¾ cup of the cheese and pour into an even layer in the prepared dish. Sprinkle alternating layers of the bread crumbs with the remaining cheese and nestle the thyme sprigs into the top of the mixture before placing into the oven. Bake for about 50 minutes, until the strata is bubbling and the cheese is nicely browned on top. Remove from the oven and allow to cool and set for 15 to 20 minutes before removing the thyme sprigs, slicing, and serving.

LEMONY VEGETARIAN CABBAGE ROLLS

Serves 10 to 12

These cabbage rolls are based on a traditional preparation called *mahshi*, an Arabic word used to describe a number of stuffed vegetable recipes. Hollowed zucchini, eggplant, or even carrots are common, as are stuffed grape or cabbage leaves. The filling may include either rice and vegetables, or ground lamb or beef and rice. Copious herbs infuse the rolls with a pleasing aroma, making the most of summer's flavorful gifts. The rolls are boiled or steamed, then served as part of an elaborate mezze meal. Making them is a fun activity for a small group of friends or family. This vegetarian version uses a lemony broth and a bright mix of carrots and radishes, but it would be great with beets as well.

FOR THE FILLING
1 cup white basmati rice
½ cup dried barberries
½ cup toasted pine nuts
¾ cup sliced scallions, white and green parts
½ cup diced carrots, or sliced if small
½ cup diced radish, or sliced if small
1 cup coarsely chopped fresh mint
1 cup coarsely chopped fresh cilantro leaves

1 cup coarsely chopped fresh flat-leaf parsley leaves
1 cup coarsely chopped fresh dill
⅔ cup tomato paste
3½ teaspoons fine sea salt
1½ teaspoons ground cardamom
1½ teaspoons ground sumac
1½ teaspoons ground Aleppo pepper
1 teaspoon crushed pink peppercorns
1 teaspoon ground cinnamon

FOR THE ROLLS
3 large sweet onions, peeled
1 head (about 2¾ pounds) savoy cabbage
About 2 quarts water
3 to 4 large russet potatoes, halved
1 quart Corn Cob Broth (page 28)
¾ cup fresh lemon juice

FOR THE GARNISH
2 to 3 tablespoons chopped fresh herbs (parsley, dill, or mint work well)

MAKE THE FILLING

Place the rice in a medium bowl and add water to cover. Allow to soak for 1 hour. Drain well.

In a large bowl, combine the remaining filling ingredients. Add the drained rice, cover with a plate or plastic wrap, and set aside. You may prepare the filling up to 1 day in advance; keep covered in the refrigerator until ready to use.

MAKE THE ROLLS

Using a sharp paring knife, cut a slit into each onion about halfway through the length of the onion. Place the onions and the head of cabbage in a stockpot and pour in enough water to cover the onions. Cover and bring to a simmer over high heat. Lower the heat to maintain a simmer and cook for about 5 minutes, until the outer leaves of the cabbage feel limp but retain their vibrant green

(recipe continues)

color. Remove the cabbage and onions from the water and set the pot aside, reserving the water in a separate bowl for later use.

Place the potatoes cut-side down into the stockpot. When the cabbage and onions are cool to the touch, separate the leaves from the core of the cabbage and peel apart the onion layers. Lay the cabbage leaves flat on a work surface and place 3 to 4 tablespoons of the rice mixture onto each leaf, making sure not to overstuff them. Roll the leaves into fat little cigar shapes, tucking the sides in as you go (similar to how you would prepare a burrito). Do the same with the onion layers, adjusting the filling to accommodate the size of the layer, and use a toothpick to secure them tightly.

Arrange the cabbage rolls and onion rolls snugly in the pot, layering them if you need to. Pour in the reserved water, stock, and lemon juice and place a heavy heatproof plate on top to keep them from floating. Cover and bring to a simmer over medium-high heat. Reduce the heat to maintain a simmer and cook for 30 minutes, or according to the package instructions for the rice.

Serve warm or at room temperature generously garnished with chopped fresh herbs. The rolls will keep in the refrigerator for up to 5 days or in the freezer well wrapped in plastic wrap for up to 3 months. Thaw in the refrigerator overnight and warm in a preheated 350°F oven for 20 to 25 minutes.

Don't be tempted to stuff the leaves of Lemony Vegetarian Cabbage Rolls too full with the rice mixture or roll too tightly, as the rice will expand while cooking.

TOK-SEL BUTTER BEANS

Serves 4

I grew up eating lima beans as many vegetables are cooked in the South: boiled to death, with a bland seasoning adding insult to injury. Lima beans are a ubiquitous legume in the Southern states with a reputation of being slightly bitter and off-putting. I always thought they were better as a cover crop than an edible celebration until I enjoyed them inspired by the Yucatán. Mellowed by fresh parsley, the savory aromas of toasted pepitas, and toasted sesame oil, and brightened with lime, I was finally able to appreciate why they are sometimes called butter beans for their smooth, creamy flesh and mild flavor. This recipe is an adaptation of one from Chef Bruce Ucán of the Mayan Café, whose family recipes have been served in this beloved restaurant on the Ohio River for almost thirty years. You can use frozen baby limas, but if you are lucky enough to have access to fresh beans, blanch them quickly before making the recipe.

1 cup fresh flat-leaf parsley leaves

½ cup fresh whole cilantro leaves

5 scallions, white and green parts

¼ cup toasted pepitas (pumpkin seeds)

1½ tablespoons Clarified Butter (page 34)

2 cups shelled lima beans

1½ tablespoons toasted sesame oil

½ teaspoon kosher salt, or to taste

1½ limes

Mound the parsley, cilantro, scallions, and pepitas on a cutting board. Using a large chef's knife, chop until the ingredients are uniform.

Heat the clarified butter in a large heavy-bottomed skillet over medium-high heat until clear. Add the lima beans and cook for 2 to 3 minutes without stirring to give them some color. Gently stir and continue cooking until the lima beans are tender and lightly browned all over, about 10 to 12 minutes. Transfer to a serving bowl, add the sesame oil, the chopped herbs and pepitas, and salt. Squeeze the juice of 1 lime over the lima beans and stir. Check for salt. Serve warm or at room temperature with the remaining lime half cut into wedges alongside.

OKROSHKA (KVASS SOUP)

Serves 2 as a meal or 4 as an appetizer

When the scorching heat of summer slows you to a snail's pace, this chilled soup will satiate your appetite with little effort. It is comparable to gazpacho, though more brothy with a slightly boozy flavor. It uses scallions and a little garlic to turn Bread Kvass (page 315) into a probiotic, savory meal. I often turn to this recipe when kvass has aged to a strong or sour flavor and (untraditionally) dilute it with cold vegetable broth. You may use all kvass instead, but I prefer the complexity and saltiness that a good clean broth can bring to this dish. If you have not brewed a batch of kvass, you can substitute a dry cider or mead.

The vegetable ingredients are flexible, but cucumber and radish are essential for their crunch and restorative properties. When tomatoes are in season, coarsely chop a cup and chill them with the broth while you prepare the rest of the ingredients. When mushrooms are abundant, consider including seared Lacto-Fermented Mushrooms (page 11). Boiled eggs add a boost of vegetarian protein, but thinly sliced leftover pork from Bacon-Wrapped Pork Loin with Charred Cabbage and Prune Sauce (page 179) would be a clever addition as well.

There are a number of different preparations and presentations; for this soup I chose to infuse the liquid with the garlic and onions before serving. Diners may choose their preferred combination of textures and flavors in a festive spread of abundance and pour the kvass over the ingredients just before eating. This refreshing soup becomes a bountiful celebration of seasonal ingredients and is sure to leave a lasting impression.

1½ cups cold Bread Kvass (page 315)

1½ cups cold vegetable stock of choice (pages 27 to 28)

3 scallions, thinly sliced, white and green parts

1 small clove garlic

½ teaspoon fine sea salt, or to taste

2 medium cucumbers, peeled, seeded, and cut into ½- to 1-inch cubes

1 large boiled new potato, cut into ½- to 1-inch cubes

4 large hard-boiled eggs, sliced

FOR THE GARNISH

½ cup sour cream

4 medium radishes, julienned

1 packed cup fresh herbs (dill, cilantro, and parsley work well)

Freshly ground black pepper

Lemon wedges

To prepare the soup, combine the kvass, vegetable stock, and scallions in a large bowl or serving pitcher. Using a Microplane, grate the garlic into the mixture. Add the salt, cover, and chill in the refrigerator for at least 30 minutes or up to 3 hours.

Ladle into bowls and serve with a platter of cucumbers, potatoes, and eggs, allowing your guests to garnish with the sour cream, radishes, and fresh herbs. Sprinkle with pepper and serve with lemon wedges.

Okroshka (cold kvass soup) can include an array of seasonal ingredients and condiments shared amongst a table of guests.

The concentrated cured flavors of Basturma appreciate the acidity of Fermented Green Tomatoes (page 287) and sweet umami of Black Garlic, Fig, and Walnut Levain (page 263).

BASTURMA

Makes 1 large piece

This traditional Armenian dried beef spiced with fenugreek, smoked paprika, and garlic is unlike any other cured meat you will ever experience. I first tasted it in Beirut in the Armenian enclave of Bourj Hammoud, where it was served with scrambled eggs. In the United States, outside of purchasing from a traditional Armenian or Lebanese butcher, it is difficult to find basturma that does not contain preservatives and artificial food colorings.

To my delight, I discovered that making basturma is rather simple and straightforward as long as you have the right conditions in which to age it. The key to a successful cure is reducing or eliminating moisture from the meat. This creates an environment that is both inhospitable to spoilage bacteria and beneficial for the halophile (salt-loving) microbes that protect the meat and add flavor. These microbes thrive in salty and dry conditions, producing lactic acid bacteria that preserve and also encourage beneficial penicillin molds. Choose a cut of beef such as filet mignon that is as tender and free of streaky fat as your wallet will allow. If you prefer a larger cut that is a little less expensive, a piece of flat-iron trimmed of excess fat will work just fine. I like to use half smoked paprika and half sweet paprika in the spice paste, but you can use any proportion.

The first time I made basturma, I closed off my bungalow before heading on vacation, prepared the meat, hung it on a hook, and ran a dehumidifier for several weeks. This approach worked beautifully, although my electric bill was rather alarming upon return! If you live in an arid environment, try making this in late summer or early fall before the rains return but the temperatures have tempered somewhat.

3½ pounds tender cut of beef

2⅓ cups kosher salt

¾ cup fenugreek seeds

1½ tablespoons toasted cumin seeds

1 tablespoon black peppercorns

1 tablespoon whole allspice berries

1 tablespoon red pepper flakes

2 heads garlic, peeled

¾ cup sweet or smoked paprika

2 tablespoons ground turmeric

3 tablespoons water

Lay a piece of wax paper or plastic wrap onto a baking sheet. Spread half of the salt onto the surface. Lay the beef on top and coat it with the remaining salt. Place another piece of wax paper or plastic on top of the meat, then add a weight, such as bricks. Place it in the refrigerator for 5 days, pouring off any liquid that pools around the meat at least once a day.

(recipe continues)

Remove the meat from the refrigerator, rinse, and place in a large bowl of water to soak. Return to the refrigerator. The surface of the meat will have transformed from red to a bleached grayish color. Change the water once every hour for 3 hours, then remove the meat from the bowl and pat dry with paper towels. Place on a wire rack and place in the refrigerator for 1 day, turning once so that the meat fully dries on both sides.

Remove the meat from the refrigerator and prepare the spice rub: Combine the fenugreek seeds, cumin seeds, peppercorns, allspice, and red pepper flakes in a spice grinder and grind to a fine powder. Transfer to a large mortar and pestle or food processor, add the garlic, paprika, turmeric, and 3 tablespoons of water, and grind to a spreadable paste, adding more water if necessary.

Record the weight of the meat. Spread a double layer of cheesecloth large enough to wrap the meat completely over a work surface. Spread half of the spice paste onto one side of the meat and lay it flat onto the cheesecloth. Spread the remaining spice paste on the other side and wrap the cheesecloth completely around the meat. Using butcher's twine, tie the cheesecloth securely around the meat four or five times around the width and once around the length. Hang in a cool, dry place for about 3 weeks, until it has reduced by at least 30% in weight. Store wrapped in plastic in the refrigerator for up to 1 month.

FERMENTED GREEN TOMATOES

Makes about 1 gallon

If you live in an area where frost lingers late and comes early but can't resist growing tomatoes regardless, this recipe is for you. I first experienced lacto-fermented green tomatoes in Brighton Beach, Brooklyn, where many Russian, Georgian, and Ukrainian shops carry these specialty pickles. They are firm and crunchy, pleasantly sour, and delightful served with cheese plates, Sweet Potato Peanut Hummus (page 90) and Smoked Paprika and Cheese Sourdough Bread (page 80), or cured meats such as Basturma (page 285). They are a surprisingly versatile ingredient that can also garnish a Fire Cider Bloody Mary (page 204) for a probiotic boost! You can make them as mild or spicy as you like and take advantage of any end-of-season flavors that suit your fancy.

You will want to use a large crock that accommodates at least 1 gallon, as you will create a salt-water brine to ferment the tomatoes under weight. The key to a successful vegetable ferment is to keep the vegetables submerged, making sure they remain in an anaerobic environment throughout the process. A crock with an airlock lid will discourage mold or slimy kahm yeast from forming on the surface that may lead to soft, unappetizing pickles. These crocks may be purchased inexpensively from homesteading or hardware stores or from specialty potters (see Resources, page 324). You may purchase or create a weight yourself using a sterilized stone or another filled jar positioned on top of the tomatoes.

An alternative version of this recipe is to use tomatillos instead of green tomatoes, following the same weight-to-salt equivalents for fermentation. If you would rather ferment small pickling cucumbers instead, increase the brine to a 7% solution. (Recipe shown on page 1.)

2270 g / about 5 pounds green
    tomatoes, cut into 1½- to
    2-inch-thick slices

120 to 180 g / 2 to 3 heads garlic,
    peeled

132 g / generous ½ cup
    kosher salt

3785 g / 4 quarts water

FOR THE SPICES (OPTIONAL)

1 tablespoon coriander seeds
    or 4 to 5 umbels green
    coriander

1 tablespoon dill seeds, 2 to
    3 large umbels of dill seeds,
    or 2 to 3 (4-inch) dill fronds

2 teaspoons black peppercorns

3 to 4 fresh or dried chilies,
    such as habanero or jalapeño,
    to taste

Place the tomatoes, garlic, spices if using, and salt in a large bowl and toss gently to coat. Cover with a plate or plastic wrap and let sit at room temperature for 30 minutes.

(recipe continues)

Transfer to a clean 1-gallon crock and pour enough water to cover the tomatoes. Submerge the tomatoes using fermentation weights, secure the lid, and ferment at room temperature for 5 to 7 days, checking periodically to make sure the tomatoes are submerged. When they have reached your preferred flavor, transfer the tomatoes and brine to a lidded container and place in the refrigerator, where they will keep for up to 1 year.

OPPOSITE *Although the smallest of these fruits may be mistaken for a tomato, these eggplants demonstrate the colorful and diverse spectrum of the nightshade family.*

THE NIGHTSHADE FAMILY

The nightshade family includes more than 2,800 species of plants—some edible, while most are poisonous, at least to some degree. It is a fascinating grouping of plants found across the world, with 13% of them estimated for extinction if current trends persist. Nightshades are not only used for food, but some types have hallucinogenic and drug-related effects. The origin of the family's scientific name, Solanaceae, alludes to the mysterious nature of its sedative properties; *solanum* comes from the Latin root *solamen*, meaning "to quiet." Tobacco (*Nicotiana tabacum*), belladonna (*Atropa belladonna*), thorn apple (*Datura stramonium*), and henbane (*Hyoscyamus niger*) all produce alkaloids that affect the human nervous system, producing mild narcotic effects at best and a permanent tranquilizer (otherwise known as death) at their worst. Although the origin of the common English name *nightshade* has been debated, it describes plants that love the dark of night.

The majority of edibles in the nightshade family—tomatoes, peppers, potatoes, and eggplant—are commonly cultivated during the warmest months of the year. These are heat-loving plants that need to be started indoors for areas with a short growing season and transplanted out after the last danger of frost. For regions with cool, damp summers, nightshades are better grown in a tunnel or hoop house where temperatures can be manipulated to extend the season.

There is an enormous variety of heirloom cultivars in the Solanaceae family, many of which have been given little attention. I am always amazed at the dazzling display of colors and shapes of those found in Asian or Indian markets. When I come across varieties I am unfamiliar with, I approach a shopper whose knowing eyes suggest they might share some pointers with me. I have discovered many new fruits and vegetables this way, from the bitter green likok eggplant used in curries to the tiny clustered *Solanum torvum* that more than a few Filipino mothers have shared their secret for mashing in a mortar and pestle with shrimp paste, ginger, and garlic to make a seasoning for fish.

GREEN TOMATO *and* EGGPLANT SHAKSHUKA

Serves 3 to 4

Shakshuka, a North African dish of eggs stewed into a spicy tomato sauce, has become highly popular throughout the Middle East, and it has recently earned its place on brunch menus across the United States as well. My devotion to farm-fresh eggs as an inexpensive protein means I will also eagerly prepare this for dinner. Using green tomatoes or a combination of green and red adds a splash of acidity to the sauce. The result isn't quite the stunning red typically associated with shakshuka, but heaps of fresh herbs give it some serious eye appeal.

3 cups coarsely chopped green (or combination of green and red) tomatoes

¾ teaspoon salt

1 teaspoon smoked paprika

1 teaspoon ground cumin

¾ teaspoon Aleppo, Urfa Biber, or another type of red pepper flakes

2 tablespoons extra-virgin olive oil

½ cup diced red onion

10 to 12 baby eggplants, halved

2 cloves garlic, minced

¼ cup heavy cream

1 small red bell pepper, diced

3 packed cups Swiss chard, kale, or spinach leaves, coarsely chopped

4 to 6 large eggs

FOR THE GARNISH

3 or 4 dollops of labneh or sour cream

2 to 3 tablespoons fresh herbs (cilantro, parsley, mint, and/or chives work well)

A sprinkling of Aleppo, Urfa Biber, or another type of red pepper flakes

Bread, to serve with, such as Table Loaf, Pita, or Nomad Bread

Place the tomatoes, salt, paprika, cumin, and red pepper flakes in the bowl of a food processor and blend on high speed until smooth. Set aside.

Heat the oil in a 10-inch skillet over medium heat. Add the onion and eggplants, and cook until the eggplants are softened and the onion is translucent, 6 to 7 minutes. Add the garlic and cook for about 1 minute, until fragrant. Add the tomato mixture and cook for 10 to 12 minutes, stirring occasionally to prevent sticking, until it is somewhat thickened. Add the cream and bell pepper and cook for

another 3 to 4 minutes, until the peppers have slightly softened. Add the chopped greens and cook until just wilted. If serving in individual cast-iron skillets, divide the mixture evenly into each before proceeding to the next step.

Using a spoon, make small divots in the mixture and break the eggs into each depression. Cover and cook until the whites are cooked through and the yolks are set or runny to your liking, about 8 minutes. Garnish with the labneh, herbs, and red pepper flakes and serve.

TOMATO COULIS, SAUCE, *or* PASTE

Makes 3½ to 4 cups

This recipe can be made into a thick paste, a chunky sauce, or a smooth, lightly seasoned coulis. It is wonderfully easy to make and then stash away in the freezer for a midwinter reprieve. When celery root arrives at the market, I will substitute one third of the weight of the tomatoes with peeled chunks for an earthy pasta sauce, or thin it to make a velvety coulis or soup base.

2 tablespoons extra-virgin olive oil

3½ pounds paste tomatoes (about 12 large tomatoes), halved

3½ pounds juicy salad tomatoes (about 3 large tomatoes), quartered

1 head garlic, peeled

8 sprigs thyme

3 sprigs oregano

3 tablespoons balsamic vinegar

1 tablespoon sugar or honey

2 teaspoons salt

½ teaspoon freshly ground black pepper

Preheat the oven to 350°F.

Grease a large roasting pan with the oil and arrange the tomatoes cut-side up on the pan. Distribute the garlic cloves among the tomatoes and nestle the thyme and oregano in between. Sprinkle with the vinegar, sugar, salt, and pepper and toss to coat. Roast, stirring occasionally, for about 1½ hours, until the tomatoes begin to take on a caramelized glow but are still swimming in their own juices. If you are using heirloom tomatoes, this may take longer, as they characteristically hold more water.

If you would like to make a rustic sauce for Fermented Pasta (page 70), cool, remove the herbs, and coarsely chop with a chef's knife. If you would like a smooth coulis for Grilled Eggplant with Buttermilk Tahini Sauce (page 294), blend in a food processor, then run through a coarse sieve or food mill, adding liquid, such as water or broth, if you would like a thinner consistency. For a thicker pizza sauce, after running the tomatoes through the sieve, continue cooking on the stovetop for another 30 minutes, or until reduced to your liking. For a more concentrated thick paste, cook for another hour, stirring often, until the juices have evaporated and the tomatoes are evenly browned, then blend. Store covered in the refrigerator for up to 1 week, or place in gallon-sized bags and freeze flat for up to 6 months. If you would like to hot-water can your sauce, add 2 tablespoons lemon juice before processing (see page 17).

GRILLED EGGPLANT *with* BUTTERMILK TAHINI SAUCE *and* TOMATO COULIS

Serves 4 to 6

Eggplant are easy-to-grow, generous plants related to tomatoes, peppers, and ground cherries, and this preparation is one of the easiest and most beloved of my summer repertoire. The smokiness of grilled eggplant pairs perfectly with tangy tahini sauce and a ladling of tomato coulis. You will make more than enough tahini for this recipe; it is a versatile condiment that can accompany a variety of sides and summer salads. It is essential for Beet Falafel (page 231) and adds a creamy savory quality to avocado toast. Choose any type of eggplant you like; I prefer a combination of heirloom lavender or purple-streaked elongated fruits or their dark-skinned Turkish cousins, as they are mild without bitterness and lend well to grilling. Soaking eggplant in a salt-water bath before grilling will not only season the flesh but leach any lingering bitterness.

FOR THE SAUCE
2 cloves garlic
¼ cup fresh flat-leaf parsley and/or mint
¼ cup fresh chives
1 teaspoon fine sea salt
1 cup tahini
1 cup whole buttermilk
¼ cup fresh lemon juice
¼ cup water
½ cup extra-virgin olive oil

FOR THE EGGPLANT
2 pounds eggplant
About 2 tablespoons kosher salt
2 tablespoons fresh lemon juice
½ cup extra-virgin olive oil
1 cup Tomato Coulis (page 293) or other tomato sauce

FOR THE GARNISH
Generous sprinkling of flaked sea salt
2 to 3 tablespoons fresh herbs (cilantro, mint, parsley, and/ or chopped chives work well)

MAKE THE SAUCE

Combine the garlic, parsley, chives, and salt in a food processor and coarsely chop. Add the tahini, buttermilk, lemon juice, and water and process until creamy. With the processor running, drizzle in the oil through the hole in the lid to emulsify. You can store the sauce in the refrigerator for up to 1 week.

MAKE THE EGGPLANT

Slice the eggplant into generous halves, smaller quarters, or thick rounds and place into a large bowl. Sprinkle the cut sides generously with salt and allow to sit for about 10 minutes, then pour in warm water to cover and add the lemon juice.

(recipe continues)

OPPOSITE *Use a combination of colorful mild-to-sweet eggplant varieties for this recipe.*

Soak the eggplant for at least 30 minutes or up to 3 hours for more bitter eggplant while you preheat the grill to medium heat.

Drain the eggplant and pat the flesh dry. Use a pastry brush to coat the eggplant in oil, then place cut-side down onto the grill grate. Close the lid and cook until softened and fork tender, 5 to 12 minutes depending on their size, flipping when the flesh shows signs of attractive grill marks. Brush with more oil, sprinkle with a pinch of salt, and finish cooking skin-side down.

Add a generous ladle of tahini to two small serving platters or one large serving platter, then add a generous ladle of tomato coulis and arrange the grilled eggplant on top. Garnish with flaked sea salt and the herbs. Serve immediately.

Author Sarah Owens preparing Buttermilk Tahini Sauce for a dinner at Edgemere Farm near her home in Rockaway Beach.

PICKLED MINI EGGPLANT

Makes 1 gallon

One of my first cooking jobs was working the line at a casual fine dining Persian restaurant where the exotic flavors of this once broad-reaching empire were revealed. My favorite condiment was torshi, a vinegar-preserved mix of eggplant, carrots, herbs, and spices that was used as a flavor enhancer for braised lamb. Although its root word comes from the Persian *torsh*, meaning "sour," this pickle is common in Turkish, Armenian, Greek, and Serbian cuisines as well. The blended, saucy version I was first introduced to required many weeks of curing to reach its proper flavor. I have since discovered that no one recipe is the same regardless of how hard I try to replicate it from memory.

This recipe pickles endearingly small, delicately flavored eggplants whole with a bold blend of spices. They are a perfect companion to grilled or braised meats. I prefer fairytale hybrid eggplants with hues of amethyst, garnet, and onyx for their creamy flesh, but you may use stronger-flavored Asian types as well. Serve on a platter drizzled with a fine-quality extra-virgin olive oil, a sprinkling of fresh herbs, and a pinch of Aleppo or Urfa Biber pepper flakes.

3½ pounds small eggplants

4 to 5 garlic scapes

6 late-season ramp bulbs (about 2 ounces) or an equivalent weight of garlic cloves

3 medium carrots, sliced

3 tablespoons kosher salt

2 to 3 tablespoons honey

3 whole bay leaves

3 whole star anise

1 teaspoon whole allspice berries

1 teaspoon whole black peppercorns

1 teaspoon whole cloves

One 4-inch stick cinnamon

3 cups red wine vinegar or sherry vinegar

Bring a large stockpot of water to a rolling boil and prepare a bath of ice and water.

Carefully place the eggplant, stems and all, into the pot. Cook for about 3 minutes (depending on their size), until they have just softened and their skins pierce easily with a fork. Using a slotted spoon, transfer the eggplant to the ice-water bath to cool, then remove from the water. Drop the garlic scapes and ramp bulbs into the hot water and heat through, 3 to 4 minutes, then transfer to a 1-gallon jar. Layer the carrots and cooled eggplant into the jar.

Make a brine by ladling 3 cups of hot water from the pot into a large bowl; add the salt, honey, and spices. Add the vinegar and stir until the salt and honey have dissolved. Pour over the contents of the jar, cool completely, then place in the refrigerator. They are ready after 8 hours but are best enjoyed after several weeks in the brine. They will keep for up to 1 year in the refrigerator.

GREEN TOMATO *and* LEMON GINGER JAM

Makes about 4 pints

Don't let the odd color of this jam fool you, as its fresh and bright flavors make it a wonderful preserve to stock away for the winter months, and it makes excellent use of hard little knobby green tomatoes. When the beans start going to seed and the roses flush a final exhalation of summer, I break out the preserving pot with the anticipation of falling leaves and mornings of freshly baked bread slathered with this preserve.

3 large lemons
10½ cups green tomatoes, cut into ½-inch pieces

One 6-inch piece fresh ginger, peeled and grated
2 cinnamon sticks

2 teaspoons ground cardamom
1 teaspoon ground allspice
6 cups sugar

Using a sharp paring knife or vegetable peeler, remove the outer layer of lemon rind, leaving behind the bitter inner pith. Cut the rind into thin slivers and juice the lemons. Place the rind, lemon juice, tomatoes, ginger, cinnamon, cardamom, and allspice into a large, wide pot. Bring to a simmer over medium heat and cook until the lemon rind is tender and the mixture has reduced by at least one quarter, 35 to 40 minutes. If you would like a better set, cool and allow the mixture to steep overnight to draw out additional pectin from the lemon. Otherwise, prepare a hot water bath at this time for sterilizing the canning jars and a separate saucepan of water for the lids (but not rings). Process for at least 10 minutes (see page 17). Dip the lids into the hot water, then remove and allow to dry. Place a small plate in the freezer.

When the lemon rind is tender, turn off the heat and stir in the sugar a little at a time until fully

dissolved. Turn the heat to medium-high and return to a rolling boil, skimming off any foam that accumulates on the surface. Cook, stirring, to keep the bottom from scorching. After about 12 minutes, check for a set by drizzling a small amount of jam onto the frozen plate. Return to the freezer for 2 minutes, then push your finger through the jam. If your finger mark remains, it is ready to be transferred to the sterilized jars, or continue cooking until the jam has thickened sufficiently. Remove the cinnamon sticks from the jam.

Transfer the sterilized jars from the hot water bath to a clean surface. Ladle the hot jam into the hot jars, leaving ½ inch headspace, and cover with lids. Screw the rings onto the jars and carefully lower them back into the hot water bath. Bring to a simmer and process for 10 minutes. Remove the jars from the hot water bath and allow to cool completely at room temperature, checking the lids within 24 hours for a seal. If the jars have not sealed properly, promptly place in the refrigerator and eat within 2 months. Properly sealed jam will keep for up to 1 year stored in a cool, dry location.

OPPOSITE *Bicolor heirloom 'Striped German' is full and sweet with a peachy texture that bruises easily. Like most heirloom tomatoes, these are best plucked from your own garden or purchased from a local farmers' market.*

SPICED GROUND CHERRY, LEMON, *and* APPLE PRESERVES

Makes about 2 pints

Although still somewhat obscure, ground cherries are making their way into farmers' markets and specialty stores for their ease of cultivation and long shelf life. I find them at their sweetest toward the end of summer and prefer the smaller ones to make this jam. Their natural pectin content creates a pleasing, thick set when allowed to steep after cooking. Serve on toast or a cheese board alongside your choice of charcuterie.

750 g / 4⅔ cups ground cherries
One 6-inch piece fresh ginger, peeled and finely grated
4 large lemons

½ cup orange juice (from 2 oranges)
2 large apples
6 star anise pods

1½ cups sugar
1 cup honey

Remove the outside husks of the ground cherries. If they are large with pronounced stem attachments, slice them in half and cut away the small core. Otherwise, leave them whole and place them in a medium pot along with the ginger. Using a sharp paring knife or a vegetable peeler, remove the outer skin from the lemons, leaving behind the bitter inner pith. Thinly slice the lemon skin into strips and place in the pot. Juice the lemons into the pot and add the orange juice in the pot, reserving any seeds. Peel and core the apples, reserving the peel and core. Finely chop the apples and stir them into the pot. Bundle the apple skins, cores, and any citrus seeds in a piece of cheesecloth and tie it securely closed. Nestle the bundle into the pot and bring to a simmer over medium heat. Reduce the heat to medium-low and cook for about 20 minutes, stirring frequently, until the apples soften and the ground cherries burst. Remove from the heat, transfer to a non-reactive bowl, and cover. Allow to steep for about 4 hours, or cool and steep in the refrigerator overnight.

Sterilize the jars according to directions on page 17. Remove the cheesecloth bundle, squeeze any absorbed juice back into the mixture, and transfer back into the pot. Bring to a simmer over medium heat and stir in the sugar and honey. Reduce the heat to medium-low and simmer for 15 to 20 minutes, stirring occasionally, until the mixture passes the set test (see page 18). Transfer to the sterilized jars and process in a hot water bath for 10 minutes. Store in a cool location for up to 1 year.

GROUND CHERRIES

Ground cherries are a general name for a small sweetly tart fruit included in the Solanaceae, or nightshade, family. They are charming golden orbs that resemble a tomato but are encompassed by a papery outer sheath much like a tomatillo, a fruit that shares the same genus, *Physalis*. The first time I tried one was in northern Italy, its delicate spidery husk pulled back to reveal a chocolate-dipped berry dusted in powdered sugar. It was a simple but decadent end to the meal that left a memorable impression on my palate.

It wasn't until I was traveling through Ecuador that I encountered them once more, this time in the form of *Physalis peruviana*. A small child in Vilcabamba approached to ask if I wanted to buy a rather large bag of Inca berries about the length of her body for a paltry few bucks. Unrecognizable by this name and in their huskless state, I poked my nose into the bag and inhaled a tropical pineapple perfume that spoke of an ancient civilization. The rest of the day I wandered around the endless spring of those evergreen hills mindlessly reaching into the bag for more, their plump seediness bursting with juicy acidity in my mouth. Their common name led me to wonder how such a mighty empire that cultivated these native fruits in abundance could fall at the hands of its conqueror, unless, perhaps, these candy-like snacks had been a desirable point of contention.

WILD CARROT SYRUP

Makes about 2 pints

Daucus carota, or wild carrot, is an introduced, edible pasture weed that is the ancestor of domesticated carrots. All parts of the plant are edible if harvested at the appropriate time, but I prefer the prolific blooms in high summer when they blanket rural hillsides and disguise abandoned urban landscapes with whispers of charming lacey blooms. The umbelliferous heads with a tiny central red dot attract a wide diversity of insect activity with fragrant nectar, signaling their potential for culinary flavor. Do be sure to properly identify the plant with hairy stems and stalk and a carrot- or parsnip-like root, as there are a few highly poisonous impostors. Harvest the blooms in a combination of stages for a wider range of flavor, ranging from freshly flowered to those that are beginning to set seed and curl.

This wild carrot syrup tastes mildly of both carrot and a sweeter, more perfumed hint of nutty caraway. It is delightful served with a sparkling beverage, such as seltzer, or a dry carbonated white wine or prosecco and a squeeze of lemon. It is an essential ingredient for A Stranger's Door Cocktail (page 147), or you may combine it with pectin following the manufacturer's directions if you would like to make a jelly.

2 packed cups (2 ounces) Queen Anne's lace blossoms, stems removed

3 cups water

1 cup sugar

⅔ cup mild honey

5 tablespoons fresh lemon juice

Place the blossoms in a large nonreactive bowl. In a medium saucepan, heat the water and sugar over medium heat, stirring until dissolved. Turn off the heat and allow to cool for 5 minutes, then stir in the honey. Pour over the blossoms and stir in the lemon juice. Cover and allow to steep for 1 to 2 hours, checking periodically for flavor. Strain into a sterilized jar, cover, and store in the refrigerator for up to 3 months.

PRESERVED STONE FRUIT *in* HERB SYRUP

One of the most beautiful sights of summer is a fruit tree burdened with the weight of apricots, peaches, or plums. When I am short on time to process this abundance, I will often turn to this recipe to preserve them for later use. These glistening beauties benefit from the creative addition of a few herbs and are quite versatile in their use in a syrup. Spoon them over ice cream, muddle them into a cocktail, whirl them with a little yogurt for a refreshing smoothie or chilled soup, or drain and toss with a little lemon zest before baking into a galette.

1 part water
1 part granulated sugar
Fresh whole stone fruits:
    peaches, nectarines, plums,
    or cherries

Three to four 4-inch sprigs
    fresh herbs (lemon thyme,
    tarragon, shiso, basil, or
    rosemary work well)

Place your fruits into a large sterilized jar and cover with water short of 2 inches. Transfer this water into a large pot and add an equal amount of sugar *by weight* to the pot. Heat over medium heat, stirring to dissolve the sugar. Bring to a boil and gently slide the fruits into the pot. If using pungent woody herbs such as rosemary, lavender, or lemon verbena, add them to the pot now. Simmer for 3 to 5 minutes, before the skins start to loosen but the flesh looks like it has softened. Using a slotted spoon, carefully transfer the fruits back into the jar. Pour the syrup over the fruit, cover, and cool completely. Slip in the herbs, then store in the refrigerator for up to 2 months.

MINI FRUIT GALETTES

Makes 5 or 6

When the markets swell with soft peaches, glistening plums, plump cherries, juicy blueberries, or tart currants, there is no better time to make these rustic, flaky desserts that sing of summer's joy. Using a Fermented Whole-Grain Piecrust (page 58) brings an added dimension of nutty, digestible flavor, and I prefer to keep the fruit somewhat simple, with the flexibility to get creative if you wish! When shopping for ingredients, it is paramount to source the best stone-ground heirloom soft wheat you can find and fruit that is at its peak of ripeness to make these easy-to-assemble tarts really shine. You can let your imagination run with potential combinations—choose to use a single fruit or pair apricots with red currants, peaches with small tomatoes, or blackberries with thinly sliced apples. For an added dimension, consider using a generous tablespoon of fresh herbs in either the crust or the fruit mixture. Two of my favorite combinations are blueberry, lime zest, cinnamon, and basil; and peach, tomato, and lemon thyme. The possibilities are endless, but do be aware that the fruit will vary from season to season, so taste before adding the sugar, adjusting to your preferred level of sweetness.

I am not a fan of fruit pies made with thickeners such as cornstarch, but if you prefer the fruit juices to run a little gooier, feel free to sprinkle a tablespoon of arrowroot powder or flour over the fruit before tossing.

1 recipe Fermented Whole-
   Grain Piecrust dough
   (page 58)
1¼ pounds fruit of your choice

¼ cup granulated sugar
2 teaspoons fresh lemon juice
1 teaspoon lemon or orange zest

FOR THE EGG WASH
1 egg yolk
1 teaspoon mild honey
Generous dash of milk or cream
2 tablespoons coarse sugar

PREPARE THE DOUGH
Make the dough the day before you plan to bake the galettes. This will allow the whole grains to fully hydrate, which will make the crust easier to roll out. For a flakier result, remove the dough from the refrigerator and roll to ¼-inch thickness. It may be somewhat crumbly at first, but with the assistance of a bench scraper to release the dough from the work surface, it will come together. Fold into thirds like a letter (top down, bottom up and overlapping). Rotate the dough and roll and fold again. Wrap it in plastic wrap and place it in the refrigerator for at least another 30 minutes before rolling to fill with fruit.

(recipe continues)

OPPOSITE *These small open-faced pies celebrate the abundance of summer fruit with a fermented whole-grain crust.*

PREPARE THE FRUIT FILLING

If using berries, simply toss them in a large bowl with the remaining ingredients, allowing to rest and macerate for at least 20 minutes or up to 3 hours before filling the crust. If using whole stone fruits or apples, slice them before tossing. I prefer stone fruits sliced ¼ to ½ inch thick; apples appreciate a thinner slice on a mandoline to ensure quick baking.

ASSEMBLE THE GALETTES

Line a baking sheet with parchment paper.

In a small bowl, whisk the egg yolk, honey, and milk for the wash and set aside.

Divide the dough into 5 or 6 even pieces and roll to a thickness of about ¼ inch. If using extra-juicy fruit such as peaches or berries, be careful not to roll too thinly so that the crust will hold up to the fruit. Place each onto the prepared baking sheet and drain the fruit of excess juice. Fill generously with fruit, leaving a 1½- to 2-inch space from the edge. Envelop the fruit with the crust, folding, overlapping, and gently pressing the creases as necessary. Apply the egg wash to the crust and sprinkle the crust and fruit generously with the coarse sugar. Place the assembled galettes in the freezer for 15 minutes to firm up before baking.

BAKE THE GALETTES

While the galettes are in the freezer, preheat the oven to 425°F.

Place the chilled galettes in the oven and bake for 22 to 25 minutes, rotating halfway. Do not be tempted to bake these too blond, as the crust will hold up better to the juiciness of the fruit if you allow it to darken to a beautiful, bold brown. Remove from the oven and allow to rest for a few minutes before transferring to a cooling rack. Serve warm or at room temperature with a dollop of vanilla ice cream, or just eat savagely straight out of hand.

BUCKWHEAT BERRY TARTLETS
with LEMON HERB CREAM

Makes 8 tartlets

Dessert often comes when you're too full to appreciate it, even if it is the most delectable creation possible. These little tartlets that combine the earthy character of a thick buckwheat crust with the light tartness of an herbed cream are a perfectly refreshing finish to a meal. Choose whatever herbs or flower blossoms are most available to you: jasmine, honeysuckle, black locust, or rose petals are all light and delightfully graceful. Or choose a bolder herb such as lemon verbena instead, tasting along the way until you've achieved your preferred flavor. Make the crust and cream a day in advance and assemble just before serving. Garnish with whatever fruit is in season. I prefer a combination of jeweled currants, gooseberries, blackberries, and currants nestled into the cream.

FOR THE HERB CREAM

470 g / 2 cups heavy cream

Four 4-inch sprigs lemon verbena or rosemary, 1 vanilla pod, split, 12 fresh jasmine blossoms, or 1 tablespoon fresh lavender blossoms

Zest and juice of 1 lemon

250 g / 1¼ cups sugar

115 g / ½ cup unsalted butter, at room temperature

Generous pinch of fine sea salt

3 large eggs

2 large egg yolks

FOR THE CRUST

125 g / 1 cup + 1½ tablespoons whole wheat pastry flour

50 g / ½ cup buckwheat flour

30 g / 3 tablespoons sugar

Pinch of salt

75 g / 5 tablespoons unsalted butter, cubed

1 large egg, beaten

10 g / about 1 tablespoon water, if needed

FOR THE GARNISH

About 1 cup fresh fruit such as blackberries, small gooseberries, sliced figs, or red or champagne currants

Handful of edible flowers

INFUSE THE CREAM

Several hours or up to a day before assembling the tarts, combine the cream and herbs in a medium saucepan and heat until steaming but not boiling. Remove from the heat and allow to steep until cool, tasting along the way for flavor strength. Remove the herbs when the mixture is cool or satisfies your palate. Store covered in the refrigerator until ready to use.

PREPARE THE CRUST

Whisk together the flours, sugar, and salt in a medium bowl. Cut in the butter using a pastry

(recipe continues)

cutter, fork, or your fingertips until the mixture resembles coarse crumbs. Add the beaten egg and toss to combine. Test to see if the mixture is fully hydrated by grabbing and squeezing a clump of the dough in the palm of your hand; if it comes together without crumbling apart, do not add the water. If it crumbles and feels dry, sprinkle in the water, adding more if needed until the dough just comes together.

BAKE THE CRUST

Preheat the oven to 400°F and lightly grease 8 holes of a muffin pan.

Press 2 to 3 tablespoons of the mixture into the prepared muffin pan, lightly pressing to achieve an even surface. Repeat until all of the mixture is used. Prick the surface of the pastry lightly with a fork and place in the refrigerator for 10 minutes, or until the pastry stiffens. Place in the oven and bake until lightly golden around the edges, about 10 minutes. Remove from the oven and allow to cool for about 10 minutes, then transfer to a wire rack.

PREPARE THE CUSTARD

Using the back of a large spoon, smoosh together the lemon zest and sugar in the bowl of a stand mixer to release the aromatic citrus oils. Add the butter and salt and beat together until thick and creamy. With the mixer running, add the eggs and yolks one at a time until fully incorporated. Pour in the lemon juice and continue mixing until homogenous.

Pour the mixture into a medium heavy-bottomed saucepan and cook over low heat for about 10 minutes, until thickened and an instant-read thermometer registers 170°F. Remove from the heat and cool completely, placing a piece of plastic flush with the surface to discourage a skin. Store in the refrigerator until ready to use.

ASSEMBLE THE TARTLETS

In a large clean bowl, whip the cream until light and fluffy but not stiff. Just before serving, fold the whipped cream into the lemon curd and fill the pastry cups almost to the top, leaving some room for the fresh fruit. Artfully nestle the fruit on top of the cream and garnish with edible flowers. Serve immediately.

PURPLE BARLEY MILK CAKE

Makes one 9 × 13-inch cake

This recipe is inspired by the Latin American milk-soaked cake *pastel de tres leches* but reimagined here as a whole-grain, slightly less sweet version. This celebration dessert revered for its silky moist texture and pleasing mouthfeel became popular in the mid-twentieth century. It is a delightfully refreshing summer cake when served chilled and topped with fresh berries and a dusting of cinnamon.

This recipe attempts to satisfy the texture and comforting experience of tres leches but using nontraditional ingredients and techniques. I use heirloom purple barley flour, a naturally sweet grain that lends a mild malted flavor to the cake and its topping, along with whole wheat pastry flour to lighten the crumb. Soft white Sonoran wheat is an excellent choice for its tender, creamy flavor as well as its historical roots tracing back to the Sonoran Desert. If you cannot source purple barley flour (see Resources, page 324), you may substitute additional whole wheat pastry flour.

Canned evaporated and condensed milks, both used in traditional tres leches cake, have had their enzymes destroyed by processing, making the lactose more difficult to digest. Making them both from scratch and adding an active culture helps to alleviate this digestive challenge. Start the night before you intend to serve the cake.

FOR THE SAUCE
230 g / 1 cup whole purple barley
635 g / 2¾ cups whole milk
128 g / ½ cup half-and-half
60 g / ¼ cup heavy cream
100 g / ½ cup sugar
One 3-inch stick cinnamon
30 g / ⅓ cup plain Milk Kefir (page 39) or equivalent weight unstrained yogurt

FOR THE CAKE
55 g / ½ cup purple barley flour
55 g / ½ cup whole wheat pastry flour
1½ teaspoons baking powder
¼ teaspoon fine salt
5 large eggs, separated
150 g / ¾ cup sugar
75 g / ⅓ cup whole milk
1 teaspoon pure vanilla extract
150 g / 1 cup fresh or frozen wild blueberries

FOR THE WHIPPED TOPPING
420 g / 1¾ cups heavy cream
15 g / 1 heaping tablespoon Pomegranate Paste (page 124) or maple syrup
Generous pinch of salt

FOR THE GARNISH (OPTIONAL)
Several handfuls of fresh berries (blueberries, blackberries, or raspberries work well)
Dusting of ground cinnamon

MAKE THE SAUCE

Preheat the oven to 350°F.

Spread the barley onto a baking sheet in an even layer and toast for 8 to 10 minutes, until it fills the kitchen with a nutty fragrance.

In a medium saucepan, combine the milk, half-and-half, heavy cream, and toasted barley and heat over medium heat until just simmering—do not let it boil. Reduce for 1 hour over low heat, stirring occasionally to prevent a skin from forming on the surface, until it thickens slightly. Turn off the heat and allow to steep for at least 1 hour, or cool, cover, and steep in the refrigerator overnight. Strain out the barley and reserve it to cook for porridge, or use in Oxtail Borscht with Sour Cherries and Purple Barley (page 176). Return the milk to the saucepan and add in the sugar and cinnamon stick. Continue to cook over low heat, reducing to a thick sauce, about 1 hour. Remove from the heat and discard the cinnamon stick.

BAKE THE CAKE

Preheat the oven to 350°F and lightly butter a 9 × 13-inch baking dish.

Sift the flours, baking powder, and salt into a medium bowl. Whip the egg whites while slowly adding in ¼ cup of the sugar until stiff peaks form. In a separate bowl, beat the egg yolks and remaining ½ cup sugar. Beat the milk and vanilla into the yolks, then add to the dry ingredients, stirring to combine. Fold the egg whites and blueberries into the batter until just combined—do not overmix or you will lose the air. Pour into the prepared baking dish and bake for 35 to 40 minutes, until a toothpick inserted into the center of the cake tests clean. Cool in the baking dish.

DRENCH AND TOP THE CAKE

When the cake has almost completely cooled, use a toothpick to generously poke small holes into the surface. Whisk the sweetened milk with the milk kefir and pour slowly and evenly over the cake, allowing it to soak the crumb.

Combine the heavy cream, pomegranate paste, and salt in the bowl of a stand mixer. Whip on medium-high speed until the topping is thick and spreadable, about 3 minutes. Spoon onto the top of the cake and use an offset spatula or knife to spread it evenly over the surface. Garnish as desired. Serve immediately, or cover and refrigerate for up to 2 days.

TRES LECHES CAKE

There is much speculation as to how, when, and where tres leches cake originated. It is enthusiastically claimed by both Mexico and Nicaragua, with various recipes found throughout their neighboring countries. Although it seems to be a fairly recent addition to the culinary repertoire of the Americas, soaked cakes are not a new phenomenon. Examples can be found all over the world, from the familiar coffee-laden tiramisu, Caribbean rum-drenched cakes, and custardy British trifle to the more exotic Middle eastern kunafa cake that whispers of honey and rosewater.

To unlock the mystery of the origin of tres leches, we must examine its ingredients—namely, condensed milk, evaporated milk, and milk or cream. The first two are highly processed, industrialized products often distributed throughout regions where refrigeration is scarce or unreliable. Evaporated milk is fresh milk that has been heated to remove 60% of its water through evaporation before it is homogenized, fortified, and sterilized in cans. Condensed milk exists in a similar concentration to evaporated milk except that it contains about 40% sugar by weight. Evidence suggests companies like Nestlé, who opened factories in Mexico in the 1940s, are responsible for popularizing tres leches by printing recipes for it on the labels of their condensed milk and evaporated milk cans.

BREAD KVASS

Makes about 3 pints

Bread kvass is a lightly effervescent lacto-fermented Slavic beverage that is typically made of stale bread, water, and a sweetener. This recipe is made with bread crusts, which imparts a depth of flavor and uses up what might otherwise be composted from making bread crumbs or Apple Charlotte (page 115). If using the crumb of a loaf, consider toasting it to encourage more flavor. You may also substitute raw honey for the sugar; I find it imparts a more vigorous fermentation. If you do so, make sure to cool the water to at least 130°F before adding the honey to maintain its raw benefits. This ferment is most successful in a warm environment; clear the top of the refrigerator or set it next to a radiator if you are brewing it in winter.

Don't be afraid to let this recipe become a direct expression of your local terroir or bread-making practice. Invite your kvass to harness the flavor of heirloom grains, wild fruits, or foraged flavors such as spicebush (see page 135). Or you can let your imagination wander to even less conventional additions—occasionally I'll slip a sprig of mint or rosemary, blueberries, or kumquats into the mix. Although not traditional at all, one of my favorite variations is to include a handful of jujube dates and a tablespoon of toasted sesame seeds!

How sour you appreciate your kvass will depend on how long you let it ferment. I prefer mine with the sugars almost completely metabolized before consuming, making it a slightly puckery experience and rather refreshing served chilled on a warm summer day. Other people prefer it only a few days old, almost like a tart cola. If you are making kvass to increase the probiotics in your diet, I suggest letting it gain flavor for at least three to four days of fermentation at room temperature before decanting and storing in the refrigerator to mellow. About a week after decanting and storing under cooler temperatures is when I prefer to drink kvass, with the funkiness of the microbial world balanced by a reduction in sugar. Kvass is also wonderful harvested mature and used as an ingredient in Okroshka (page 282), to braise sausages, or in a marinade for meats such Pork Loin (page 179). Once strained, you may recycle the spent crusts to make Probiotic Granola Bars (page 318), giving your bread several cycles of life!

150 g / 2 cups bread crusts, cut or torn into 2- to 3-inch pieces

1380 g / 6 cups water

225 g / 1 cup sugar or equivalent volume of honey

(recipe continues)

Stale bread is recycled to make a refreshing fermented and carbonated beverage called kvass.

Place the crusts into a clean 2-quart jar with a noncorrosive lid. Heat the water to a simmer, then turn off the heat. Stir in the sugar until it dissolves and allow it to cool to at least 130°F. Pour over the crusts and give it a gentle stir. Cover loosely, place the jar on a small plate to catch any overflow, and tuck it away in a warm location. After 1 to 2 days, you will notice fermentation activity in the form of bubbles rising to the surface. These are the wild yeasts metabolizing the sugar and exhaling carbon dioxide gas as a by-product of fermentation. Dip a spoon into the fermenting mixture every few days to check on its flavor; strain it whenever it tastes pleasing to you or when you begin to notice its activity slowing down. To create another batch after decanting, simply use a few tablespoons of your last batch to inoculate and jump-start your new one, adding it to the jar once you stir in the cooled sugar water. You may find that after the third or fourth batch, you can decrease the amount of sugar by at least ¼ cup.

KVASS

Kvass is a low-alcohol, high-vitamin B probiotic drink with Russian origins, dating back to 989 A.D. when Prince Vladimir's baptism was recorded. The beverage was preferred as a more hygienic alternative to water, much like the origins of beer's popularity. Likewise, what we know of original kvass recipes is similar to how beer's ancient history was unveiled—recorded mostly by the literate (namely, monks). They described kvass using the term *zhivoi*, meaning "live," a word that appears much like *cheers* when enthusiastically toasting any alcoholic beverage in the Serbian language. Once you witness its exuberant performance, you will be reminded of the power of the invisible microbial world as it gurgles away, a gregarious companion whispering bubbles of primordial vitality tucked into a warm corner of your kitchen.

Kvass was historically made with many variations, including wheat or rye sourdough bread, flour only, sourdough starter only, beets only, sprouted grains, or any combination thereof along with a sugar source to activate carbonation by feeding the wild yeasts and bacteria. Birch sap water or honey was most likely used until granulated sugar became more widely available, and each household is famed to have had its own recipe. I have been told that raisins often make an appearance, as do other creative variations, including herbs, spices, or fresh fruit to flavor and sweeten the sourness of this fortifying beverage. More modern expressions of kvass range widely and enjoy an identity as a health drink in Slavic cultures as well as more adventurous Western fermenting trends. It is still poured from large tanks on the streets of the former Soviet Republic, enjoyed in frosty glass mugs—or more frequently, plastic cups—as a refreshing beverage on hot summer days.

PROBIOTIC GRANOLA BARS

Makes one 9½ × 14½-inch pan

One of the most important habits of the heirloom kitchen is avoiding food waste, and this recipe makes the most from by-products of two others in this book: Bread Kvass (page 315) and Hazelnut Milk (page 137). You may use any presoaked nut; toast the pulp first in a preheated 350°F oven for about 10 minutes for a touch of flavor before working it into this moist raw bar. I prefer these after they have been aged for a week or dehydrated at a very low temperature for a few hours, but you may enjoy them while still moist and somewhat sticky. As with most granola bars, the ingredients are fairly flexible, especially the nuts and seeds, so think of this recipe as a suggestion more than a fixed recipe.

160 g / ¾ cup pitted dried dates

215 g / 1 cup leftover bread from making Bread Kvass (page 315), strained of excess moisture

95 g / 1¼ cups leftover pulp from making Hazelnut Milk (page 137), toasted

170 g / ½ cup mild honey

60 g / ¼ cup smooth or chunky peanut butter

1 teaspoon ground cinnamon

250 g / 2 cups rolled oats, toasted

155 g / 1 cup almonds, toasted and coarsely chopped

60 g / ½ cup pepitas, toasted

35 g / ¼ cup black sesame seeds, toasted

30 g / ½ cup coconut flakes, toasted

1 teaspoon flaked sea salt

Combine the dates, bread, nut pulp, honey, peanut butter, and cinnamon in the bowl of a food processor and process on high speed until a thick paste forms. Transfer to a large bowl and stir in the oats, almonds, pepitas, and sesame seeds.

Line a 9½ × 14½-inch baking pan with parchment paper, wax paper, or plastic wrap and firmly press the oat mixture into the pan. Use the palms of your hands to compact the mixture; this will ensure that it will cut easily once chilled. Sprinkle the coconut flakes and flaked sea salt on top and firmly press them into the surface. Cover with plastic wrap and allow to sit at room temperature overnight. Cut into squares or rectangles the size of your choice and wrap in wax paper or plastic wrap. Store at room temperature or in the refrigerator for up to 2 weeks.

Acknowledgments

My deepest and sincerest gratitude is extended to David Selig, a slow food advocate whose insatiable appetite for bread led to our introduction and my occupation of The Castle Rockaway's basement, where I developed many of the baking recipes included in this book. The images included in *Heirloom* were captured both at The Castle and in the beautiful home of Matthew and Jessie Sheehan, both advocates for better food systems (and vintage baked goods!). I am continually beholden to Ngoc Minh Ngo for not only her tireless collaboration on the images for my past three projects but her commitment to revealing the peculiar beauty of the natural world. Many thanks to Brett Regot, whose talented skills, keen eye, and cooperative demeanor made the styling of both *Heirloom* and *Toast and Jam* a refreshing and inspired experience. Thank you also to stylist Mira Evnine, who stepped in with heroic resourcefulness for some cantankerous falafel! Sincerest gratitude for the use of Mako Nishimori's handmade ceramics made with profound reverence to the natural elements. Edgemere Farm is deeply appreciated for its continued commitment to providing fresh, seasonal food, honey, and eggs for the Rockaway table and sourcing farm-fresh products from other nearby producers. To Fabrizia Lanza of Anna Tasca Lanza Cooking School and Linda Sarris of Snack Sicily, my deepest gratitude for revealing the soul of Sicilia in her ancient grains. Thank you to the many friends and strangers who have written with enthusiasm to share your recipes or have invited me into your homes to reveal your traditions and family secrets for delicious, nourishing meals, including EunYoung Sebazco, Brant Stewart, Boshko Boskovic, Karim Massoud, George Pisegna, and Doris Loechle. And, of course, without the love and support of my family who taught me the social and nutritional value of small farms, I would not have the perspective that led me to investigate this book. I am deeply grateful for the many who have dedicated their livelihoods to bringing good grains back into our kitchens, including the many farmers and grain alliances who work so tirelessly in the face of environmental and economic challenges. Together we are making the changes that are needed to bake the world a better place.

Deepest thanks are extended to the whole team and especially to the editors at Roost Books, Jennifer Urban-Brown and Breanna Locke, for their fastidious attention to detail. And, of course, to my literary agent, Coleen O'Shea, for nudging me forward on the undefined path as an author. Finally, to anyone who has taken a class with me, thank you for your participation, as this dialogue only helps to increase the effectiveness of the recipes included here.

Appendix

BREAD BAKING BASICS

The following is a quick-reference guide of alphabetical terms related to the bread-baking recipes in this book.

Essential Equipment

Baker's Couche: A type of baker's linen that can be used to shape dough during final proofing, giving support to the loaves as well as preventing them from sticking together.

Bench Knife or Dough Scraper: Ideal for lifting bread dough and pastries from your work surface, this helpful tool will also assist in shaping wet dough.

Dutch Oven: These versatile baking pots are constructed of heavy, heat-retaining materials, such as cast iron or enamel-coated cast iron, allowing you to balance the heat and humidity needed to produce quality loaves in your own home kitchen. When used properly, they produce a hearty and rustic loaf with a thick, crispy crust and moist interior crumb. See individual recipes for complete instructions.

Hearthstone: A heavy slab made from ceramic, stone, or steel to retain heat, increasing the overall performance of your home oven in the production of hearth-style breads. It is useful in baking freeform breads or other breads that do not fit inside a Dutch oven. A hearthstone must be used in combination with steam in order to achieve a thick and crusty loaf. See "Baking with Steam" for complete instructions.

Lame: A double-sided blade used to score bread, often attached to the end of a handle. If making your own, use a thin, flexible blade and attach it to the end of an ice pop stick, chopstick, or whittled-down branch.

Loaf Pans: Two types of loaf pans are used in this book—most often a 2-pound, 9-inch standard pan, but sometimes an 8-inch, 1-pound pan. Choose a heavy gauge, preferably of aluminized steel made with a corrugated bottom.

Proofing Basket: A round or oblong basket used to shape and support dough in the final stages of bread proofing. Also called a brotform or banneton. If you are using a Dutch oven to bake your loaves, make sure the shape of the basket fits within the diameter of the Dutch oven.

Scale: If you are serious about becoming a home baker and fermentationist (if you bought this book, I assume you are!), please do purchase an inexpensive scale that measures in grams and ounces. Most of the baking recipes and ferments in this book are formulated by weight, with the percentages of ingredients calculated according to their biochemical interactions. (All ingredients in these recipes, including liquids, are measured in grams to prevent you from having to switch display screens mid-mix.) Although cultivating intuition in response to environmental and ingredient variables is key, using an accurate scale helps to eliminate guesswork in measuring by volume and ensures that your time invested yields successful results.

Thermometer: An instant-read thermometer removes the guesswork from gauging water temperature in dough mixing as well as if a dense loaf is ready to pull from the oven. An oven thermometer is also incredibly helpful for determining appropriate bake times, as every oven (particularly electric ovens) will behave differently.

Basic Techniques and Bread Vocabulary

Autolyze: A resting period in the initial stages of dough mixing, during which the flour is allowed time to hydrate and gluten proteins assemble to build dough strength.

Baking with Steam: The introduction of steam that ensures that the crust of bread remains soft during the first 15 to 20 minutes of baking, allowing the bread to expand freely. Place a heavy-gauge roasting pan in the oven while preheating a baking stone. Carefully pour warm water into the pan, covering to ½ inch, after loading the loaves into the oven. Make sure your oven's fans are turned off during this time. Remove the pan after 15 to 20 minutes of baking time if there is remaining water to allow the crust to set and become crisp.

Bench Rest: A resting period used most often after pre-shaping dough. This allows the dough to relax before being shaped into its final, tighter form.

Bulk Proof/Ferment: The period after mixing and working the dough either through kneading or a series of slap-and-folds. During this time, yeast consume the sugars present in the flour and release a by-product of carbon dioxide gas that leavens the dough. If using a sourdough culture, bacterial fermentation also occurs, releasing flavor compounds referred to as acetic and lactic acids. This is most often done at room temperature, but it may be performed in a colder, refrigerated environment as well.

Crumb: The interior of a loaf, defined by the holes or alveolation in the bread. A well-developed crumb is judged not necessarily by the size of the holes but rather by their consistency in relation to one another, indicating fermentation was thorough and shaping was done correctly. Depending on the type of flour used and its relative hydration, crumb performance will vary dramatically.

Crust: The exterior of the loaf where sugars concentrate and caramelize to produce a light golden to deep and dark brown toothsome outer layer. Generally, hearth-style loaves are baked *bien cuit*, or "well done," to allow full emancipation of steam from the crumb and to achieve a thick and bold dark crust. Other doughs include butter or oil and eggs to tenderize the loaf and are baked to have a thin, more delicate skin. Both methods produce rich flavor compounds, each quite different in character.

Kneading: Working the dough by hand to gain strength and elasticity. Done most often with doughs that are moderately hydrated to develop the gluten structure necessary to trap the gases that leaven bread.

Leaven: The intermediate step between your starter and mixing dough. Leaven is made from a small amount of refreshed starter with flour that may be the same or different from what you use to feed your starter. Likewise, the hydration of your leaven may be the same or different from how you maintain your starter, making it more stiff or more liquid. Although you may use the same amount of refreshed starter (fed 8 to 12 hours before you mix your dough) in place of leaven, following the recipe for leaven allows you to explore choices in flavor and texture in the resulting dough that may be different from when using your refreshed starter to make dough.

Mixing Dough: Mixing dough by hand brings together all the wet ingredients including leavening with all the dry ingredients to initiate dough fermentation. The leavening is often simply a 100% hydration sourdough starter (equal parts flour and water by weight) that has been refreshed for 8 to 12 hours previously or a customized leaven according to the recipe that includes specific flours. Commercial yeast may also be used. These leavening agents work with additional flour and a source of hydration, often water but sometimes juice, dairy, or eggs and also sweeteners that are mixed well until no dry lumps remain. When making one or two loaves it helps to work in a rhythmic squeezing motion, rotating the bowl with one hand while mixing with the other. Be sensitive to the textural feeling and temperature of the dough as you work, as this will help you to gauge fermentation during the succeeding steps.

Poke Test: Using a floured finger, gently push into the surface of the shaped dough. If the indentation springs back, the dough needs more time to proof before baking. If the indentation lingers, it is ready to bake.

Refresh: Often referred to as a "feed" when maintaining a sourdough starter. For the purposes of this book, starter is fed with equal parts flour and water by weight to the starter. This is done at room temperature 8 to 12 hours before the intended use, allowing it time to become active and visibly bubbly.

Retard: Slowing fermentation by cooling the dough in the refrigerator at temperatures ideally held between 36°F and 41°F. This encourages the development of acetic acids (recognized as a complex sour flavor in the baked bread) as well as the digestibility of the grain.

Scoring: Cutting into the surface of a loaf before loading it into the oven to be baked. This is done most often with a straight or curved razor blade or with a special baker's tool called a lame. Scoring is performed so that the loaf may expand in a controlled fashion, releasing steam in the process. To adequately score a loaf, all you need is one slash performed with an even motion halfway to three quarters from the edge of the loaf to a ¼- to ⅓-inch depth. Once you get the hang of it, you may want to play with more decorative patterns, adding shallow cuts for visual appeal.

Shaping: The handling of dough to form it into a particular shape for baking. This is typically done before the final proofing and involves two steps: pre-shaping with a short bench rest and a final shaping that pulls the dough into a tighter, more coercive form.

Specialized shaping procedures are described in the recipe instructions themselves, but the following are instructions to create a basic boule shape used for the Dutch oven method in this book: Remove the dough from the bowl and divide it on a floured work surface. Fold the edges of the dough ball into the center to create a circular shape, using your bench knife to assist with wet dough. Place the dough seam-side down on the work surface, cover it with plastic wrap or a damp kitchen towel, and allow it to visibly relax and bench rest for 10 to 20 minutes before final shaping. To final shape, use your bench scraper to turn the pre-shaped dough over seam-side up and repeat this process with greater coercion of the dough to create surface tension. Do not tear, rip, or over-fondle the dough, as this will lead to a heavy, dense bread. With naturally leavened dough, especially if it is more highly hydrated, it is important to create surface tension in the loaf to trap the gases in final proofing without deflating the dough in the process. If you are used to making bread with commercial yeast, do not punch down bread leavened solely with sourdough before shaping. This final step is a delicate balance that requires intuitive practice, using the dough's fermentation activity to guide your movements.

Slap-and-Fold: A way to work and develop wet dough shortly after mixing, in place of kneading. This encourages further strength in the dough that can trap leavening gases and will result in a more aerated, open crumb once baked. To perform the slap-and-fold technique, remove the dough from the bowl and slap it against a clean work surface, dragging the dough to stretch it before folding it over itself. This step is repeated in a rhythmic fashion until the dough transforms from a shaggy mass into a more cohesive, smooth form, 5 to 7 minutes. If the dough begins to tear on the surface, cover it with plastic wrap or a damp kitchen towel and allow it to rest for a few minutes before returning to the movement.

Stretch-and-Fold: A way to work wet dough in its mixing bowl in place of kneading on the work surface. Reach to the bottom of the bowl and gently pull a handful of the dough up and over itself, folding it to the center. Rotate the bowl with a series of turns until all of the dough has been stretched.

Resources

ETHICALLY FARMED AND PROCESSED LIVESTOCK

Backyard Terroir
www.backyardterroir.com
A working farm in Sebastopol, California, dedicated to heritage pigs, goats, and cows to produce delicious and mindfully crafted products available through their Share Forward program. Their website includes a considerable amount of knowledge on and observation of cheese making, charcuterie, and sourdough breads.

Eatwild
www.eatwild.com
Promotes the benefits—to consumers, farmers, animals, and the planet—of choosing meat, eggs, and dairy products from 100% grass-fed animals or other non-ruminant animals fed their natural diets. Eatwild is the number one clearinghouse for information about pasture-based farming and features a state-by-state directory of local farmers who sell directly to consumers.

Heritage Foods USA
www.heritagefoodsusa.com
A farm-to-table online butcher based in Brooklyn, New York, dedicated to supporting family farmers raising livestock with old-school genetics on pasture. These farmers cannot rely on the commodity market for sales because their animals take too long to grow. Turkeys, pigs, lamb, goats, chickens, ducks, and geese are all purchased nose-to-tail and sold online in cuts to customers in all 50 states as well as 130 of America's best restaurants. Heritage genetics are famous globally for their gastronomic attributes and are raised with no antibiotics, using traditional farming methods.

Local Harvest
www.localharvest.org
An online resource for connecting consumers to local farms and their products as well as CSAs.

Slow Food USA
www.slowfoodusa.org
Slow Food USA is part of the global Slow Food movement that is creating dramatic change in more than 160 countries. In the United States, there are more than 150 local chapters and 6,000 members connecting the pleasures of the table with a commitment to the communities, cultures, knowledge, and environment that make this pleasure possible.

FLOURS, GRAINS, AND LEGUMES

The following abbreviated list is continuously expanding with the demand for organic flour milled with integrity. Check with your local food cooperative or green market for the best sources in your area.

Anson Mills, Columbia, South Carolina
www.ansonmills.com
An incredible resource of heirloom grains, flours, seeds, and legumes shipped with astute attention to quality and freshness. Founder and visionary Glenn Roberts works with growers to bring back ingredients of pre-Civil War larder, making near-extinct varieties of heirloom corn, rice, and wheat available to chefs and home cooks alike.

Barton Springs Mill, Austin, Texas
www.bartonspringsmill.com
Organic stone-milled heirloom and landrace grains, many of which were grown in Texas in the early 1900s. Milled on demand for wholesale and retail customers.

Bluebird Grain Farms, Winthrop, Washington
www.bluebirdgrainfarms.com
Certified organic ancient grains, fresh-milled flour, and whole-grain handcrafted blends.

The Buckwheat Project,
Fort Kent, Maine
www.ployes.com
Mills tartary buckwheat flour for preparation of a
crepe called "Ployes," a recipe based on one created by
French Acadian exiles who settled in Northern Maine.

Camas Country Mill,
Junction City, Oregon
www.camascountrymill.com
Committed to building a strong, sustainable, and
vibrant regional grain economy, the mill is the natural
extension of the Hunton family's third-generation
farm.

Capay Mills, Rumsey, California
www.capaymills.com
David Kaisel, founder, farmer, and miller, is bringing
back the forgotten qualities and nutritional advantages
of freshly milled flour in northern California.

Carolina Ground, Asheville,
North Carolina
www.carolinaground.com
Female-owned and run mill shipping products grown
regionally with fine attention to quality and freshness.
Linking the farmer, miller, and baker together with
cold stone–milled flour of regional distinction,
province, and quality.

Central Milling, Logan, Richmond,
and Collinston, Utah; and Petaluma,
California
www.centralmilling.com
Employee-owned-and-operated mill working with
farmers to grow sustainable grains with exceptional
flavor, nutrient content, color, and tested baking
performance.

Community Grains, Oakland, California
www.communitygrains.com
Whole-grain products grown with integrity and
whole-milled to preserve the essential nutrients and
robust flavors lost to industrial milling.

Eat Grain
www.eatgrain.ca
Farm-direct Canadian dry goods including whole
wheat berries, farro, quinoa, lentils, and chickpeas to
make the hummus of your dreams.

Farmer Ground Flour via Cayuga Pure
Organics, Brooktondale, New York
www.farmergroundflour.com
A farmer and miller cooperative business that stone
mills organic grain harvested in the Finger Lakes
region of New York.

Four Star Farms,
Northfield, Massachusetts
www.fourstarfarms.com
A family farm providing locally grown grains, freshly
milled flour, hops, and turf.

Great River Milling, Arcadia, Wisconsin
www.greatrivermilling.com
Organic, milled-to-order stone-ground flours grown
and harvested with dedication to building and
maintaining soil integrity. Kosher approved.

Greenmarket Regional Grains Project
Brooklyn, New York
www.grownyc.org/grains
A Northeast regional collective of growers and millers
providing heirloom and conventional whole grains,
legumes, and freshly stone-ground flours. Wholesale
pricing available.

Grist and Toll, Los Angeles, California
www.gristandtoll.com
LA's first urban flour mill in more than 100 years
dedicated to stone grinding wheat, corn, barley, and
alternative grains such as teff, buckwheat, and oats.

Hayden Flour Mills, Phoenix, Arizona
www.haydenflourmills.com
A family business devoted to making the freshest and
most flavorful flours from some of the world's oldest
varieties of wheat, corn, farro, durum, and chickpeas
grown by small Arizona farms.

Honoré Farm and Mill,
Marin County, California
www.honoremill.org
Grows and sources dry-farmed heirloom wheat
varietals, such as Sonora, Red, Fife, and Turkey Red,
without the use of pesticides. Stone-milled flour is
sold as a nonprofit business model dedicated to the
education and service of the Honoré community.

Lindley Mills,
Graham, North Carolina
www.lindleymills.com
A family-owned milling operation that roller mills
organic wheat with low-heat processes to maintain
multinutritional integrity as much as possible. Stone-
ground grits, sprouted wheat, and North Carolina
bread flour are their specialty products. Kosher
approved.

Louismill, Louisville, Kentucky
www.louismill.com
Stone-ground organic wheat and rice flours and
grits supporting local farmers through personal
relationships and dedicated partnerships.

Maine Grains, Skowhegan, Maine
www.mainegrains.com
A gristmill featuring traditional stone milling operating from a repurposed historic county jail house in Central Maine. Locally sourced, organic, and heritage grains.

Migrash Farm, Randallstown, Maryland
www.migrashfarm.com
Small-batch, stone-milled flours grown locally and organically in the Chesapeake Bay region on family farms.

The Mill, San Francisco, California
www.themillsf.com
A bakery and mill dedicated to naturally leavened, whole-grain deliciousness.

Morganics Family Farm, Hillsborough, New Jersey
www.morganicsfamilyfarm.com
A family farm dedicated to the revitalization of the local grain shed, providing organically grown, sun-dried oats and dry beans.

Nitty Gritty Grain Co., Shelburne and Charlotte, Vermont
www.nittygrittygrain.com
A small family-owned, certified-organic farm that mills and mixes cornmeal, cornmeal mixes, and flours.

Palouse Heritage, Endicott, Washington
www.palouseheritage.com
Landrace grains originally grown by fur traders and early settlers of the Pacific Northwest and colonial American farmers. Grown with sustainable practices for the sake of environmental preservation and restoration.

Stutzman Farms, Millersburg, Ohio
Phone: 330.674.1289
Family-owned farm providing organically grown granolas, flours, and sprouted grains.

Upinngil, Gill, Massachusetts
www.upinngil.com
Growers of wheat, rye, and buckwheat in rotation with forage and row crops. Available as whole grains or freshly milled flour in their farm store.

Wheat Montana, Three Forks, Montana
www.wheatmontana.com
Sustainably grown wheat flours, including 'Rouge de Bordeaux,' milled with a steel-cut process using minimal heat and no tempering.

Wild Hive Community Grains Project, Clinton Corners, New York
www.wildhivefarm.com
Stone-ground, heritage grains in small batches. They are dedicated to creating high-quality grain products from the region where they are grown.

INGREDIENT RESOURCES

Bourbon Barrel Foods
www.bourbonbarrelfoods.com
Specialty Southern ingredients, including bourbon barrel–aged sorghum, sourced from small artisanal farmers and craftsmen.

Cultures for Health
www.culturesforhealth.com
Reliable starter cultures and fermentation equipment with excellent tutorials.

Dual Specialty Store, New York, New York
www.dualspecialtystorenyc.com
Providing ground and whole spices, herbs, rice, and grains to the Lower East Side of New York City and via mail order.

Kalustyan's, New York, New York
www.kalustyans.com
Global spices sold in prepackaged form with some bulk item choices.

Oliver Farm Artisan Oils
www.oliverfarm.com
Cold-pressed, unrefined, non-GMO oils, including green peanut, pecan, and pumpkin.

Sahadi's, Brooklyn, New York
www.sahadis.com
An affordable and well-curated collection of bulk items as well as spices, condiments, and Middle Eastern specialty ingredients. A Brooklyn, family-owned-and-operated tradition since 1948, now shipping worldwide.

Turkey Hill Farm, Tallahassee, Florida
Phone: 850.980.2485
turkeyhilltlh@gmail.com
Small growers of Texas gourdseed cornmeal and grits, small-batch sugar cane syrup, and roselle, among other heirloom and culinary oddities.

BOOKS

Bernardin, Tom. *The Ellis Island Immigrant Cookbook: The Story of Our Common Past Told Through the Recipes and Reminiscences of Our Immigrant Ancestors*. New York, NY: Tom Bernardin Inc., 1995.

Boutard, Anthony. *Beautiful Corn: America's Original Grain from Seed to Plate*. Gabriola, British Columbia, Canada: New Society Publishers, 2012.

Chaplin, Amy. *At Home in the Whole Food Kitchen*. Boulder: Roost Books, 2014.

Duggar, John Frederick. *Agriculture for Southern Schools*. New York: The Macmillan Company, 1921.

Fallon, Sally, and Mary G. Enig. *Nourishing Traditions*. Washington D.C.: New Trend Publishing Inc., 1999.

Howard, Sir Albert. *An Agricultural Testament*. New York, NY: Oxford University Press, 1943.

Katz, Sandor. *The Art of Fermentation*. White River Junction, VT: Chelsea Green Publishing, 2012.

Lutz, Henry Frederick. *Viticulture and Brewing in the Ancient Orient*. Carlisle, MA: Applewood Books, 2007.

McGee, Harold. *On Food and Cooking: The Science and Lore of the Kitchen*. New York, NY: Scribner, 1984.

Nosrat, Samin. *Salt Fat Acid Heat: Mastering the Elements of Good Cooking*. New York, NY: Simon and Schuster, 2017.

Percival, Bronwen. *Reinventing the Wheel: Milk, Microbes, and the Fight for Real Cheese* (California Studies in Food and Culture). Oakland, CA: University of California Press, 2017.

Wigginton, Eliot, ed. The Foxfire Book Series, 12 vols. Anchor Press/Doubleday/Foxfire Fund, 1972–2004.

EQUIPMENT

Etsy
www.etsy.com
Handcrafted fermentation crocks, and vintage and custom kitchen items.

Lodge Cast Iron
www.lodgemfg.com
Long-lasting, heirloom-quality Dutch ovens, griddles, and cookware.

Quitokeeto
www.quitokeeto.com
Rare finds in the culinary realm picked by Heidi Swanson and Wayne Bremser with an eye toward longevity, usefulness, authenticity, and beauty.

Stone Creek Trading
www.stonecreektrading.com
Traditional products, including fermentation crocks, for a modern, natural home.

Villagers
www.forvillagers.com
An urban homestead supply store located in Asheville, North Carolina, offering quality tools, supplies, and classes to support healthy lifestyle activities, including organic gardening, food preservation, home cooking, medicinal herbalism, and keeping chickens.

Index

About the Author

SARAH OWENS is a New York City–based cookbook author, baker, professional horticulturist, and instructor. She was awarded a James Beard Award for her first book, *Sourdough*, and released her second book, *Toast and Jam*, in 2017. Sarah believes strongly in the power of baking to foster community and social change; she is an advocate of sustainable agricultural practices to rebuild global grain sheds and believes stone milling can bring good bread back to the table. As a teacher of nourishing food traditions, she travels globally to encourage an interest in fermentation and has helped establish a bakery in Tripoli, Lebanon, working with Syrian refugees, as well as an annual Fermentation Summit in Oaxaca, Mexico. Her own subscription-based business and workshop space is Ritual Fine Foods (formerly BK17 Bakery), located at The Castle in Rockaway Beach, New York, where she teaches the alchemy and digestive benefits of natural leavening.

Roost Books
An imprint of Shambhala
Publications, Inc.
4720 Walnut Street
Boulder, Colorado 80301
roostbooks.com

9 8 7 6 5 4 3 2 1

First Edition
Printed in China

♾This edition is printed on
acid-free paper that meets
the American National
Standards Institute Z39.48
Standard.
♻Shambhala Publications
makes every effort to print
on recycled paper. For more
information please visit
www.shambhala.com.
Roost Books is distributed
worldwide by
Penguin Random House, Inc.,
and its subsidiaries.

Designed by Toni Tajima

Library of Congress Cataloging-
in-Publication Data
Names: Owens, Sarah, 1978–
author. | Ngo, Ngoc Minh,
photographer.
Title: Heirloom: time-honored
techniques, nourishing
traditions, and modern recipes
/ Sarah Owens; photographs by
Ngoc Minh Ngo.
Description: First edition. |
Boulder: Roost Books, 2019. |
Includes index.
Identifiers: LCCN 2018034654 |
ISBN 9781611805420
(hardcover: alk. paper)
Subjects: LCSH: Seasonal
cooking. | LCGFT: Cookbooks.
Classification: LCC TX714 .O956
2019 | DDC 641.5/64—dc23
LC record available at https://
lccn.loc.gov/2018034654